A Short Guide to Writing about Biology

FIFTH EDITION

JAN A. PECHENIK
Tufts University

PEARSON
Longman

New York   Boston   San Francisco
London   Toronto   Sydney   Tokyo   Singapore   Madrid
Mexico City   Munich   Paris   Cape Town   Hong Kong   Montreal

Senior Vice President and Publisher: Joseph Opiela
Acquisitions Editor: Susan Kunchandy
Assistant Editor: Rebecca Gilpin
Senior Supplements Editor: Donna Campion
Media Supplements Editor: Nancy Garcia
Executive Marketing Manager: Ann Stypuloski
Production Manager: Eric Jorgensen
Project Coordination, Text Design, and Electronic Page Makeup:
    UG / GGS Information Services, Inc.
Cover Design Manager: John Callahan
Cover Illustration/Photo: Cover images courtesy of Photodisc
Manufacturing Manager: Dennis J. Para
Printer and Binder: RR Donnelley & Sons Company—Crawfordsville
Cover Printer: The Lehigh Press, Inc.

Library of Congress Cataloging-in-Publication Data
    Pechenik, Jan A.
    A short guide to writing about biology / Jan A. Pechenik.—5th ed.
        p. cm.—(The short guide series)
    Includes bibliograpical references and index.
    ISBN 0-321-15981-0 (alk. paper)
    1. Biology—Authorship. 2. Report writing. I. Title.

QH304.P43 2004
808'.06657—dc21

                                            2003047686

Visit us at *http://www.ablongman.com*

ISBN 0-321-15981-0

12345678910–DOC–06 05 04 03

PEARSON
Longman

To Oliver,
wise guy and b.p.

Contents

PART II
Guidelines for Specific Tasks

Preface

Careful thinking cannot be separated from effective writing. With the dramatic innovations in molecular techniques and information technology, students can easily lose sight of what being a biologist is all about. It is not just about memorizing facts and esoteric terminology, or about mastering an increasing array of computer software and molecular techniques. Biology is a way of thinking about the world. It is about making careful observations, asking specific questions, designing ways to address those questions, manipulating data thoughtfully and thoroughly, interpreting those data and related observations, reevaluating past work, asking new questions, and redefining older ones. It is also about communicating information—accurately, logically, clearly, concisely, and unambiguously. The hard work of thinking about biology is at least as important as the work of doing it. Writing provides a way to examine, to evaluate, to refine, and to share that thinking. Writing is both a product and a process.

Biology instructors are increasingly concerned about their students' writing for two reasons. First, bad writing often reflects fuzzy thinking, so questioning the writing generally guides students toward a clearer understanding of the biology being written about. Secondly, effective communication is such a key part of the biologist's trade that our students really must learn to do it well. The difficulty, of course, is finding the time to teach both biology and writing when there is barely enough time in the semester to cover the biology. This book allows instructors to guide their students' writing without taking up valuable class time. And as the writing improves, so, too, will the students' understanding of what they are writing about.

Although the book covers every sort of writing assignment that biologists face—both as students and as professionals—it is brief enough to be read along with other, more standard assignments, and straightforward enough to be understood without additional instruction. Although intended especially for undergraduate use in typical lecture and laboratory courses at all levels, the book is also appropriate for undergraduate and graduate seminars. Many long-established colleagues tell me that they have also found much in the book that was new and helpful in their own writing, and in their teaching.

I have included examples from all fields of biology. However, because the book is intended for use even at introductory levels, I have avoided examples that assume substantial specialized knowledge or terminology. Instructors in advanced courses may wish to amplify basic principles with examples chosen from papers published in their own fields; students benefit in particular from studying good models.

ORGANIZATION

The first 5 chapters cover general issues that apply to all types of writing (and reading) in biology. In Chapter 1, I emphasize the benefits of learning to write well in biology, describe the sorts of writing that professional biologists do, and review some key principles that characterize all sound scientific writing. Chapter 2 emphasizes the struggle for understanding that must precede any concern with *how* something is said. In it, I explain how to locate research articles using computerized indexing services, on-line journals, and the World Wide Web; how to read the formal scientific literature, including graphs and tables; and how to take useful notes, and take them in ways that prevent unintentional plagiarism. Chapter 3 talks about the use and interpretation of statistical analyses, while Chapter 4 explains how to cite references and how to prepare Literature Cited sections. Chapter 5 focuses on the process of revision—for content, organization, clarity, conciseness, grammar, word use, and spelling. It emphasizes the benefits of peer review, and explains both how to be an effective reviewer of other people's writing and how to interpret criticism. Many readers have found Chapter 5 to be one of the most important chapters in the book. Most students learn very little in preparing the first draft of anything. They can learn much, however—about biology and about writing—through properly guided revision.

The rest of the book covers all of the specific writing tasks encountered in biology coursework and in professional life: writing summaries and critiques (Chapter 6), writing essays and term papers (Chapter 7), writing laboratory and other research reports (Chapter 8), writing research proposals (Chapter 9), answering essay questions on examinations (Chapter 10), preparing poster presentations (Chapter 11), writing for general audiences (Chapter 12), giving oral presentations

(Chapter 13), and writing letters of application, for jobs or for graduate school (Chapter 14).

"Writing summaries and critiques" merits a separate chapter (Chapter 6) because most students seem not to have had much practice summarizing information accurately and concisely, and in their own words. An inability to summarize effectively is a serious obstacle to both synthesis and critical evaluation. Writing summaries is also a particularly effective way for students to self-test their understanding and to prepare for examinations.

The chapter on writing laboratory and other research reports (Chapter 8) emphasizes that the results obtained in a study are often less important than the ability to discuss and interpret those results convincingly in the context of basic biological knowledge, and to demonstrate clear understanding of the purpose of the study. It emphasizes the variability inherent in biological systems and how that variability is dealt with in presenting, interpreting, and discussing data. This chapter will also be useful to anyone preparing papers for publication.

My inclusion of Chapter 12, on writing for a general audience, has apparently baffled some reviewers. Many readers, however, are finding that such assignments help students dejargonize their writing, and help instructors tell just how much their students understand about the material they are writing about. You cannot write clearly and accurately for a general audience without thoroughly understanding the material. For some students, such assignments have led to useful and interesting careers.

There are also a number of appendices, including one that lists commonly used abbreviations for lengths, weights, volumes, and concentrations. Other appendices note computer software particularly useful for biologists, list Web sites that both students and instructors will find useful in both writing and data presentation, and provide sample forms for guiding peer review. I have also included an appendix summarizing how to use the paper versions of the leading indexing services; this will be particularly useful for searching the older literature.

CHANGES MADE FOR THE FIFTH EDITION

For this edition of the not-so-short guide, I have added a new section on developing and supporting arguments (thesis statements). I have also added 2 new checklists, one for oral presentations and one for research proposals, and have added page references to checklists closing the longer chapters, to help students locate information on particular topics. The section on statistical analysis and interpretation has been expanded, in part to introduce some of the current controversy concerning hypothesis testing (more detailed discussions are given in several new appendix references). The discussion of how (and when) to search the World Wide Web has also been enlarged. I have also increased my focus, throughout the book, on the importance of learning to summarize.

Perhaps the most conspicuous change for the fifth edition is the addition of 5 Technology Tips, helping students to take better advantage of the computer technology available to them for writing, graphing, and oral presentation.

Users of the previous edition will notice many smaller improvements throughout this book, including greater use of boldfacing and bulleting to emphasize key points.

ACKNOWLEDGMENTS

This revision has benefited greatly from the suggestions of many people who took the time to read and comment on the fourth edition: Dr. Christine E. Jungklaus, Clarkson University; Scott Kinnes, Azusa Pacific University; Chris Maher, University of Southern Maine; Kay McMurry, University of Texas at Austin; William R. Morgan, The College of Wooster; Regina Raboin, Tufts University; Linda L. Tichenor, University of Arkansas; and Cheryl L. Watson, Central Connecticut State University.

The fourth edition, in turn, was improved by the sage advice given by reviewers of previous editions: Virginia Anderson, Tina Ayers, Sylvan Barnett, Arthur Buikema, Edward H. Burtt, Robert Chase, Maggie de Cuevas, Robert Curry, John R. Diehl, George F. Edick, Stephen Fuller, Louis Gainey, Jr., Sharon Hanks, Marcia Harrison, Jared Haynes, Joseph Kelty, Scott Kinnes, Anne Kozak, George Labanick, Martin Levin, Sara Lewis, Barbara Liedl, John W. Munford, Colin Orians, Peter Pederson, Laurie Sabol, Carl Schaefer, Christopher Schardl, Stephen van Scoyoc, Barbara Stewart, Marcia Stubbs, and David Takacs.

I am grateful to all of these people for their comments and suggestions and am much cheered by their dedication to the cause. And who could ask for a more attentive reader than Victoria McMillan?

It is also a pleasure to thank those involved in producing this new edition: Susan Kunchandy and Rebecca Gilpin at Longman, and Sondra Greenfield at UG / GGS Information Services, Inc.

Finally, I have learned much about writing and teaching from correspondence and conversation with enthusiastic readers of previous editions—both instructors and students—and from working for so many years with colleagues from all disciplines in the Writing Across the Curriculum program at Tufts University. I welcome additional comments from readers of the present edition. Forward into battle. . . .

JAN A. PECHENIK

`jan.pechenik@tufts.edu`

I

GENERAL ADVICE ABOUT WRITING AND READING BIOLOGY

1

INTRODUCTION AND GENERAL RULES

What appears as a thoroughly systematic piece of scientific work is actually
the final product: a cleanly washed offspring that tells us very little about the
chaotic mess that fermented in the mental womb of its creator.

Auner Treinin

The logical development of ideas and the clear, precise, and succinct
communication of those ideas through writing are among the most difficult, but most important, skills that can be mastered in college. Effective
writing is also one of the most difficult skills to teach. This is especially
true in biology classes, where there is often much writing to be done but
little time to focus on doing it well. The chief message of this book is that
developing your writing skills is worth every bit of effort it takes, and that
biology is a splendid field in which to pursue this goal.

WHAT DO BIOLOGISTS WRITE ABOUT, AND WHY?

The sort of writing that biologists do (lectures, grant proposals, research
papers, literature reviews, oral and poster presentations for meetings, letters of recommendation, committee reports, and critiques of research papers, research proposals, and books written by other biologists) is similar
in many respects to the sort of writing (essays, literature reviews, term
papers, and laboratory reports) you are asked to do while enrolled in a
typical biology course. Basically, we must all prepare arguments.

Like a good term paper, research report, oral presentation, or thesis,
a lecture is an argument; it presents information in an orderly manner
and seeks to convince the audience that this information fits sensibly into
some much larger story. Few students are aware of the time and effort
required to write a coherent lecture, but the sad fact is that putting together a string of 3 or 4 lectures on any particular topic is the equivalent
of preparing one 20- to 30-page term paper weekly.

In addition to preparing lectures, many of us spend quite a bit of time writing grant proposals in the hope of obtaining the funding that will enable us to pursue our research programs (and possibly hire one of you for a summer in the process). A research proposal is unquestionably an argument; success depends on our ability to convince a panel of other biologists that what we wish to do is worth doing, that we are capable of doing it, that we are capable of correctly interpreting the results, that the work cannot be done without the funds requested, and that the amount of funding requested is appropriate for the research planned. Research money is not plentiful. Even well-written proposals have a difficult time; poorly written proposals generally don't stand a chance.

When we are not writing grant proposals or lectures, we are often preparing the results of our research for publication or for presentation at meetings. Research articles are really just laboratory reports based on data collected over a period much longer than the typical laboratory session; in research articles, as in laboratory reports, the goal is to present data clearly and to interpret those data thoroughly and convincingly in the context of previous work and basic biological principles. The preparation of research reports typically involves the following steps:

1. Organizing and analyzing the data
2. Preparing a first draft of the article (following the procedures outlined in Chapter 8 of this book)
3. Revising and reprinting the paper
4. Asking one or more colleagues to read the paper critically
5. Revising the paper in accordance with the comments and suggestions of the readers
6. Reprinting and proofreading the paper
7. Sending the paper to the editor of the journal in which we would most like to see our work published

This is not the end of the story. The editor then sends the manuscript out to be reviewed by 2 or 3 other biologists. Their comments, along with those of the editor, are then sent to the author, who must again rewrite the paper, often extensively. The editor may then accept or reject the revised manuscript, or may request that it be rewritten again prior to publication.

Oral presentations involve similar preparation. The data are organized and examined, a draft of the talk is prepared, feedback on the talk is solicited from colleagues, and the presentation is revised.

Biologists obviously write about biology, but they also write about other things. One of the other things college and university biologists write about is you; letters of recommendation are especially troublesome for us because they are so important to you. Like a good laboratory report, literature review, essay, or term paper, a letter of recommendation must be written clearly, developed logically, and proofread carefully. It must also support all statements of opinion with facts or examples if it is to argue convincingly on your behalf and help get you where you want to go.

And then there are the progress reports, committee reports, and internal memoranda. All this writing involves thinking, organizing, nailing down a convincing argument on paper, revising, retyping, and proofreading.

Clearly, effective writing is not irrelevant in a scientific career. When students in a biology course receive criticisms of their writing, they often complain that "this is not an English course." These students do not understand that clear, concise, logical writing is an important tool of the biologist's trade, and that learning how to write well is at least as important as learning how to use a balance, extract DNA, use a taxonomic key, measure a nerve impulse, run an electrophoretic gel, or clone a gene. And, unlike these rather specialized laboratory techniques, mastering the art of effective writing will reward you regardless of the field in which you eventually find yourself.

In preparing the cover letter that accompanies a job application, for example, you are again building an argument. You are trying to convince someone that you understand the position you are applying for, have the skills necessary to do the job well, and that, in fact, you want to do the job well. Similarly, in constructing a business plan you must write clearly, concisely, and convincingly if you are to get your project funded. The fact that you may not become a biologist is no reason to cheat yourself out of the opportunity to become an effective writer.

THE KEYS TO SUCCESS

> It's always easier to learn something than to use what you've learned.
> Chaim Potok, *The Promise*

There is no easy way to learn to write well in biology, or in any other field. It helps to read a lot of good writing, and not just in biology. Whenever you read a sentence or a paragraph or a page or even the caption to a graph that seems especially clear or easy to follow, examine that writing carefully to see what made it work so well for you. Reading well-written sentences aloud can also help to plant good patterns in your brain. But mostly, you just have to work hard at writing, and keep working hard at it, draft after draft, assignment after assignment. That will be much easier to do if you have something in mind that you actually want to say. Much of this book is about how to get to that point.

All good writing involves 2 struggles: the struggle for understanding and the struggle to communicate that understanding to readers. Like the making of omelettes or crepes, the skill improves with practice. There are no shortcuts. However, being aware of certain key principles will ease the way considerably. Each of the following rules is discussed more fully in later chapters (note relevant page numbers). This listing is worth reading at the start of each semester, or whenever you begin a new assignment.

Ten Major Rules for Preparing a First Draft

1. **Work to understand your sources (pp. 21–28).** When writing laboratory reports, spend time wrestling with your data until you are convinced you see the significance of what you have done. When taking notes from books or research articles, reread sentences you don't understand and look up the words that puzzle you. Try to take notes in your own words; extensive copying or paraphrasing usually means that you do not yet understand the material well enough to be writing about it. Too few students take this struggle for understanding seriously enough, but all good scientific writing begins here. You can excel—in college and in life after college—by being one of the few who meet this challenge head on. Do not be embarrassed to admit (to yourself or to others) that you do not understand something after working at it for a while. Talk about the material with other students or with your instructor. If you don't commit yourself to winning the struggle for understanding, you will end up with nothing to say, or worse, what you do say will be wrong. In both cases, you will produce nothing worth reading.

2. **Don't quote from your sources.** Direct quotations rarely appear in the formal biological literature. Describe what others have done and the ideas they have presented, but do so in your own words. Consider this sentence:

   > Shell adequacy was measured by the "shell adequacy index," defined by Vance (1972) as "the ratio of the weight of the hermit crab for which the shell was of preferred size to the actual weight of the hermit crab examined."

   When I see writing like this, I assume that the writer did not understand the material being quoted; when you understand something thoroughly you should be able to explain it in your own words. Perhaps I'm being unfair: perhaps this student just couldn't think of how to explain this better than the author already did. But if the student were explaining the shell adequacy index to a fellow student, would he or she have used that wording? I don't think so. Always put yourself in the position of explaining things to others, and do so using your own words.

3. **Don't plagiarize (p. 29).** Whenever you restate another writer's ideas or interpretations, you must do so in your own words and credit your source explicitly. Note, too, that simply changing a few words here and there or changing the order of a few words in a sentence or paragraph is still plagiarism. Plagiarism is one of the most serious crimes in academia: it can get you expelled from college or cost you a career later. With practice and conscientious effort, you will find yourself capable of generating your own good ideas and presenting them in perfectly fine prose of your own devising.

4. **Think about where you are going before you begin to write (pp. 132–135, 220–221).** Much of the real work of writing is in the thinking that must precede each draft. Effective writing is like effective sailing; you must take the time to plot your course before getting too far from port. Your ideas about where you are going and how best to get there may very well change as you continue to work with and revise your paper, since the act of writing invariably clarifies your thinking and often brings entirely new ideas into focus. Nevertheless, you must have some plan in mind even when you begin to write your first draft. This plan evolves from thoughtful consideration of your notes. Think first, then write; thoughtful revision follows.

   Some people find it helpful to think at a keyboard or with pen in hand, letting their thoughts tumble onto paper. Others prefer to think "inside," writing only after their thoughts have come together into a coherent pattern. Either way, the hard work of thinking must not be avoided. If, when you sit down to write that last draft of your paper, you still don't know where you are heading, you certainly won't get there smoothly and you may well not get there at all. Almost certainly, your readers will never get there.

5. **Practice summarizing information (p. 28).** The longer I work with writing issues, the more I realize the central importance of being able to summarize information effectively. If you can't summarize the results of 1 research paper in your own words, you can't possibly see the relationship between 3 or 4 such papers; summary is an

essential prelude to synthesis. The more practice you get summarizing information in your own words the better. After you hear a lecture, take 10 minutes to summarize the major points in your notebook. After you see a movie, or read a book or short story or even a newspaper article, try writing a one-paragraph summary every now and then. From time to time, after reading even a single paragraph of something, try writing a one-sentence summary of that paragraph (see pp. 28–29 for an example). The ability to summarize is an underappreciated and largely neglected, but essential, skill for professional life.

6. **Write to illuminate, not to impress (p. 202).** Use the simplest words and the simplest phrasing consistent with that goal. Avoid acronyms, and define all specialized terminology. In general, if a term was recently new to you, it should be defined in your writing. And if you can talk about "zones of polarizing activity" instead of "ZPAs," please do so. Your goal should be to communicate; why deliberately exclude potentially interested readers by trying to sound "scientific"? Don't try to impress readers with big words and a technical vocabulary; focus instead on getting your point across.

7. **Write for your classmates and for your future self (pp. 84, 202).** It is difficult to write effectively unless you have a suitable audience in mind. It helps to write papers that you can imagine being interesting to and understood by your fellow students. You should also prepare your assignments so that they will be meaningful to *you* should you read them far in the future, long after you have forgotten the details of coursework completed or experiments performed. Addressing these 2 audiences—your fellow students and your future self—should help you write clearly and convincingly.

8. **Support all statements of fact and opinion with evidence (pp. 66–70, 183–184).** Remember, you are making an argument. In any argument, a statement of fact or opinion becomes convincing to the critical reader only when that statement is supported by evidence or explanation; provide it. You might, for instance, write:

```
Among the vertebrates, the development of sperm
is triggered by the release of the hormone
testosterone (Gilbert, 1997).
```

In this case, a statement of fact is supported by reference to a book written by Scott Gilbert in 1997. In the following example, a statement is backed up by reference to the writer's own data:

```
Some wavelengths of light were more effective
than others in promoting photosynthesis. For ex-
ample, the rate of oxygen production at 650 nm*
was nearly 4 times greater than that recorded for
the same plants when using a wavelength of 550 nm
(Figure 2).
```

References to papers or books written by 2 authors must include the names of both authors (for example, Burns and Allen, 1946). When there are more than 2 authors, only the first author's name is written out (for example, Fried *et al.*, 1995). Note that an author's first name is never included in the citation. A statement made by your instructor should be cited as a personal communication (for example, "Professor Rachel Merz, personal communication, October 2002"). Refer to a laboratory manual or handout by the author of that handout (for example, Wendt, 2000), or as follows: (Bio 13 Laboratory Manual, 2000).

Statements can also be supported by reference to the results of statistical analyses, as in the following example:

```
The blue mussels produced significantly thicker
shells in the presence of crustacean predators
(t = 4.65; d.f. = 23; P < 0.01).
```

Here, the statement is supported by the results of a t-test. The meaning of the items in parentheses is further explained in Chapter 3.

9. **Always distinguish fact from possibility**. In the course of examining your data or reading your notes, you may form an opinion. This is splendid. But you must be careful not to state your opinion as though it were fact. "The members of species X lack the ability to respond to sucrose" is a statement of fact and must be supported with a reference. "Our data suggest that adults of species X lack the ability to respond to sucrose" or "Adults of species X seem unable to respond to sucrose" expresses your opinion and should be supported by drawing the reader's attention to key elements of your data set.

---

*nm = nanometers; that is, 10^{-9} meters

Similarly, consider the following statement:

```
The data suggest that "vestigial wings" is an au-
tosomal recessive trait whereas "carnation eyes"
is a sex-linked recessive trait.
```

The addition of that one phrase, "the data suggest," makes all the difference; basing an opinion solely on his or her own data, the writer would be on far shakier ground beginning the sentence with " 'Vestigal wings' is an autosomal recessive trait."

10. **Allow time for revision (pp. 75–76).** Accurate, concise, successfully persuasive communication is not easily achieved, and few of us come close in a first or even a second draft. Although the act of writing can itself help clarify your thinking, it is important to step away from the work and reread it with a fresh eye before making revisions; a "revision" is, after all, a re-vision: another look at what you have written. This second (or third, or fourth) look allows you more easily to see if you *have* said what you had hoped to say, and whether you have guided the reader from point to point as masterfully as you had intended. Remember, you are constructing an argument. It takes thoughtful revision to make any argument fully convincing. Start writing assignments as soon as possible after receiving them, and always allow at least a few days between the penultimate and final drafts; if you follow this advice, the quality of what you submit will improve dramatically, as will the quality of what you learn from the assignment.

Seven Major Rules for Developing Your Final Draft

Once you have nailed together the basic framework of your presentation or argument, it is time to tighten the construction.

11. **Stick to the point (p. 135).** Delete any irrelevant information, no matter how interesting it is to you. Snip it out and put it away in a safe place for later use if you wish, but don't let asides interrupt the flow of your writing.

12. **Say exactly what you mean (pp. 81–92).** Words are tricky; if they don't end up in the right places, they can add considerable ambiguity to your sentences. "I saw 3 squid SCUBA diving last Thursday" conjures up a very interesting image. Don't make readers guess what you're trying to say; they often guess incorrectly. Good scientific

writing is precise. Write to mean what you mean to say, and be sure you say what you mean. It often helps to read aloud what you have written and to listen carefully to what you say as you read.

13. **Never make the reader back up (pp. 99–103).** You should try to take the reader by the nose in your first paragraph and lead him or her through to the end, line by line, paragraph by paragraph. Avoid making the reader flip back 2 pages, or even 1 sentence. Link your sentences carefully, using such transitional words as "therefore" or "in contrast," or by repeating key words, so that a clear argument is developed logically. Remind the reader of what has come before, as in the following example:

```
In saturated air (100% relative humidity), the
worms lost about 20% of their initial body weight
during the first 20 hours but were then able to
prevent further dehydration. In contrast, worms
maintained in air of 70-80% relative humidity ex-
perienced a much faster and continuous rate of
dehydration, losing 63% of their total body water
content in 24 hours. As a consequence of this
rapid dehydration, most worms died within the
24-hour period.
```

Note that the second and third sentences in this example begin with transitions ("In contrast," "As a consequence of"), thus continuing and developing the thought initiated in the preceding sentences. A far less satisfactory last sentence might read, "Most of these animals died within the 24-hour period."

Link your paragraphs in the same way, using transitions to continue the progression of a thought, reminding the readers periodically of what they have already read.

Avoid casual use of the words *it, they,* and *their.* For example, the sentence, "It can be altered by several environmental factors" forces the reader to go back to the preceding sentence, or perhaps even to the previous paragraph, to find out what *it* is. Changing the sentence to "The rate of population growth can be altered by several environmental factors" solves the problem. Here is another example:

```
Our results were based upon observations of
short-term changes in behavior. They showed that
```

```
feeding rates did not vary with the size of the
caterpillar.
```

The word *they* could refer to "results," "observations," or "changes in behavior." Granted, the reader can back up and figure out what *they* are, but you should work to avoid the "You know what I mean" syndrome. Changing *they* in the second sentence to "These results" avoids the ambiguity and keeps the reader moving in the right direction.

Do not be afraid to repeat a word used in a preceding sentence; if it is the right word and avoids ambiguity, use it.

14. **Don't make readers work harder than they have to (pp. 88–92, 184).** If there is interpreting to be done, you must be the one to do it. For example, never write something like:

```
The difference in absorption rates is quite
clearly shown in Table 1.
```

Such a statement puts the burden of effort on the reader. Instead, write something like:

```
Clearly, alcohol is more readily absorbed into
the bloodstream from distilled beverages than
from brewed beverages (Table 1).
```

The reader now knows exactly what you have in mind and can examine Table 1 to see if he or she agrees with you.

15. **Be concise (pp. 92–99).** Give all the necessary information, but avoid using more words than you need for the job at hand. By being concise, your writing will gain in clarity. Why say:

```
Our results were based upon observations of
short-term changes in behavior. These results
showed that feeding rates did not vary with the
size of the caterpillar.
```

when you can say:

```
Our observations of short-term changes in behav-
ior indicate that feeding rates did not vary with
the size of the caterpillar.
```

In fact, you might be even better off with the following sentence:

```
Feeding rates did not appear to vary with cater-
pillar size.
```

With this modified sentence, 50% of the words in the first effort have been eliminated without any loss of content. The savings are not merely esthetic. It costs something like 20 cents a word to publish a scientific paper, and authors are often asked to bear some of this cost; in the real world of biological publications, it pays, quite literally, to be concise. Besides, cutting out extra words means you will have less to type. You'll have your paper finished that much sooner. Finally, your readers can digest the paper more easily, reading it with pleasure rather than with impatience.

16. **Don't be teleological (p. 103).** That is, don't attribute a sense of purpose to other living things, especially when discussing evolution. Giraffes did not evolve long necks "in order to reach the leaves of tall trees." Birds did not evolve nest-building behavior "in order to protect their young." Insects did not evolve wings "in order to fly." Plants did not evolve flowers "in order to attract bees for pollination." Natural selection operates through a process of differential survival and reproduction, not with intent. Long necks, complex behavior, and other such genetically determined characteristics may well have given some organisms an advantage in surviving and reproducing unavailable to individuals lacking those traits, but this does not mean that any of these characteristics were deliberately evolved in order to achieve something.

Organisms do not evolve structures, physiological adaptations, or behavior out of desire. Appropriate genetic combinations must always arise by random genetic events, by chance, before selection can operate. Even then, selection is imposed on the individual by its surroundings and, in that sense, selection is a passive process; natural selection never involves conscious, deliberate choice. Don't write, "Insects may have evolved flight in order to escape predators." Instead, write, "Flight among insects may have been selected for in response to predation pressure."

17. **Proofread.** Although it is a crucial part of the writing process, none of us likes to proofread. By the time we have arrived at this point in the project, we have put in a considerable amount of work and are certain we have done the job correctly. Who wants to read the paper yet another time? Moreover, finding an error means having to make a correction. But put yourself in the position of your instructor. Your instructor must read perhaps 100 or more papers each term. He or

she starts off on your side, wanting to see you earn a good grade. Similarly, a reviewer or editor of scientific research manuscripts starts off by wanting to see the paper under consideration get published. A sloppy paper—for example, one with many typographical errors—can lose you a considerable amount of goodwill as a student and later as a practicing scientist. For one thing, sloppy work may suggest to the reader that you are equally sloppy in your thinking, or that you take little pride in your own efforts. Furthermore, it's insulting: failure to proofread your paper and to make the required corrections implies that you don't value the reader's time; that is not a flattering message to send, nor is it a particularly wise one. Never forget: there is often a subjective element to grading and to decisions about the fate of manuscripts and grant proposals. Lastly, a carelessly proofread paper may suggest to the reader that the research itself was carelessly performed. For all these reasons, shoddily prepared material can easily lower a grade, damage a writer's credibility, reduce the likelihood that a manuscript will be accepted for publication or that a grant proposal will be funded, or cost an applicant a job or admission to professional or graduate school. Why put yourself in such jeopardy for a mere half-hour saved? Turn in a piece of work that you are proud to have produced.

Eight Finer Points: One Last Pass

Once you have come up with something to say and are convinced that you have said it effectively, you need to look closely at your work one last time before producing the final version.

18. **Abbreviate units of measurement that are preceded by numbers.** Do not put periods after unit symbols, and always use the same symbol for all values regardless of quantity: 1 mm (millimeter), 50 mm; 1 hr (hour), 50 hr; 1 g (gram), 454 g.

19. **Always underline or italicize species names, as in *Homo sapiens*.** Note also that the generic name (*Homo*) is capitalized, whereas the specific name (*sapiens*) is not. Once you have given the full name of the organism in your paper, the generic name can be abbreviated; *Homo sapiens*, for example, becomes *H. sapiens*. There is no other acceptable way to abbreviate species names. In particular, it is not permissible to refer to an animal using only the generic name, since most genera include many species. Note that the plural of "genus" is "genera," not "genuses."

20. **Do not capitalize common names:** monarch butterfly, lowland gorillas, pygmy octopus, fruit fly.

21. **Capitalize the names of taxonomic groups (clades) above the level of genus, but not the names of the taxonomic categories themselves.** For example, insects belong to the phylum Arthropoda and the class Insecta. Do not capitalize informal names of animals: insects are arthropods, members of the phylum Arthropoda.

22. **Remember that the word *data* is plural.** The singular is *datum*, a word rarely used in biological writing. "The data are lovely" (not "The data is lovely"). "These data show some surprising trends" (not "This data shows some surprising trends"). You would not say, "My feet is very large"; treat *data* with the same respect.

23. **Pay attention to form and format: appearances can be deceiving.** Your papers and reports should give the impression that you took the assignment seriously, that you are proud of the result, and that you welcome constructive criticism of your work. Type or computer-print your papers whenever possible, using only one side of each page. Leave margins of about an inch and a half on the left and right sides of the page, leave about an inch at the top and bottom of each page, and double-space your typing so that your instructor can easily make comments on your paper. Make corrections neatly. Never underestimate the subjective element in grading.

24. **Put your name and the date at the top of each assignment, and number all pages.** Pages should be numbered so that readers can tell immediately if a page is missing or out of order and so that the readers can easily point out problems on particular pages ("In the middle of page 7, you imply that. . . .").

25. **Always make a copy of your paper before submitting the original to your instructor.** Even instructors sometimes lose things.

ON USING COMPUTERS IN WRITING

Computers are a biologist's best friend when it comes to analyzing data, making graphs, and revising advanced drafts of manuscripts and reports, and it is here that you can exploit those disk drives to best advantage. When I read drafts of my work back in the days of typewriters, I would often see places where rearranging a few paragraphs, adding a phrase or sentence, or even simply replacing one word with another, would have substantially improved the final product. But if I had already typed several drafts, I rarely made those additional changes; the benefits of increased clarity of expression usually seemed minor in comparison with the unbearable thought of retyping one or more pages yet again. With word processing, however, perfection is within your immediate grasp. It is now easy to change a word, modify or delete a sentence, or reorganize a paragraph or an entire paper, and the computer will produce the revised version at the touch of a button.

In fact, because even major revisions no longer require much time-consuming retyping, using a computer places increased responsibility on you to make the revisions. Instructors find it increasingly annoying when students turn in computer-printed reports that are carelessly written and not proofread. Word processing has become a two-edged sword.

Even though computers have in some ways simplified the task of revision, you may still be better off writing your first drafts with pencil and paper. First drafts serve primarily to get ideas on paper, where they can't escape; the form, order, and manner of expression are not major concerns at this early stage of creation. Consequently, the first revision is often so extensive that it may be far less time consuming to revise this draft by hand than to do so with a computer. In fact, putting a first draft on the computer can actually inhibit you from making the extensive revisions that are called for. Moreover, if there is a power failure, you can lose everything; if you use a pencil or pen instead, you will still have your first, handwritten draft to work from. For me, it's the second draft that gets entered into the computer.

On the other hand, if you are one of those people who are intimidated by a blank sheet of paper but not by a blank video screen, ignore my advice about not using a computer for first drafts. If composing directly on the computer works for you, stick with it. But if it hasn't been working for you, try the pencil or pen method for first drafts and see what happens.

Regardless of when you begin entering your work into the computer, **save your work frequently**, at least every few paragraphs, and always make a backup copy.

Let me end this section with some warnings about what you cannot expect a computer to do for you. Advertisers suggest that owning a computer will take the work out of your writing. Armed with a personal computer, they say, you will see your spelling improve, your sentences make sense, your paragraphs become well organized, your ideas seem brilliant, and your grades soar. As the ever-optimistic reader of many computer-printed laboratory reports and papers, I must inform you that computers—no matter how fast they operate or how much you pay for them—do not work these kinds of miracles.

In particular, computers can do little to help you in that all-important first struggle—the struggle for understanding. Neither (unfortunately) can they think, organize, or revise for you. Computerized spelling checkers are of some use in catching your typographical and spelling errors, but you cannot expect them to catch all of your mistakes. Biology is a field with much specialized terminology, much of which is of no use to nonbiologists; these terms, therefore, do not find their way into the dictionaries that accompany computerized spelling programs. Although you can easily add words to the computer's dictionary, the terminology in your papers will be changing with every new assignment; many of the words you add for today's assignment will probably not be used in next week's assignment. Moreover, a spelling-checker program will not distinguish between *to* and *too*, *there* and *their*, or *it's* and *its*, and the program will miss typographical errors that are real words; using the program will not spare you the chore of proofreading for spelling mistakes. Suppose, for example, that you typed *an* when you intended to type *and*, or you typed *or* when you should have typed *of*, or you typed *rat* instead of *rate*. To catch these errors, you would have to use a program that catches grammatical mistakes, but be aware that such programs will not catch every error and do not always suggest the proper correction when mistakes are recognized. By all means use spelling- and grammar-checking programs if they are readily available, but then use your own sharp eyes and keen intellect—moving word by word and sentence by sentence—to complete the necessary process of proofreading your work.

TECHNOLOGY TIP   1
Getting the most from your word-processing program

The field of biology contains much specialized terminology, a number of abbreviations that require superscripts or subscripts, and many long, tongue-twisting species names (which always need to be italicized—Rule 19). Here are some ways to save time and avoid typographical errors when you deal with any of these problems repeatedly.

- **For italicizing**, instead of highlighting and then clicking on the I selection in the bottom line of the Word menu system (to the right of the B symbol, for boldfacing), press the Ctrl key and type an "i" (or " _ " underscore) before and after the word(s) that you want italicized; leave no space between the "i" (or underscore) and the letters of the word. You can **boldface** terms in a similar way, by typing Ctrl b before and after the word.

- **For long words**, such as complicated chemical names (eg., fructose 1,6 diphosphate) that you need to type repeatedly, use the AutoCorrect feature of Word. With AutoCorrect, you need to type the full expression only once. To work this miracle, begin by selecting Tools in the Word tool bar, and then select AutoCorrect. Think of a few letters you can use in place of "fructose 1,6 diphosphate." You are about to instruct Word to replace those few letters with the longer word whenever you type those code letters, so be sure that the simple combination of letters that you choose is not part of any other words that you type.

  For the previous edition of this book, the production department decided to replace the word "one" with the numeral "1" wherever those 3 letters occurred in my manuscript. In consequence I found myself reading, in the page proofs, such oddities as "some1 might notice," and cautioning writers to consider their "t1 of voice."

  The letters frc seem safe. Type those 3 letters into the Replace space in AutoCorrect. Then type "fructose 1,6 diphosphate" (without the quotation marks) into the With space. **Double-check your spelling before proceeding!** Then click Add, and then OK. Now, every time that you type the letters "frc" and hit the space bar, Word will automatically "correct" this to the name of the sugar that you programmed in.

  Keep a list—on a large index card, perhaps—of all the codes that you program in. Note that the AutoCorrect feature is case-sensitive; if you type "Frc" nothing will happen. You could separately program Frc to stand for "Fructose 1,6 diphosphate," something you might use at the start of a sentence.

- You can also train AutoCorrect to **automatically italicize** words for you.° Suppose you need to mention the sea urchin genus *Strongylocentrotus* many times in a report. This word must always be italicized because it is a formal

  (Continued)

Latin name. To have this happen automatically in Word, first click on the I symbol in the Word tool bar (to the right of the B for "boldface") to turn on italics and type the word on your screen. Then click on I again to turn italicizing off. Alternatively, you can type the word, highlight it, and then click the I symbol. Once the word is italicized, click Tools, and then Autocorrect. The generic name will already be visible in the With space. Click the "Formatted text" circle to the right of the With space, then click in the Replace space.

You could type the entire word "Strongylocentrotus" into the Replace space, but let's come up with a simpler code word instead, so that you'll never have to type this word again. "Sts" seems safe. Type those 3 letters into the Replace space of AutoCorrect (leaving out the quotation marks). Click on Add (double-check the spelling before you do this), and then on OK to exit the procedure. From now on, type Sts and you will instantly see *Strongylocentrotus* on your screen, spelled correctly and beautifully italicized, as soon you hit the space bar.

- You can also use AutoCorrect to **automatically format subscripts and superscripts**, as in the expression K_m, associated with enzyme kinetics. To automate this, first type Km, and then highlight just the "m." Then click on Format in the toolbar, select "Font" (probably the last place you'd look for help with subscripts and superscripts!), and then click "Subscript." Then click Tools and then AutoCorrect, select "Formatted text," and type Km in the Replace space. Then click Add, and then OK. From now on, whenever you type Km and hit the space bar you will automatically see K_m on your screen.

- You can play the same trick with **other specialized symbols** such as μm (micrometer), °C (degrees Centigrade), and ‰ (parts per thousand, referring to salinity). You might, for example, program AutoCorrect to print "μm" whenever you type "umc," or to print "‰" whenever you type "ppt." These and many other specialized symbols can be found by first clicking on Insert on the Word toolbar and then Symbol.

Note that if you program "um" as a default abbreviation for "μm," you will get μmbrella whenever you type the word "umbrella." The letters "umc" are a much safer choice. Again, be sure to keep a list of the codes that you have programmed.

Thanks to Karen Knisely for pointing this out.

ON USING COMPUTERS FOR DATA STORAGE, ANALYSIS, AND PRESENTATION

In addition to their use as word processors, computers are also used by many biologists for storing and retrieving literature references and for storing and analyzing data. Some data sets, particularly in ecology, are often too complex to analyze any other way. But undergraduate Biology majors will probably find that a set of notecards and a $30 scientific calculator will be perfectly adequate for anything they will be asked to do in most courses.

On the other hand, computers can be a real help in preparing your graphs and tables, as discussed in Chapter 8. Even so, you should not feel compelled to generate your figures and tables by computer; unless told otherwise by your instructor, hand-drawn graphs and tables should earn you as good a grade, provided they are carefully planned, sensible, and neatly executed.

Computers are also being used with increasing frequency in formal presentations in classes and at conferences. With appropriate software, you no longer have to prepare slides. All of your visual displays can now be created on and displayed from a laptop computer, in brilliant color, with palm tree backgrounds, and with titles and pointers sliding in from the sidelines at the push of a button as you talk. But again, unless teaching you how to use the technology is one of your instructor's goals, you can give a perfectly wonderful talk using the chalkboard or using simple overheads in black and white. **The substance of what you say and the extent to which you communicate that substance to your audience are what really matter.** Effective communication should always be your primary goal. For many of us, the more technologically impressive the presentation, the more skeptical we become about the quality of the work being presented. If you aren't careful, a high-tech presentation can be a barrier to effective communication, as discussed in Chapter 13.

SUMMARY

1. Acknowledge the struggle for understanding, and work to emerge victorious; read with a critical, questioning eye (pp. 5, 21–28, 122–123, 132–133, 220–221).

2. Think about where you are going before you begin to write, while you write, and while you revise (pp. 6, 76–81, 99–101, 132–133, 200–221).

3. Never miss an opportunity to practice summarizing information in your own words (pp. 6, 28, 30–37, 122–126).

4. Write to illuminate, not to impress (pp. 7, 76, 255).

5. Write for an appropriate audience: for example, your classmates and your future self (pp. 7, 84, 202).

6. Back up all statements of fact or opinion (pp. 7–8, 66–70, 183–185, 192, 202).

7. Always distinguish fact from possibility (pp. 9–10, 193–195).

8. Don't quote and don't plagiarize (pp. 5–6, 29–30).

9. Allow adequate time for revision (pp. 9, 75–76).

10. Stick to the point (pp. 9, 76, 135, 204, 254).

11. Say exactly what you mean (pp. 9–10, 81–92).

12. Never make the reader back up (pp. 10–11, 88–92, 99–103).

13. Be concise: avoid unnecessary words, unnecessary jargon, weak verbs, and unnecessary prepositions (pp. 11–12, 88–90, 92–99).

14. Avoid teleology (pp. 12, 103).

15. Save your computer work frequently—at least every few paragraphs—and always make a backup copy before ending a session.

16. Proofread all work before turning it in, and keep a copy for yourself.

17. Underline or italicize the scientific names of species.

18. Remember the word *data* is plural, not singular.

19. Make your papers neat in appearance, double-space all work, and leave margins for the instructor's comments and suggestions.

20. Put your name and the date at the top of each assignment, and number all pages.

21. When giving talks, never let style and technology become more important than the substance of what you are presenting (pp. 19, 252–262).

2

GENERAL ADVICE ON READING AND NOTE-TAKING

> The truth is that badly written papers are most often written by people who are not clear in their own minds what they want to say.
>
> John Maddox

WHY READ AND WHAT TO READ

Partly you are reading about biology to learn the facts that form the foundation of your field—what we know and how we know it. That's certainly why we read textbooks and other such "**secondary sources**"—sources that summarize the research findings of others. But for most writing assignments in upper-level biology courses, you are being asked to go beyond the factual foundations. You are being asked to interpret, to evaluate, to analyze, to synthesize, to ask new questions, and maybe even to design experiments to address those questions. This means that you will mostly be reading papers that describe the results of original observations and experiments—the so-called **primary literature** of biology.

EFFECTIVE READING

Too many students think of reading as the mechanical act of moving the eyes left to right, line by line, to the end of a page, and repeating the process page after page to the end of a chapter or an assignment. I call this "brain-off" reading. When the last page has been "read," the task is over and it's on to something else. This is, after all, the way we typically watch television: We sit transfixed before the television until the program has ended, and then either change the channel or turn the set off; we've "seen" the program. In the same way, students typically "listen" to a lecture by furiously copying whatever the instructor writes or says, without really thinking about the information as it is presented.

However, **if you hope to develop something worth saying in your writing, you must *interact* intellectually with the material**; you must become a "brain-on" reader, wrestling thoughtfully with every sentence, every graph, every illustration, and every table *as you read*. If you don't fully understand any element of what you are reading (including your lecture notes), you must work through the problem until it is resolved rather than skipping over the difficult material and moving along to something more accessible.

This is inevitably a time-consuming process, but you can do a number of things to smooth the way. Whether you are writing an essay or term paper, the introduction or discussion section of a laboratory report or research article, or the introduction to an oral presentation, always begin by carefully reading the appropriate sections of your textbook and class notes to get a solid overview of the general subject of which your topic is a part. It is usually wise to then consult 1 or 2 additional textbooks before venturing into the primary literature that reports the results of original research; a solid construction requires a firm foundation. Your instructor may have placed a number of pertinent textbooks on reserve in your college library. Alternatively, you can consult the library filing system, looking for books listed under the topic you are investigating. I will say more about locating appropriate sources at the end of this chapter (pp. 37–47). Science encyclopedias, such as the *McGraw-Hill Encyclopedia of Science and Technology*, are also excellent sources of factual information.

Armed with this background information, you are now prepared to delve into more advanced textbooks, review papers, and the primary research literature.

Reading a formal scientific paper is unlike reading a work of fiction or even a textbook or review article. The primary scientific literature must be read slowly, thoughtfully, and patiently, and a single paper must usually be reread several times before it can be thoroughly understood; don't become discouraged after only 1 or 2 readings. As with playing tennis or sight-reading music, reading the primary literature gets easier with practice. If, after several rereadings of the paper, and if, after consulting several textbooks, you are still baffled by something in the paper you are reading, ask your instructor for help.

As you carefully read each paper, pay special attention to the following:

- What specific questions were asked?
- How was the study designed, and how does the design of the study address the question posed?
- What are the controls for each experiment?
- What are the specific results of the study? How convincing are they? Are any of the results surprising?
- What contribution does this study make toward answering the original question?
- What aspects of the original question remain unanswered?

You can answer many of these questions just by studying the figures and tables in the Results section, as described below.

If you were planning to write a research proposal (Chapter 9) you would ask one additional question:

- What question(s) would I ask next?

READING DATA: PLUMBING THE DEPTHS OF FIGURES AND TABLES

Data—the most important parts of any book or journal article—are displayed either as figures or tables; it is important to develop the skills needed to examine these elements critically. Your goal here is to come to your own interpretation of the data so that you can better understand or evaluate the author's interpretation. To do this, you must study the data and ask yourself some questions about how the study was done, why it was done, and what the major findings were.

Consider the example shown in Figure 1, modified from a 1990 review paper entitled "Peptide regulation of mast-cell function," by David E. Cochrane. From your background reading or class lecture notes, you would probably know that mast cells release into the blood a variety of substances involved in provoking allergic and inflammatory responses. If you didn't already know this, you would do some background reading in your textbook before proceeding.

Looking at Figure 1, let us see if we can figure out what the researchers did to collect their data. By reading the axis labels, we learn that the graph shows how blood histamine concentrations changed

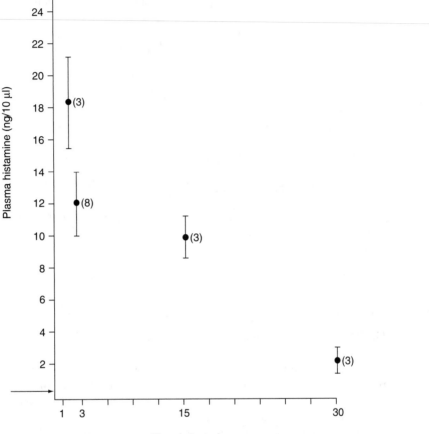

Figure 1. Plasma histamine concentrations in response to neurotensin (NT) given at t = 0. Rats were anesthetized and given NT (5 nmol/kg) or saline (0.3 ml) intravenously. Blood samples were collected at the indicated times. Each point represents the mean (± one standard error about the mean) of n values (given in parentheses). The horizontal arrow (lower left) shows the mean histamine concentration before addition of NT. Intravenous injection of saline did not alter this concentration over the 30-minute observation period. From Cochrane, D. E., 1990. Peptide regulation of mast-cell function. In *Progr. Medicinal Chemistry*, Vol. 27; G. P. Ellis and G. B. West, eds.; Elsevier Science Publ. (Biomedical Division), pp. 143–188.

over time, and we learn from the figure caption that these changes were provoked by a particular peptide called neurotensin (NT). The study was done on anesthetized rats, and all the action seems to have occurred rather quickly since the x-axis extends only to 30 minutes. Looking more closely, we see that histamine concentrations were initially quite low (less than 1 nanogram° per 10 microliters°° of blood plasma), as indicated by the arrow (at the lower left side of the graph), and that they rose impressively by the time the first blood sample was taken 1 minute into the study. Other blood samples were taken 3, 15, and 30 minutes after neurotensin was administered, and 3 to 8 separate samples were taken at each time period. Even without reading the figure caption and without seeing the numbers alongside each data point, we would know that replicate samples were taken, since the thin lines extending vertically from each point indicate the amount of variation seen about the mean value recorded for each sampling time; obviously one can see variation about a mean value only when multiple samples are taken.

What were the controls for this experiment? Apparently a number of rats were injected with a saline solution instead of with neurotensin, and blood samples were also taken from these rats at appropriate times.

So, we know quite a bit about how this aspect of the study was conducted just by scrutinizing the graph. It helps considerably that the graph and figure caption were carefully constructed. What additional information might you wish to have? Here are a few questions that might arise as you think about the figure.

1. How did Dr. Cochrane decide to inject NT at a concentration of 5 nmol/kg? Is this a physiologically realistic concentration?
2. How was histamine concentration determined?
3. How many rats served as controls for each time interval?
4. How old were the rats? What sex were they? Where were they obtained from?
5. How were the rats anesthetized, and might this pretreatment affect the response to NT?
6. With regard to the replicate samples, were 3 to 8 blood samples taken simultaneously from a single rat at each sampling time, or were

---

°1 nanogram (ng) = 10^{-9} gram.
°°1 microliter (μl) = 10^{-6} liter.

blood samples taken from 3 to 8 different rats each time? Blood samples were *probably* taken from a number of different individual rats, but we can't be sure from the graph.

7. Were different rats sampled at each time interval, or were the same individuals sampled repeatedly, for example, at 15 minutes and again at 30 minutes? One might guess that the same individuals were sampled repeatedly. On the other hand, there may be technical limitations to drawing blood from any individual rat more than once. Suppose, for instance, that a very large volume of blood was required to determine the histamine concentration. This issue leads to my last 3 questions.

8. What volume of blood was withdrawn for each sample?

9. How were the blood samples obtained?

10. Does drawing blood influence the production of histamine? How could one tell?

Asking such questions puts you in a good position to interpret the results illustrated and provides a framework for your later reading of the Materials and Methods section of the report; you can now enter the methodology section of the paper looking for the answers to specific questions.

If asked to describe how this aspect of the study was conducted and why the study was probably undertaken, how might you respond? Even without reading anything else in the paper, you could write the following summary:

```
      This study was apparently undertaken to deter-
mine the ability of the peptide neurotensin to
elicit histamine secretion from mast cells. A num-
ber of rats were anesthetized and then injected
intravenously with 5 nmol/kg* of neurotensin,
whereas others (control rats) received intravenous
injections of saline solution to control for the
possibility that the act of injection itself pro-
voked histamine release. Some quantity of blood
was withdrawn from a number of rats 1, 3, 15, or
30 minutes after injections were made, and the
histamine concentration in each blood sample was
somehow determined.
```

---

*nmol/kg = nanomoles per kilogram.

Now, in a few short sentences, let us try to summarize the results beginning with the most general statements we can make.

1. Neurotensin had a dramatic and rapid effect on histamine concentrations in the blood of laboratory rats, with histamine concentration increasing by about 20 times within 1 minute after injection.
2. The effect seems rather short-lived; only 2 minutes into the study the histamine concentrations had already fallen considerably from the peak level recorded 1 minute earlier.
3. By 30 minutes after the injection, the mean histamine concentration approached initial levels.
4. The effect shown is clearly due to the peptide rather than to the procedure itself, because histamine concentrations in the blood of control rats receiving saline injections did not change appreciably during the study.

You can approach tabular data in the same way, first reading the accompanying legends and column headings, and then asking yourself *how* the study was done, *why* it might have been undertaken, and *what* the key general results seem to be; if the tables were prepared with as much care as the figure we just looked at, you should be able to answer each of these questions.

Apply the same procedure figure by figure, table by table, until you reach the last bit of data. Now it is safe to actually read the text of the paper. Perhaps you will find the author reaching conclusions different from your own. You may have missed some crucial element in studying the data yourself, or perhaps you will learn something crucial in the text of the paper that was not made clear in the figure. If so, you can then happily leave your own opinion behind and embrace the author's. On the other hand, you may genuinely disagree with the conclusion reached by the paper's author (or authors), or you may object to the author's interpretation because of some concern you have about the method used. This is, in fact, how new questions often get asked in science, and how new studies get designed, each new step building on the work of others. Most of us will never have the final say in any particular research area, but we can each contribute a valuable next step, even if our individual interpretation of that step turns out to be mildly or even dramatically wrong.

Thinking about figures and tables in these ways, you may be on your way to a productive scientific career, research project in hand. At the very least, you will be in an excellent position to *discuss* the paper, on its own or in relationship to other studies that you will go on to scrutinize as thoroughly.

If you don't go through these steps in "reading" the data, you will be all too accepting of the author's interpretation. In consequence, you will have considerable difficulty avoiding the book report format in your writing, simply repeating what others did and what they say they found. You can move your work to a higher, more interesting plane (more interesting for you and the reader) by becoming a brain-on reader. It's tough slogging, and although it becomes considerably easier with practice, it never becomes trivial. But it does become fun, and satisfying, in the same way that a good tennis game can be fun and satisfying, even when played in hot, humid weather.

READING TEXT: SUMMARIZE AS YOU GO

Resist the temptation to copy your source's words verbatim, or simply to highlight them. Instead, try to summarize chunks of material as you read along. In that way, you will be processing the information as you read, and you will be one major step closer to having something interesting to write about later.

To summarize effectively, you must first determine the most important points in the material you wish to summarize. Consider the following paragraph from Rachel Carson's landmark book *Silent Spring*.° First published in 1962, this book marks for many people the start of the environmental movement.

> Water, soil, and the earth's green mantle of plants make up the world that supports the animal life of the earth. Although modern man seldom remembers the fact, he could not exist without the plants that harness the sun's energy and manufacture the basic foodstuffs he depends upon for life. Our attitude toward plants is a singularly narrow one. If we see any immediate utility in a plant we foster it. If for any reason we find its presence undesirable or merely a matter of indifference, we may condemn it to destruction forthwith. Besides the various plants

---

°I have not altered the original wording, with its anachronistic use of what is now generally considered to be sexist writing. If Rachel Carson was writing this today, she would most likely replace "modern man" with "people," and "he" with "we." This would actually strengthen the paragraph, by pointing the finger clearly at all of us.

that are poisonous to man or his livestock, or crowd out food plants, many are marked for destruction merely because, according to our narrow view, they happen to be in the wrong place at the wrong time. Many others are destroyed merely because they happen to be associates of the unwanted plants.

What are the key points in this paragraph? What information would upset Ms. Carson were we to leave it out?

- All animals, including people, depend on plants for food.
- People think little about the consequences of destroying plants that annoy them or don't seem to do anything useful.

Here is a possible one-sentence summary that incorporates both of these points:

```
People destroy any plant that happens to annoy
them or doesn't seem to do anything useful, for-
getting the extent to which all animal life ulti-
mately depends on photosynthesis.
```

This summary is (1) **accurate**, (2) **complete**—it incorporates all major points, (3) **self-sufficient**—it makes good sense even if the reader has never read the original text, and (4) **in my own words**. Get in the habit of writing such summaries as you read and as you take notes in lecture. It is a real challenge, but one that gets easier with practice. Persist: the eventual payoff is tremendous.

PLAGIARISM AND NOTE-TAKING

Plagiarism

The paper or report you submit for evaluation must be original: it must be *your* work. **Submitting anyone else's work under your own name is plagiarism**, even if you alter some words. **Presenting someone else's ideas as your own is also plagiarism.** Consider the following 2 paragraphs:

```
    Smith (1991) suggests that this discrepancy in
feeding rates may reflect differences in light in-
tensities used in the two different experiments.
Jones (1994), however, found that light intensity
```

> did not influence the feeding rates of these ani-
> mals and suggested that the rate differences re-
> flect differences in the density at which the ani-
> mals were held during the two experiments.
>
> This discrepancy in feeding rates might reflect
> differences in light intensities. Jones (1994),
> however, found that light level did not influence
> feeding rates. Perhaps the difference in rates re-
> flects differences in the density at which the ani-
> mals were held during the two experiments.

The first example is fine: every idea is clearly associated with its source. In the second example, however, the writer takes credit for the ideas of Smith and Jones; the writer has plagiarized.

Plagiarism is theft. It is one of the most serious offenses that can be committed in academia, where original thought is the major product of one's work—often months, sometimes years of physical and mental work. At the very least, an act of plagiarism will result in an F on the assignment, or for the entire course. Repeated plagiarism (but sometimes even a single offense) can get you expelled from college.

Take notes in ways that minimize the likelihood of plagiarism, as discussed below. An added benefit of these note-taking techniques is that you will come away with a much greater understanding of what you read, and much more substantive things to talk and write about.

Take Notes in Your Own Words

Plagiarism sometimes occurs unintentionally through faulty note-taking. Photocopying an article or book chapter does not constitute note-taking; neither does highlighting or even copying a passage by hand, occasionally substituting a synonym for a word used by the source's author. Take notes using your own words; you must get away from being awed by other people's words and move toward building confidence in your own thoughts and phrasings.

Note-taking involves critical evaluation; as you read, you must decide either that particular facts or ideas are relevant to your topic or that they are irrelevant. As Sylvan Barnet says in *A Short Guide to Writing about Art* (2003, Pearson Longman, seventh edition, p. 251), "You are not doing stenography; rather, you are assimilating knowledge and you are thinking, and so for the most part your source should be digested rather than engorged whole." If an idea is relevant, you should **jot down a summary using your own words**. Try not to write complete sentences as you take notes; this will help you avoid unintentional plagiarism later and will encourage you to see through to the essence of a statement while note-taking. For the same reason, try not to take notes or write while you are looking at the source.

Sometimes the authors' words seem so perfect that you cannot see how they might be revised to best advantage for your paper. In this case, you may wish to copy a phrase or a sentence or two verbatim, but be sure to enclose this material in quotation marks as you write, and clearly indicate the source and page number from which the quotation derives. If you modify the original wording slightly as you take notes, you should indicate this as well, perhaps by using modified quotation marks: ⸙. . .⸙. If your notes on a particular passage are in your own words, you should also indicate this as you write. I precede such notes, reflecting my own ideas or my own choice of words, with the word "*Me*" and a colon. If you take notes in this manner, you will avoid the unintentional plagiarism that occurs when you later forget who is actually responsible for the wording of your notes or who is actually responsible for the origin of an idea.

If you find yourself copying verbatim or paraphrasing your source, be sure it is not simply because you do not understand what you are reading. Be honest with yourself. **It is always best to summarize in your own words as you read along**; at the very least you should think your way to some good questions about what you are reading and write those questions down. Sooner or later, serious intellectual engagement is required; there are no shortcuts available here I'm afraid.

Here is an example of some notes taken using the suggested system of notation. These notes are based on a paragraph from Charles Darwin's *The Origin of Species* published in 1859. Accompanying the notes is the selection from Darwin's work on which the notes were based (Fig. 2). The notes (Fig. 3) were being taken for an essay on the mechanism of natural selection. Note that **the student has avoided using complete sentences**, focusing instead on getting the basic points and pinning down a few words and phrases that might be useful later. Notice also that **the student has taken notes selectively**, has found it unnecessary to quote any of the material directly, and **has clearly distinguished his or her own thoughts** from those of Darwin (by preceding such thoughts with "Me"). This student will not have to worry about accidental

It may be worth while to give another and more complex illustration of the action of natural selection. Certain plants◄―① excrete sweet juice, apparently for the sake of eliminating something injurious from the sap: this is effected, for instance, by glands at the base of the stipules in some Leguminosæ, and at the backs of the leaves of the common laurel. This juice, though small in quantity, is greedily sought by insects; but their visits do not in any way benefit the plant. Now, let us◄―② suppose that the juice or nectar was excreted from the inside of the flowers of a certain number of plants of any species. Insects in seeking the nectar would get dusted with pollen, and would often transport it from one flower to another. The flowers of two distinct individuals of the same species would thus get crossed; and the act of crossing, as can be fully proved, gives rise to vigorous seedlings which consequently would have the best chance of flourishing and surviving. The◄―③ plants which produced flowers with the largest glands or nectaries, excreting most nectar, would oftenest be visited by insects, and would oftenest be crossed; and so in the long-run would gain the upper hand and form a local variety. The flowers, also, which had their stamens and pistils placed, in relation to the size and habits of the particular insects which visited them, so as to favour in any degree the transportal of the pollen, would likewise be favoured. We might have taken◄―④ the case of insects visiting flowers for the sake of collecting pollen instead of nectar; and as pollen is formed for the sole purpose of fertilisation, its destruction appears to be a simple loss to the plant; yet if a little pollen were carried, at first occasionally and then habitually, by the pollen-devouring insects from flower to flower, and a cross thus effected, although nine-tenths of the pollen were destroyed it might still be a great gain to the plant to be thus robbed; and the individuals which produced more and more pollen, and had larger anthers, would be selected.

Figure 2. Taken from Charles Darwin's *The Origin of Species*, published in 1859, from which notes on the mechanism of natural selection were taken (see Fig. 3).

plagiarism when writing a paper based on these notes. Moreover, the student is well on the way to preparing a solid essay because the style of note-taking indicates clearly that the student has been thinking while reading.

Here is another example of good note-taking, based on a 1999 paper by William Biggers and Hans Laufer. Figure 4 shows an excerpt from the paper, and Figure 5 shows some notes based on that excerpt. As shown in Figure 5, the note-taker has clearly distinguished between his or her

Plant evolution tied to insect behavior. Flowers now = effective in attracting insects for pollen exchange; how did this system originate?

(1) Some plant sap apparently toxic (Me: no evidence given). Plant nectar makes sap less nasty. Insects attracted to the sweet nectar, even though produced by plant originally to protect plant.

(2) If plant produces nectar in flower, insects attracted to flower, thus transport pollen, facilitate cross-fert. Me: note that selection for nectar prod. in flower can occur only if a few plants accidentally start secreting nectar in flowers. Note that nectar not orig. prod. to attract insects; selected to protect plant, but once being produced, can evolve different function, sez Darwin.

(3) Those flowers that have the greatest success attracting insect will spread the most pollen. Me: now know that the genes of these flowers would thus have increased prob. of successful representation in next generation.

(4) Nectar prod. not essential to explain evol. of insect-mediated cross pollination. Suppose insect feeds on pollen (as some spp. do). Some pollen would stick to legs and be transferred to another flower. Again, flowers most successful in attracting insects would incr. chance of spreading genes, even though most of the pollen gets eaten.

Figure 3. Handwritten notes based on the passage shown in Fig. 2. Numbers in the margin correspond to the indicated portions of Figure 2.

thoughts and the authors' thoughts, and between what the authors have done and what the student thinks could be done later or might have influenced the results. Perhaps the most important points are that the note-taker clearly *thought* while reading and took notes in his or her own words.

Introduction

The chemoreception by marine invertebrate larvae of chemical "cues" that are present in the ocean environment and induce settlement and metamorphosis is important for the recognition of habitats that favor growth and reproduction (Chia and Rice, 1978; Rittschof and Bonaventura, 1986; Scheuer, 1990). These settlement signals appear to be specific for different species, as evidenced by findings that larvae of the abalone *Haliotis rufescens* respond to specific chemicals in red algae (Morse *et al.*, 1984), larvae of the nudibranch *Phestilla sibogae* respond to chemicals in corals (Hadfield, 1978, 1984), larvae of the polychaete annelid *Phragmatopoma californica* respond to chemicals present in the burrows of adult worms (Pawlik, 1988, 1990; Jensen and Morse, 1990), and larvae of the sand dollars *Dendraster excentricus* (Burke, 1984) and *Echinarachnius parma* (Pearce and Scheibling, 1990) respond to chemicals produced by adult sand dollars.

In previous studies, we have found that juvenile hormones (JH), which are known morphogens that regulate reproduction and development of insects and crustaceans (Laufer and Borst, 1983, 1988; Laufer *et al.*, 1987), as well as chemicals with juvenile hormone activity in insect cuticle bioassays, are able to induce settlement and metamorphosis of metatrochophore larvae of the polychaete annelid *Capitella* sp. I (Biggers and Laufer, 1992, 1996). In nature, larvae of *Capitella* sp. I are stimulated to settle and metamorphose when they come into contact with chemical inducers present in sediments (Butman *et al.*, 1988); although the identity of these chemicals remains in debate (Cuomo, 1985; Dubilier, 1987), they appear to have JH-activity (Biggers, 1994).

We have now investigated the signal transduction process through which the *Capitella* larvae respond to JH-active compounds. Our results presented in this paper indicate that JH-active compounds stimulate settlement and metamorphosis of these larvae through the activation of protein kinase C (PKC) and subsequent modulation of ion channels.

Materials and Methods

Capitella *larval settlement bioassays*

Stock cultures of *Capitella* sp. I were maintained at 18°C in artificial seawater (Utikem Co.) and washed sea sand (Fisher Scientific) and were fed Tetramin fish food flakes. Brood tubes containing adult females along with their developing eggs and larvae were then separated from the cultures and placed into 60-mm glass petri dishes containing seawater. The dishes were checked daily for hatched, swimming larvae to be used for bioassays. Stock solutions of juvenile hormone III (JH III), MF, phorbol-12,13 dibutyrate (PDBU), 1-(5-isoquinolinyl-sulfonyl)-2-methylpiperazine (H-7), arachidonic acid, elaidic acid, verapamil, 4-aminopyridine, and nigericin were prepared in 95% ethanol. Settlement and metamorphosis bioassays were conducted at 18°C using 60-mm glass petri dishes that were pre-baked at 250°C to remove contaminants (Biggers and Laufer, 1996). For the assays, 10 to 100 μl of the test chemical stock solutions were added by micropipet into petri dishes containing 10 metatrochophore larvae less than 1 day old (1 day post-release), and 10 ml of artificial seawater. The dishes were then observed. After 1 h, the amount of settlement and metamorphosis was assessed by placing each dish under a dissecting microscope and counting the number of settled larvae crawling on the bottom of the dish. Metamorphosis after 1 hour was also more critically assessed by using a compound microscope and noting the loss of cilia, elongation, and development of capillary setae.

Protein kinase C assays

Assays for the presence of protein kinase C were carried out essentially as described by Yasuda *et al.* (1990), by measuring phosphorylation of an 11-residue synthetic peptide from myelin basic protein (MBP_{4-14}). This method is specific for measurement of PKC, and permits selective measurement in crude tissue prepar-

Figure 4. Modified excerpt from "Settlement and metamorphosis of *Capitella* larvae induced by juvenile hormone-active compounds is mediated by protein kinase C and ion channels," by William J. Biggers and Hans Laufer (pp. 187–188) as reprinted from *The Biological Bulletin* 196 (1999):187–198. Reprinted with permission of *The Biological Bulletin* and the authors, William J. Biggers and Hans Laufer.

1. Marine larvae do not metamorphose until contact chemicals that indicate juveniles will do well here.

2. Larvae of different species respond to different chemicals.
   Me: How many diff. species have been looked at?
       Do we know what the chemical cues are? How (and where?) do the larvae sense them?

3. Larvae of the polychaete <u>Capitella</u> sp. I metamorphose in response to a juvenile hormone-like chemical in mud.
   Me: odd that same chemical works on both insects and worms?
       What distinguishes polych. from other annelids?
       And how big are these larvae? Microscopic I think ...

   Purpose of this study: How does the juvenile hormone make the larvae metamorphose?

4. Apparently the chem. cue activates "protein kinase C," which then either opens or closes ion channels somewhere (Me: calcium channels maybe?).

5. Methods: Collect larvae $\rightarrow$ expose to very small amounts of chemical ($\leq 100\ \mu l^*!$) $\xrightarrow{1\,hr}$ count number of larvae that have metam.'d.
   Nine chemicals tested (Me: must find out what each one does).
   * microliters

Figure 5. Handwritten notes based on the article by Biggers and Laufer (see Fig. 4). Numbers in the margin correspond to the indicated portions of Figure 4.

You cannot take notes in your own words if you do not understand what you are reading. Similarly, it is difficult to be selective in your note-taking until you have achieved a general understanding of the material. I suggest that you first consult at least one general reference textbook and read the material carefully, as recommended earlier. Once you have located a particularly promising scientific article, read the entire paper at least once without taking any notes. **Resist the (strong) temptation to annotate and take notes during this first reading** even though you may feel that without a pen in your hand you are accomplishing nothing. Put your pencils, pens, notecards, paper, or laptop computer away, and read. Read slowly and with care. Read to understand. Study the illustrations, figure captions, tables, and graphs carefully, and try to develop your own interpretations before reading those of the author(s). Don't be frustrated by not understanding the paper at the first reading; understanding scientific literature takes time and patience—and often many rereadings, even for practicing biologists. Concentrate not only on the results reported in the paper but also on the reason the study was undertaken and the way the data were obtained. The results of a study are real; the interpretation of the results is always open to question. And the interpretation is largely influenced by the way the study was conducted. Read with a critical, questioning eye. Many of the interpretations and conclusions in today's journals will be modified in the future. It is difficult, if not impossible, to have the last word in biology; progress is made by continually building on and modifying the work of others.

By the time you have completed your first reading of the paper, you may find that the article is not really relevant to your topic after all or is of little help in developing your theme. If so, the preliminary read-through will have saved you from wasted note-taking.

People differ in their note-taking styles. Some people suggest taking notes on index cards, with one idea per card so that the notes can be sorted readily into categories at a later stage of the paper's development. If you prefer taking notes on full-size paper, begin a separate page for each new source and write on only one side of each page to facilitate sorting into categories later. Similarly, if you enter notes directly into a computer, be sure to leave a few lines of space above and below each entry. Whatever system works best for you, that's the one to use. If your present system of note-taking is not working, experiment until you find one that does.

Split-Page Note-Taking: A Can't-Fail System

> Perfectly organized notes that cover everything are beautiful, but they live on paper, not in your mind.
>
> Peter Elbow

If you have trouble taking notes in your own words and thinking as you read, try split-page note-taking. With this system you divide a piece of paper into left and right halves, either by folding the paper in half lengthwise or drawing a line down the middle. On the left side of the page, write factual information as you read—preferably in your own words, but it's also okay to quote directly. Then on the right side of the page, write your response to the entry you just made on the left side. Try to respond to everything that you write on the left as you read. Your response could be a simple question ("What on earth is protein kinase C?"), a more thoughtful question ("How can they know that? First they would have had to measure. . . ."), a reminiscence ("That reminds me of what Professor Bolker said in lecture last week about. . . ."), or a comparison ("Interesting: the freshwater species have very different life histories."). Write whatever you happen to think of when you look at what you wrote on the left. See Figure 6 for an example of split-page note-taking in action, based on the first few paragraphs of the material presented in Figure 4.

Split-page note-taking may seem like a gimmick. Well, actually it is a gimmick, but it's a gimmick that works. It works by slowing you down, forcing you to think as you read. Split-page note-taking is also a very effective way to read tables and figures. Try it, for example, in looking at Figure 1 and its caption. Even experienced note-takers often find that they learn something new by taking notes this way.

Final Thoughts on Note-Taking: Document Your Sources

As you take notes, be sure to make a complete record of each source used: author(s), year of publication, volume and page numbers (if consulting a scientific journal), title of article or book, publisher, and total number of pages (if consulting a book). It is not always easy to relocate a source once it has been returned to the library stacks; in fact, the source you forgot to record completely is always the one that vanishes as soon as you realize that you need it again. Furthermore, before you finish with a source, it is good practice to read the source through one last time to be sure that your notes accurately reflect the content of what you have read.

LOCATING USEFUL SOURCES

Once you have carefully read the appropriate sections of your textbook and the relevant portions of your class notes to get a solid foundation, you are ready to delve into more specialized material. When seeking relevant books, you may have to become a little devious before you can convince your library's online catalog system to satisfy

Facts	Responses
marine invert. larvae are induced to metam. by chemical cues	True for _all_ larvae? How many species have been studied? The larvae are awfully tiny — what body parts "smell" the cues? What _are_ the cues?
Different species respond to diff. chem. cues	Must be pretty widespread. Examples given incl. a variety of species from very different groups.
Juvenile hormone (JH) regulates insect development, but also makes polychaete annelid larvae metamorphose	Why would juvenile hormone be floating around in seawater? Maybe it's not — maybe it's not the chem. cue discussed in first paragr. but rather something that acts inside the larva? Why would an insect chemical work on a worm? Are worms and insects closely related?

Figure 6. An example of split-page note-taking, based on the first 2 paragraphs of material presented in Figure 4. The student has recorded factual information on the left side of the page and her response to that information on the right.

your request for information. Suppose, for example, that you wish to find material on reptilian respiratory mechanisms. You might try, to no avail, looking under Respiration or Reptiles, but looking under Physiology or Comparative Physiology will probably pay off. Similarly, in researching the topic of annelid locomotion, you might try, unprofitably, searching under Annelids, Locomotion, or Worms; looking under Invertebrate Zoology will probably turn up something useful. Using a library's online catalog is like using the Yellow Pages of the telephone book; the phone number of the local movie house isn't found under a heading of Movies or Movie Theaters, but under Theaters, not the first place I'd look. If at first you don't succeed . . . consult with a reference librarian.

The references given in textbooks often provide good access to the primary research literature, as do those given in review articles. Especially good sources of reviews include *The American Zoologist, Biological Reviews, BioScience, Scientific American, Quarterly Review of Biology*, and the *Annual Reviews* series (e.g., *Annual Review of Ecology and Systematics; Annual Review of Genetics*). Once you locate a review on the topic you wish to explore, look carefully at citations used to support statements of particular interest. For example, consider this brief excerpt from a paper published recently in *Biological Reviews**:

> Chimpanzees perhaps make the most frequent and diverse use of tools in the wild (Goodall, 1973; Tomasello, 1990). Chimpanzees living in one region of West Africa use a pair of stones (a hammer and an anvil) to open oil-palm nuts (e.g., Sugiyama and Koman, 1979; Boesch and Boesch, 1983). The nut-cracking process is thought to be one of the most difficult learned tasks performed by any animal in the wild. Chimpanzees place a nut on a suitable stone or sometimes a root (the 'anvil') and hit it with a carefully chosen stone or piece of wood ('the hammer'). Chimpanzees not only transport hammers; some wooden hammers are made by the chimpanzees (Boesch and Boesch, 1990). One possibility is that the chimpanzees understand the logical structure of the task (Byrne, 1994) and the behaviour sequence (taking the stone into the hand, putting the nut on the . . .)

A student interested in the manufacture of tools by animals might add Boesch and Boesch 1990 to his or her list of papers to read. The title and complete reference for that paper will be found at the end of the article, in the Literature Cited section.

It is also profitable to browse through recent issues of specialized journals relevant to your topic; ask your instructor to name a few journals worth looking over, or ask your reference librarian for help in finding core journals in your research area. **If you find an appropriate article in the recent literature, examine the literature citations at the**

---

*Miklósi, A. 1999. The ethnological analysis of imitation. *Biol. Rev.* 74: 347–374.

end of the article for additional references, particularly those used to support statements of special interest made in the text of the article. This is an especially easy and efficient way to accumulate research material; the yield of good references is usually high for the amount of time invested.

Using Indexes

In 1968, over 130,000 biological research papers were published. In 1998, over 350,000 such papers were published. Thumbing through journals at random is not an efficient—or even feasible—way to conduct a thorough search of the literature. **For thorough and efficient searches on particular topics, use one or more indexing services.** These are currently available in both print and computerized form, although I wouldn't be surprised if the print versions of some services were terminated in the next few years because of cost and space considerations.

I will concern myself here primarily with computerized indexing services. In a matter of seconds, the computer will examine from 10 to 30 years or so of source material and give you a list of all references relevant to the information you provided; knowing how to input your search terms in a way the computer "understands" is the key. If your library has only the paper version of the services I discuss, ask your reference librarian for instruction on how to use them most efficiently, or consult the previous edition of this book (or the summary in Appendix I).

The most widely used indexing services are *Science Citation Index* (published by the Institute for Scientific Information), *Current Contents* (also published by ISI), *Medline* (produced by the U.S. National Library of Medicine), *Biological Abstracts* (published by BIOSIS), and *Basic BIOSIS*, a subset of *Biological Abstracts*. The distinctions among the computerized versions of these services are not nearly as great as those among the print versions. In particular, most now provide full abstracts of articles when these are made available by the journals. Another long-running indexer is *Zoological Record*, published jointly by BIOSIS and the Zoological Society of London. The main distinguishing feature of *Zoological Record* is that it provides a means of looking up articles by taxonomic group, geographic location, or geological time period. Because it is now possible to do some of these searches by keyword entry in other indexing programs, *Zoological Record* may be of greatest use in tracking down older references using the older printed volumes.

Using *Science Citation Index*

Science Citation Index (one of the products available within the ISI Web of Science, or the ISI Web of Knowledge) is a unique tool for locating recent references on a specific topic. To use this tool, you must first have located a key paper on the topic that was published at least 2 to 3 years ago. It might be a major review paper, for example, or a particularly interesting article in a major research journal. *Science Citation Index* allows you to find out what has happened subsequently, in that exact area, by listing more recent publications, with full citations, that cite your key paper in their Literature Cited sections. A paper that cites your key paper is likely to have built closely on your topic of special interest. So, through this means, you can quickly track a particular topic forward in time, from a paper published even 30 or 40 years ago to related papers published within the past year. Coverage extends back to 1945 (although many libraries do not have all years available), and about 17,750 new entries are added to the database each week, covering nearly 6,000 journals. But *Science Citation Index* can also help you to follow a topic even further back in time, since it will also list all of the papers that are cited in each of the references in its database.

Science Citation Index also allows you to search the database by subject (e.g., "parasite behavior"), author name, or journal title. But the ability to track particular topics forward (and backward) in time from an older key reference is what sets this service apart from others.

Using *Current Contents*

Current Contents essentially puts the best library in the world at your fingertips. Each weekly issue includes the complete table of contents for scientific journals published a few weeks earlier; nearly 1,000 different journals are covered by the publication, so you are not likely to miss much of the relevant literature, no matter how meager the holdings in your institution's library. If you encounter a paper of particular interest while browsing the latest issue of *Current Contents*, you can try to find that article in your library, or request a copy from your library's Document Delivery Service, if available. Failing that, you can request a copy of the paper from its author, as *Current Contents* lists the complete mailing addresses for authors of each article. You can also search the database by keyword, title, author, or journal name. As the title implies, the online database extends back only about 1 year.

Using Medline, Biological Abstracts, Basic BIOSIS, and BioDigest

Medline offers complete coverage of the biomedical literature back to 1966. *Biological Abstracts* offers broader coverage of biological topics. *Basic BIOSIS* covers the primary research literature using a smaller subset of journals. *BioDigest* indexes popular articles in a variety of fields. Search in each of these indexes by entering a keyword (e.g., coughing), phrase ("coughs induced by parasites"), or Boolean search string ("coughs and parasite and induced"); the name of an author; or the title of a particular journal or article.

Other useful computerized databases are:

- *Oceanic Abstracts*, which focuses on marine-related topics, including aquaculture, fisheries, and the effects of pollution
- *Agricola*, a database offered through the U.S. Department of Agriculture, including over 3 million records on agriculture and related topics from over 1,400 journals
- *Environment* and *Environment Abstracts*, both of which provide multidisciplinary coverage of publications in the environmental sciences
- *Toxline*, which focuses on the toxicological literature
- *Pollution Abstracts*
- *Geobase*, which indexes the geological and ecological literature
- *Index to Scientific Reviews*, which indexes more than 30,000 newly published review articles each year
- *Index to Scientific Book Contents*, which indexes the individual chapters of multiauthored scientific books
- *CAB Abstracts*, which covers the fields of forestry, agriculture, animal health, human health and nutrition, and the conservation of natural resources.

Please note that computer databases rarely include references to papers published before 1965; in most areas of biology, **the older literature is a valuable and important resource** that should not be overlooked. Thus, thorough searches of the literature must never be limited to computer-based services.

Your university librarian can tell you which of these services is available at your school, and how to access each of them.

Prowling the Internet

Although there are many ways to cruise the information superhighway, the World Wide Web (www) probably offers the easiest access. There is a phenomenal amount of information out there in the ether, and the amount is growing at a truly astounding rate. In 1998 about 200,000 Web sites were available. Now there are well over 500 million sites, and thousands of new sites are added weekly. There are over 100 billion pages of information currently on the Web.

This abundance of information creates both opportunities and problems. Prowling the Web can eat up your time the way a vacuum cleaner sucks up dirt. And that is a rather good analogy, because much of what is on the Web is not worth reading. Information presented in formal scientific journals and many books has gone through a rigorous peer-review process; other scientists have evaluated and often shaped the information that is ultimately presented, and in some cases, kept it from being published. But most of the information available through the Internet has not been checked for accuracy. The old adage "Don't believe everything you read" applies with a vengeance to most of what you will find on the Web. **Don't use any information presented on the Web that isn't offered by a recognized authority on the subject or that you can't verify using other sources**.

Some Web sites are well worth visiting, but you must choose your sites carefully. The most reliable information can be found through the Web sites of museums, recognized research organizations (e.g., the Marine Biological Laboratory in Woods Hole, MA, and major research universities), scientific societies, and government agencies (e.g., The World Health Organization, and the National Oceanic and Atmospheric Administration[NOAA]).

See Appendix H for additional information about evaluating Web sites.

In addition, the past few years have seen the birth—and rapid growth—of on-line journals. Papers published in these "virtual" journals are generally subjected to the same review procedures that are applied to papers published in hard-copy journals. Nevertheless, there are many uncertainties about the future of on-line journals, including who will pay for them, how to prevent people from altering the data after they have been presented, and how to determine whether individual papers will be maintained in a permanent database.

In the meantime, many existing print journals have begun offering additional full-text on-line access through the Web. A listing of all journals currently offered on-line can be found at *www.scicentral.com*. This site also provides access to numerous other biological databases, including organism-specific gene sequences and a range of standard protocols in molecular biology. In addition, the American Institute of Biological Sciences (AIBS) now provides Internet full-text access to more than 60 biological and environmental journals in a project called BioOne (*www.bioone.org*), first released in 2001. Every journal article in BioOne is linked to other relevant articles within the database, making it very easy to assemble related references on particular topics.

In addition, the special collections area at the Northern Light Web site (*www.northernlight.com*) provides immediate access to articles (for a small fee) in *Ecology, The Lancet,* and many other leading scientific journals. A Web site offered by Encyclopaedia Britannica, Inc. (*www.britannica.com*) provides links to numerous biology Web sites, each of which is rated with a star system for accuracy and relative value. First Search's NetFirst also provides links to numerous biology-related Internet resources, including individual Web pages, all screened for quality. Finally, Elsevier Science launched an interesting new site in 2001 called Scirus (*www.scirus.com*), a search engine focused exclusively on science-related information and providing access not only to research article citations but also to the home pages of individual university and government researchers. Check with your instructor or reference librarian to find out what is available and recommended at your school.

Conducting Web Searches: Developing Productive Search Strategies

There are two other ways to search for information on the Web. To conduct a "directory" search, start with a main topic area (e.g., Biology) and gradually narrow your search down step by step. From Biology, for example, you might click on the subtopics Neurobiology or BioDiversity, and then narrow the topic further within each of those subtopics. Yahoo! (*www.yahoo.com*) and the Librarian's Index to the Internet (*www.lii.org*) are particularly good sites for conducting this type of "directory" search.

Alternatively, you might want to conduct a keyword search, in which you enter terms or phrases related to your subject of interest. The trick here is to limit your search so that you bring back a manageable number of references (See Table 1). Entering "Effects of para-

Table 1. Commonly used terms for limiting your computer searches. Check the help pages within specific search engines for additional information.

Term	Example	Effect
AND	parasites AND flatworm	Returns only sites referring to both terms
OR	parasites OR flatworm	Returns sites referring to either term
NOT	parasites NOT flatworm	Returns sites referring to parasites, except those referring to flatworms
°	paras°	Returns sites referring to parasite, parasites, parasitism, parasitic—all terms that begin with "paras," no matter how they end
" "	"parasites in amphibians"	Returns only entries containing the exact phrase

sites on salmon growth rates" for a search using AltaVista (*www. altavista.com*), for example, brought up listings for over 26 million Web pages! That's ridiculous! If I were interested in finding out more about the effects of parasites on salmon growth rates, I might conduct an advanced search and enter the following to better advantage: Parasites AND salmon AND "growth rate." The "AND" is a connector telling the search engine that I am interested only in pages covering all 3 issues. In place of "AND," you could instead enter a plus sign before each term. The quotation marks around "growth rate" tell the search engine to look for that entire phrase, not just the isolated words "growth" and "rate." This entry hauled in only 102 Web pages, a far more manageable number. The most relevant pages are usually the first ones on the list, assuming that you chose the right keywords to search with. Similarly, when I typed "pollution" as a keyword, I unearthed hundreds of thousands of Web pages. But limiting my search using connectors and entering terrestrial AND vertebrates AND pesticides AND NOT frogs, I found 159 Web pages. The "AND NOT" tells the search engine to ignore everything concerned with frogs. Alternatively, I could have conducted the same search using plus and minus signs (e.g., + terrestrial + vertebrates − frogs). Google (*www. google.com*) and Scirus (*www.scirus.com*) are also excellent engines for conducting keyword searches. Each of these search engines monitors millions of different Web sites. As mentioned earlier, Scirus is focused exclusively on scientific material. By clicking on the Advanced Search feature of Scirus you can selectively search journal sources or Web sites, can select the types of sources to be searched for (e.g., articles, abstracts, conference materials, books, researcher home pages), and restrict your search to particular subject areas (e.g., Life Sciences) and years.

At most sites, including Yahoo!, you can begin with a directory search, and then, once you get the topic sufficiently focused, you can switch to a keyword search. For example, starting with a directory search and clicking first on Science and then on Biology (or Life Sciences), I could then type the keyword "journals" in the search box and gain access to on-line journals in the area of interest.

Use several different search engines to conduct each Web search, as the different engines cover remarkably different databases.

For highly specialized searches on rather obscure topics, you may want to use a "metasearch" engine that explores the catalogues of Web sites offered by a variety of other search engines. Metacrawler (*www.metacrawler.com*), for example, explores the databases of dozens of other search engines simultaneously, while All in One (*www.allinone.com*) allows you to choose particular search engines in sequence. Using Metacrawler, I entered the term "echiuran," the name of a very small and somewhat obscure group of marine worms, and got 29 hits. Narrowing the search to "feeding AND echiurans," I narrowed the list to 4 Web pages.

The Web is growing in size and complexity with such rapidity that I can give only very general advice about Web searches here. For more specific information, visit any of the sites listed in Appendix H. I am guessing that they will be updated more frequently than this book.

In addition, AltaVista, Google, Yahoo!, and most other search engines provide detailed advice about how best to conduct searches using their databases. You can access this advice from their home pages.

Final Thoughts about Efficient Searching: Technology Isn't Everything

Cruising the Web is fascinating and a lot of fun, and it's always exciting to be using the latest technology. But you can easily spend hours prowling the Internet and return with little of value, especially compared with what you could have gained from spending the same amount of time reading books or looking through current issues of relevant journals. Not only is much on the Web not worth reading, but most of it is also ephemeral. Web sites appear and disappear, and the information at any particular site can change daily. How can you substantiate any statement of fact or opinion with anything so impermanent? You can't. Searching the Web is a great way to find inexpensive airfares and textbooks and reviews of the latest movies. It's also an excellent way to learn about particular graduate programs and the research being done by the faculty in those programs. But it's a generally untrustworthy source of information for formal papers and research reports. Unless your instructor says otherwise, or asks you to visit specific Web sites relevant to your course, do not cite Web pages as references, other than those of on-line journals and the other sources mentioned earlier (pp. 43–44).

Remember, **your goal in conducting a literature search is generally to collect a small number of high-quality references that you will then read carefully** so that you can discuss them with conviction. Returning from a voyage on the Internet bearing hundreds or thousands of references creates only an illusion of accomplishment. Yes, you've downloaded many gigabytes of information. But the real work, and the really useful work, comes after you select your references and sit down to read them. Make sure you give yourself plenty of time for that job.

CLOSING THOUGHTS

Printed indexing services, *Current Contents*, and computerized databases are all good sources of references, but there is a major catch: your library will probably not subscribe to all the journals included in the literature searched by the various services. Although *Current Contents* provides a partial solution to this problem for very recent literature, you must wait from one to many weeks before having the actual research paper in hand. You may thus spend considerable time accumulating a long list of intriguing references, creating the comforting illusion that you are getting something done, only to discover that most of the listed journals are not to be found on your campus or in any other nearby library. **Consulting recent issues of available, appropriate journals may thus be the most efficient way to find promising research topics and associated references for most undergraduate writing projects.**

SUMMARY

1. Become a brain-on reader: work to understand your sources fully, sentence by sentence, figure by figure, and table by table.

2. Take notes thoughtfully. In particular, practice summarizing information as you go along. Your summary must be accurate, complete, self-sufficient, and in your own words.

3. In your note-taking, be careful to distinguish your words and thoughts from those of the author(s) to avoid unintentional plagiarism. Be sure to record the complete citation information for everything on which you take notes.

4. Be efficient in exploring the primary scientific literature: browse the list of references given in your textbook and in other relevant books and the papers published in recent issues of relevant scientific journals.

5. Become familiar with the major abstracting and indexing services, including computerized databases, and use these as necessary to complete your literature search. Be cautious about the validity of information posted on the Internet, and don't be so dazzled by the Internet that you confuse downloading information with reading and understanding it.

3

READING AND WRITING ABOUT STATISTICAL ANALYSES

It is difficult to read the primary biological literature without running into statistics. And it is virtually impossible to draw conclusions from most laboratory or field studies involving numerical data without subjecting those data to statistical analysis. In this brief chapter I explain why biologists use statistics, what is meant by the terms *statistical analysis* and *statistical significance*, how to interpret the probability values ("P values") reported in formal research reports, and how to incorporate the results of statistical analyses into your own reports. This chapter is no substitute for a full course in biostatistics, but it will get you off to a good start. Appendix E lists some additional references on this topic.

STATISTICAL ESSENTIALS

Variability and Its Representation

Variability is a fact of biological life: Student performance on any particular examination varies among individuals; the growth rate of tomato plants varies among seedlings and from place to place and year to year, or even week to week; the toxicity of a particular concentration of a particular pollutant varies among species, and among individuals within a species; the respiration rate of mice held under a given set of environmental conditions varies among individuals; the number of snails occupying a square meter of substrate varies from place to place and from one year to the next; the extent to which a particular chemical enhances or suppresses the transcription of a particular gene varies from test tube to test tube; the amount of time a lion spends feeding varies from day to day and from lion to lion. Some of the variability we inevitably see in our data reflects unavoidable imprecision in the making of measurements. If you measure the length of a single bone 25 times to the nearest millimeter (mm), for example, you will probably not end up with 25 identical measurements. But much of the variability recorded in a study reflects real biological differences among the individuals in the sample population. Put identical meals in front of 20 people at a restaurant, and few of these people will finish their meals at the same time. Moreover, the amount of food consumed will probably also vary quite a lot among individuals. This sort of natural variability is referred to as "error" by statisticians, but it isn't "error" in the sense of "making mistakes." It's better to think of such variation as natural "scatter" in the data (Motulsky, 1995; see Appendix E).

Variability, whether it be in the responses you measure in an experiment or in the distribution of individuals in the field, is no cause for embarrassment or dismay, but it cannot be ignored in presenting or interpreting results.

Suppose you have 2 samples of 4 rats each. The rat tail lengths in samples A and B are

$$A = 7.2, 7.0, 6.8, 7.0 \text{ cm}$$

$$B = 3.6, 12.5, 3.3, 8.6 \text{ cm}$$

Both samples have the same mean value (7.0 cm), but the tails in sample A are much less variable in length than those in sample B. Simply listing the mean value, then, would omit an important component of the story contained in the data.

Listing the mean and the range of values obtained in each sample would help, but presenting the variance (σ^2) about the mean would give an even better indication of how much the data vary from one observation to the next. These days, variance is usually calculated using a statistical calculator or computer, but for small sample sizes the variance is not difficult to calculate by hand. Here is the formula:

$$\sigma^2 = \frac{\sum_{i=1}^{N}(X_i - \overline{X})^2}{N - 1}$$

N is the number of observations made, X_i is the value of the ith observation, and $\overline{X}$ is the mean value of all the observations made in a sample.

Σ is the symbol for summation. In this case, you are to sum the squared differences of each individual measurement from the mean of all the measurements. As an example, suppose you have the following data points:

$$5 \text{ cm}$$
$$4$$
$$4$$
$$6 \quad N = 5$$
$$5$$

$$\overline{X} = \frac{\sum\limits_{i=1}^{N}}{N} = \frac{24}{5} = 4.8 \text{ cm}$$

$$\sigma^2 = \frac{(5 - 4.8)^2 + (4 - 4.8)^2 + (4 - 4.8)^2 + (6 - 4.8)^2 + (5 - 4.8)^2}{4}$$

$$= 0.7$$

All we are doing is seeing how far each observation is from the mean value obtained and adding all these variations together. The squaring is done simply to eliminate minus signs so that we have only positive numbers to work with. Clearly, 100 measurements should give a more accurate estimation of the true mean tail length than only 10 measurements, and, if we had the time and the patience, 1,000 measurements would be better still. We thus divide the sum of the individual variations by a factor related to the number of observations made. Increasing the sample size will reduce the extent of experimental uncertainty. Variance, then, is a measure of the amount of confidence we can have in our measurements. The smallest possible variance is zero (all samples were identical); there is no upper limit to the potential size of the variance.

People do not generally report variance per se, but rather something related to the variance—either the standard deviation, the standard error, or the "95% confidence interval."

To calculate the standard deviation (SD), simply take the square root of the variance.

To calculate the standard error of the mean (SEM), simply divide the standard deviation by the square root of N.

Unlike standard deviations and standard errors, the related "95% confidence interval" has inherent meaning. If you were to repeat an experiment 100 times and calculate a mean result for each one, you can expect 95 of those means to fall within the calculated confidence interval. For sample sizes larger than about 15, the 95% confidence interval is approximately twice the standard error of the mean.

When Is a Difference a Meaningful Difference?
What You Need to Know about Tomatoes,
Coins, and Random Events

Suppose we plant 2 groups of 30 tomato seeds on day 0 of an experiment, and the individuals in group A (N = 30) receive distilled water, whereas those in group B (N = 30) receive distilled water plus a nutrient supplement. Both groups of seedlings are held at the same temperature, are given the same volume of water daily, and receive 12 hours of light and 12 hours of darkness (12L:12D) each day for 10 days. Twenty-six of the seeds sprout under the group A treatment, and 23 of the seeds sprout under the group B treatment. At the end of 10 days, the height of each seedling is measured to the nearest 0.1 cm, and the data are recorded on the data sheet, as shown in Figure 7. Note that the units (cm; sample size) are clearly indicated on the data sheet, as is the nature of the measurements being recorded (height after 10 days). The number of samples taken, or of measurements made, is always represented by the symbol N.

The question now is this: did the mineral supplement affect the seedlings' growth rates? That is, did it make a difference in the height of seedlings by the 10th day after planting?

If all the group A individuals had been 2.0 cm tall and all the group B individuals had been 2.4 cm tall, we would readily conclude that growth rates were increased by adding nutrients to the water. If each group A individual had been 2.3 cm tall and each group B individual had been 2.4 cm tall, we might again suggest that the nutrient supplement improved the growth rates of the seedlings. In the present case, however, there was considerable variability in the heights of the seedlings in each of the 2 treatments, and the difference in the average heights of the 2 populations was not large with respect to the amount of variation found within each treatment. The heights of group A seedlings differed by as much as 1.0 cm (2.8 − 1.8), and the heights of group B seedlings differed by as much as 0.8 cm (2.8 − 2.0), whereas the average height differences between the 2 groups of seedlings was only 0.1 cm (2.4 − 2.3).

The average height of the seedlings in the 2 populations is certainly different, but does that difference of 0.1 cm in average height reflect a real, biological effect of the nutrient supplement, or have we simply not planted enough seeds to be able to see past the variability inherent in individual growth rates? If we had planted only one seed in each group, the 2 seedlings might have both ended up at 2.6 cm; some seedlings reached this height in both treatment groups, as seen in Figure 7. On the other hand, the one seed planted in group A might have been the one that grew

Group A seedlings: water only
(height, in cm, after 10 days)

2.1 cm, 2.1, 2.0, 2.8, 2.7, 2.4, 2.3, 2.6,
2.6, 2.5, 2.1, 2.8, 2.0, 1.9, 2.8, 2.0,
2.2, 2.6, 1.8, 2.0, 2.2, 2.5, 2.4, 2.3, 2.1, 2.

Average = 2.3 cm; N = 26 measurements

Group B seedlings: water plus
nutrients (height, in cm, after
10 days)

2.6 cm, 2.1, 2.0, 2.4, 2.8, 2.6, 2.2, 2.7,
2.4, 2.4, 2.3, 2.2, 2.4, 2.6, 2.4, 2.8,
2.6, 2.5, 2.6, 2.4, 2.6, 2.3, 2.4

Average = 2.4 cm; N = 23 measurements

Figure 7. Data sheet with measurements recorded. Note that units of measurement are indicated clearly.

to 2.8 cm, and the one seed planted in group *B* might have been one of the seeds that grew only to 2.2 cm. Or it might have turned out the other way around, with the tallest seedling appearing in group *B*. Clearly, a sample size of one individual in each treatment would have been inadequate to conclusively evaluate our hypothesis. Perhaps 30 seeds per sample is also inadequate. If we had planted 1,000 seeds, or 10,000 seeds, in each group, the differences between the 2 treatments might have been even less than 0.1 cm—or the differences might have been substantially greater than 0.1 cm. If only we had planted more seeds, we might have more confidence in our results. If only we had measured 100,000 individuals, or 1,000,000 individuals, or. . . .

But wishful thinking has little place in biology; we have only the data before us, and they must be considered as they stand. Is the difference between an average height of 2.3 cm for the group *A* seedlings and 2.4 cm for the group *B* seedlings a real difference? That is, is the difference statistically significant? Or have we simply conducted too little sampling to see through the variability in individual results?

Here is another way to look at the problem. Suppose you stand at the doorway to the Biology or Science building on campus, and measure the heights of the first 10 men and the first 10 women to enter the building after you arrive at your post. You want to determine whether the men and women on your campus differ, on average, in height. You calculate the mean height for each of the 2 groups and find that the means differ. But then you measure the average heights of the next 10 men and the next 10 women who enter the building, and you find that the average heights of the first and second groups of men also differ from each other, as do the average heights of the first and second groups of women. How can you trust the measured difference in heights between men and women when you get different averages from one group of men to the next and from one group of women to the next? That's why we need statistics. We need statistics whenever we are subsampling from a population in which individuals vary naturally in the traits that we are measuring, or whenever individual measurements—of size, reaction rates, survival, growth, amounts of transcription or translation . . . anything that can be measured— vary from replicate to replicate. Statistics now infiltrate nearly every area of biology.

As an additional example, suppose we have crossed plants producing yellow peas with other plants also producing yellow peas, and, from knowledge of the parentage of these 2 groups of pea plants, we expect their offspring to produce yellow or green peas in the ratio of 3:1. Suppose we actually count 144 offspring that produce yellow peas and 45 offspring that produce green peas so that slightly more than 3 times as many of the offspring produce yellow peas. Do we conclude that our expectations have been met or that they have not been met? Is a ratio of 3.2:1 close enough to our expected ratio of 3:1? Is the result (144 yellow-producing plants + 45 green-producing plants) statistically equivalent to the expected ratio?

As one final example, suppose we wish to know whether there is a pronounced relationship (a "correlation") between the weight of hermit crabs of a particular species and the size of the shells they occupy in the field. We carefully remove 12 hermit crabs from their shells, weigh the crabs, and then measure the shells they had been living in. The data are shown in Figure 8. Is there a relationship between hermit crab weight and shell size or not? How confident can we be in predicting shell size if we know only a hermit crab's weight?

Establishing a Null Hypothesis

Biologists use statistical tests to determine the significance of differences between sampled populations, or differences between the results expected and those obtained. To begin, we typically define a specific issue (hypothesis) to be tested. The hypothesis to be tested is called the null hypothesis, H_0. The null hypothesis usually assumes that nothing unusual will happen in the experiment or study; that is, it assumes that the treatment (addition of nutrients, for example) will have no effect, or that there will be no differences between the results we observe and the results we expect to observe. Examples of typical null hypotheses are:

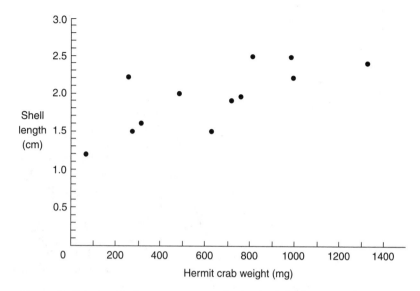

Figure 8. Relationship between wet weight (mg) of the hermit crab *Pagurus longicarpus* and the size of the periwinkle shells (*Littorina littorea*) occupied at Nahant, MA, on September 23, 2002 (N = 12).

H_0: The seedlings in groups *A* and *B* do not differ in height (or the addition of nutrients does not alter growth rates of the seedlings).

H_0: The seed color of offspring does not differ from the expected ratio of 3:1.

H_0: There is no relationship between hermit crab weight and the size of the shells they occupy in the field.

H_0: Juniors did not do better than sophomores on the midterm examination.

H_0: Activation of a particular intracellular enzyme does not alter neuronal survival rate in cell culture.

H_0: There is no relationship between wing mass and body mass in the locust *Schistocerca gregaria*.

H_0: The amount of the steroid corticosterone released into the blood by starlings in response to stress does not vary seasonally.

It may seem surprising that the hypothesis to be tested is the one that anticipates no unusual effects; why bother doing the study if we begin by assuming that our treatment will be ineffective, or that there will be no differences in eye color, or that wing lengths will not differ from population to population? For one thing, the null hypothesis is chosen for testing because scientists must be cautious in drawing conclusions. **Hypotheses can never be proved; they can only be discredited or supported**, and the strongest statistical tests are those that discredit null hypotheses. Therefore, the cautious approach in testing the effect of a new drug is to assume that it will not cure the targeted ailment. The cautious approach in testing the effects of different diets on the growth rate or survival rate of a test organism is to assume that all diets will produce equivalent growth or survival—that is, that one diet is not superior to the others tested. The cautious approach in testing the effects of a pollutant is to assume that the substance is not harmful. Only if we can discredit the null hypothesis (the hypothesis of no effect) can we tentatively embrace an alternative hypothesis—for example, that a particular drug *is* effective, or that wing lengths *do* differ among populations, or that a pollutant *is* harmful.

Please understand that **evidence against the null hypothesis does not *prove* that it is incorrect**. Neither does it *prove* that the alternative hypothesis is correct. Similarly, **failure to reject the null hypothesis does not *prove* that the null hypothesis is correct**, or that the alternative hypothesis is incorrect. Therefore, **we must choose our words with great care when reporting the results of statistical tests**. This is tricky business, which I will try to clarify in the next section.

Conducting the Analysis and Interpreting the Results

Once we have established our null hypothesis and collected the data for our study, statistical analysis of the data can begin. A large number of statistical tests have been developed, including the familiar chi-square test, the Student's t-test, and tests for correlation. The test that should be used to examine any particular set of data will depend on the type and amount of data collected and the nature of the null hypothesis being addressed. If you are asked to conduct a statistical analysis of your data, your laboratory instructor will undoubtedly specify the test for you. Once the appropriate test is chosen, the data are maneuvered through one or more standard, prescribed formulas to calculate the desired test statistic. This test statistic may be a chi-square value, a t-value, an F-value, or any of a variety of other values associated with different tests; in all cases, the calculated test value will be a single number, such as 0.93 or 129.8. A calculated value close to 0 suggests that the data from the experiment are consistent with the null hypothesis (little deviation from the outcome expected if the null hypothesis is true). A value very different from 0 indicates that the null hypothesis may be wrong, because the data obtained are very different from those that would be expected if the null hypothesis were true.

Returning to our seedling experiment, we wish to determine if the addition of certain nutrients alters seedling growth rates; the null hypothesis states that the nutrients have no effect. The appropriate test for this hypothesis is the t-test. Applying the formula provided in statistics books, the value of the t-statistic calculated for the data obtained in our tomato seedling experiment turns out to be 1.62 (or -1.62; the sign makes no difference). This particular value has some probability of turning up if the null hypothesis is true. Here the argument gets a bit tricky. If we repeated the experiment exactly as before, using another set of 60 seeds, we would most likely obtain a somewhat different result and the t-statistic would have a different value, even though the null hypothesis might still be true. If we did 5 identical experiments, we would probably calculate 5 different t-values from the data. In other words, a statistic may take on a broad range of values even if the null hypothesis is correct, and each of these values has some probability of turning up in any single experiment. But some values are more likely to turn up than others.

Suppose the null hypothesis stating that the addition of nutrients does not alter the growth of tomato seedlings over the first 10 days of observation is actually correct. If we ran our experiment (with 30 seeds planted in each of the 2 treatment groups) 100 times, we might actually find no measurable difference between the average heights of the seedlings in some of the experiments; our calculated t-values for these data would then be 0. In most of the experiments, we would probably record small differences between the average sizes of seedlings in the 2 populations (and, for each of these experiments, calculate a t-value close to 0), and in a few experiments, purely by chance, we would probably record large differences (and calculate t-values very different from 0, either much larger or much smaller). All these results are possible if we do enough experiments, even though the null hypothesis is correct, simply because the growth of seedlings varies even under a single set of experimental conditions. The oddball result may not come up very often, but there is always some probability that it will pop up in any given experiment. If we do only one experiment, we have no way of knowing whether we got an odd result, or how odd our result is.

The important point here is that the outcome of an experiment or study can vary quite a lot, regardless of whether or not the null hypothesis is correct. A nonbiological example may help clarify this point. In coin tossing, a fair coin should, on average, produce an equal number of heads and tails. Yet experience tells us that 10 tosses in a row will often produce slightly more of one result than the other. Every now and then, we will actually end up tossing 10 heads in a row, or 10 tails in a row, even though the coin is perfectly legitimate; neither of these results will occur very often, but each will occur eventually if we repeat the experiment enough times.

Yes, the fact of the matter is that there is considerable morphological, physiological, and behavioral variability in the real world, and that the only way to know, with certainty, that our one experiment is a true reflection of that world is to measure or count every individual in the population under consideration (for example, plant every tomato seed in the world, and measure every seedling after 10 days) or conduct an infinite number of experiments. This is not a practical solution to the problem. The next best alternative is to use statistical analysis. Statistics cannot tell us whether we have revealed THE TRUTH, but they can indicate just how convincing our results are (or aren't), and guide the direction of future studies.

The numerical value of any calculated test statistic has some probability of turning up when the null hypothesis is true. Statisticians tell us, for example, that values of t are distributed as in Figure 9, and that values of chi-square (χ^2) are distributed as in Figure 10. **If the null hypothesis is correct, values of each statistic will usually fall within a certain range**, as indicated; these values will have the greatest probability of turning up in any individual experiment. If the t-value calculated for our experiment falls within the range indicated as "very common," we are probably safe in accepting the null hypothesis; at least we have no reason to disbelieve it. However, even if the null hypothesis is correct, very unusual values of t or of χ^2 will occasionally occur. We are, after all, randomly picking only a few seeds to plant out of a bag that may contain many thousands of seeds; it could be just our bad luck to have picked only those seeds that are most unlike the average seed.

If we calculate a very unusual (very far from 0) value for t using the data from our experiment, how can we decide to reject the null hypothesis when we know there is still some small chance that H_0 is correct and that we have simply witnessed a very rare event? Well, we must admit that we are not omniscient. **We must be willing to take a certain amount of risk in drawing conclusions from our data; the amount of risk taken can be specified.** Typically, researchers assume that if their very unusual (that is, far from 0) value of t (or of some other statistic) would turn up fewer than 5 times in 100 repetitions of the same ex-

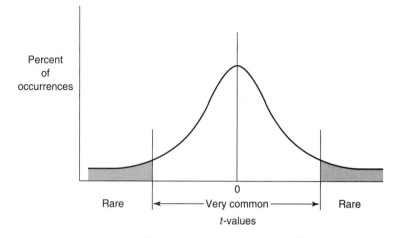

Figure 9. The distribution of t-values expected when the null hypothesis (H_0) is true. The exact shape of the distribution depends on the number of degrees of freedom, which increases with sample size. A wide range of values may occur, but some values will occur more commonly than others. Obtaining a common value for t causes us to provisionally accept H_0. Obtaining a rare value for t causes us to doubt the validity of H_0.

periment when the null hypothesis is true, then this oddball value of t is a strong argument *against* the null hypothesis being correct; H_0 is then tentatively rejected. That is, the large calculated value of t would be so rarely encountered if the null hypothesis is true that the null hypothesis is *probably* wrong. However, there is still the 5 in 100 chance that the null hypothesis is correct and that the researchers, through random chance, happened upon atypical results in their experiment. Tossing 10 heads in a row using a fair coin won't happen very often, but it *will* happen. Tossing 100 heads in a row is an even rarer event, but it could happen. If you conducted only one tossing experiment of 100 flips and tossed only heads, you could tentatively reject the null hypothesis that the coin is fair. But you wouldn't know with certainty that you were correct. Would you bet your car, your savings account, your little finger, or your stereo that you would get all heads if you did another round of 100 tosses? Only if the coin has 2 heads.

Sometimes researchers will be even more cautious in rejecting H_0 and reject it only when there is less than a 1 in 100 chance of doing so incorrectly. Then you will need a very unusual value of t indeed (unusual if

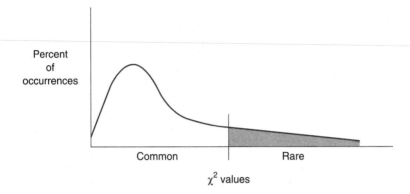

Figure 10. The distribution of χ^2 values expected when H_0 is true. The exact shape of the distribution depends on the number of degrees of freedom. A wide range of values may occur, but some values will occur more often than others. The rarer the value obtained, the less confidence we can have in the validity of H_0.

H_0 is true) before rejecting the null hypothesis. The downside, of course, is that by making it harder to reject H_0, you make it more likely to accept H_0 when in fact H_0 is wrong. There is no win–win situation available in this game.

It is, I hope, becoming clear why experiments must be repeated many times, and with much replication within an experiment, before the results become convincing. Such is the challenge of doing biology. Only when large values of a test statistic appear many times can we become fully confident that the null hypothesis deserves to be rejected. Only when low values appear many times can we become confident that the null hypothesis is most likely correct.

Degrees of Freedom

The exact shape of statistical distributions like those shown in Figures 9 and 10 varies slightly with something called "degrees of freedom" (abbreviated "d.f."), which is related to sample size and/or the number of treatments included in the study. As a simple example, consider a t-test comparing the means of 2 columns of numbers (e.g., the final heights of seedlings with and without added nutrients, or the number of moles of product formed after 5 minutes of an enzymatic reaction at 2 temperatures). Suppose we have 10 replicates in one column and 9 replicates in the other—somebody dropped one test tube and lost that sample. For the first column of data, if we know 9 of the numbers and the mean of all 10, then the 10th number has no freedom to vary—knowing the mean locks that last number into a particular value. Thus, each time we calculate a mean we lose one degree of freedom. In calculating 2 means, we lose 2 degrees of freedom; in our example, then, the number of degrees of freedom is $(10 + 9) - 2 = 17$. For the data shown in Figure 7, d.f. = $(26 + 23) - 2 = 47$. The important point is that the exact shapes of the t and χ^2 distributions shown in Figures 9 and 10 (and those for other statistics as well) are different for different degrees of freedom. Thus, the cutoff between common and unusual values for any statistic if H_0 is true differs among experiments with different sample sizes. As discussed earlier, in using statistical tables to determine the numerical cutoff value, then, you need to know the number of degrees of freedom in your analysis as well as the degree of risk you are willing to assume for incorrectly rejecting H_0.

SUMMARY: DOING STATISTICS

In performing a statistical test you first decide on a reasonable degree of risk (usually 5% or less) of incorrectly rejecting the null hypothesis (and incorrectly accepting an alternative hypothesis). Then you perform the study, plug the data into the appropriate formula to calculate the value of the appropriate statistic, and end up with a single number. You then look in the appropriate statistical table (using the correct number of degrees of freedom) to see whether this number is within the range of values expected when the null hypothesis is correct. If your number lies within the expected range of values, your data support (but do not prove) the null hypothesis. If your number lies outside the range of commonly expected values, your data do not support H_0; they support (but do not prove) the alternative. Remember, there is always some small chance that you are making the wrong decision by rejecting H_0. Similarly, when your number lies within the range of commonly expected values, there is always some chance that you are making the wrong decision by accepting H_0. For this reason, biologists never seek to *prove* any particular hypothesis; we can only accumulate data that either favor or argue against the null hypothesis.

READING ABOUT STATISTICS

When you read the results of statistical analyses in a published research paper, you don't need to understand how the particular calculations were made in order to understand what the results mean. A small P-value means that if the null hypothesis were true, we would find a difference as large as the one found in that study very rarely. "$P < 0.001$" means that such a large difference would be expected by chance fewer than 1 time in 1000 repeats of the study, if H_0 is true. Thus, the null hypothesis is probably wrong. A large P-value means that the researchers obtained a difference about the size expected if the null hypothesis were true. "$P = 0.28$," for example, means that the results would turn up at least 28 times out of 100 repeats of the experiment if H_0 is true. Thus, the researchers can't reject H_0 with confidence, and must retain it for the time being as part of a work in progress.

WRITING ABOUT STATISTICS

If you have analyzed your data using appropriate statistical procedures, the products of your heavy labor are readily and unceremoniously incorporated into the Results section of your report to support any major trends that you see in your data, as in the following 3 examples. **Note that in Example 1, the author reports the sample size (N = 30 caterpillars), the test statistic and its value, the number of degrees of freedom (d.f.) associated with the test, and the size of the associated P-value.** Note also that the writer focuses on the biology being studied—the biological question being addressed—rather than on the statistics themselves.

EXAMPLE 1

For 30 caterpillars reared on the mustard-flavored diet and subsequently given a choice of foods, the caterpillars showed a statistically significant preference for the mustard diet ($\chi^2 = 17.3$; d.f. = 1; $P < 0.05$). For 30 caterpillars reared on the quinine-flavored diet, however, there was no significant influence of previous experience on the choice of food ($\chi^2 = 0.12$; d.f. = 1; $P > 0.10$).

In this example, H_0 states that prior experience does not influence the subsequent choice of food by caterpillars; "$P < 0.05$" means that if we were to conduct the same experiment 100 times and H_0 were true, such a high value for χ^2 would be expected to occur in fewer than 5 of those 100 studies. In other words, the probability of making the mistake of rejecting H_0 when it is, in fact, true is less than 5%. You can therefore feel reasonably safe in rejecting H_0 in favor of the alternative: that prior experience did influence subsequent food selection for caterpillars reared on the mustard diet.

Different results were obtained, however, for the caterpillars reared on the quinine-flavored diet; $P > 0.10$ means that if the experiment were repeated 100 times and H_0 were true, you would expect to calculate such a small value of χ^2 in at least 10 of the 100 trials. In other words, the probability of getting this χ^2-value with H_0 true is rather high; certainly the χ^2-value is not unusual enough for you to mistrust H_0 and run the risk of rejecting the null hypothesis when it might, in fact, be true. **This does not mean that H_0 is true, only that we do not have enough evidence to reject it**. The quinine-flavored diet may have altered dietary preference—the variability in response may simply have been too great for us to perceive the effect with the small number of caterpillars used in our study. It is also possible, of course, that the diet on which caterpillars were fed affected food choices in ways that we did not test for. Thus, the wording in Example 1 was very carefully chosen to say no more than it is safe to say.

EXAMPLE 2

```
Over the first 10 days of observation, growth of
seedlings receiving the nutrient supplement was
not  significantly  faster  than  the  growth  of
the seedlings receiving only water (t = 1.62;
d.f. = 47; P = 0.11).
```

In this second example, the writer has chosen to report the actual P-value, rather than writing "$P > 0.10$." The null hypothesis (H_0) states that the nutrient supplement does not influence plant growth; "$P = 0.11$" means that if the experiment were repeated 100 times and H_0 were true, you would expect to calculate such a low value of t in 11 of the 100 trials. As before, you have obtained a value of t that would be fairly common if H_0 were true and so have no reason to reject H_0. It is, of course, possible that H_0 is actually false and the nutrients really do promote seedling growth, and that you just happened upon an unusual set of samples that gave a misleadingly small t-value. If such is the case, repeating the experiment should produce different results and larger t-values. But with only the data before you, you cannot reject H_0.

EXAMPLE 3

The hermit crabs in our sample (N = 12) showed a significant relationship between their wet weights and the size of the shells they occupied in the field (r^2 = 0.477; test for zero slope: F = 9.104; d.f. = 1.12; P = 0.013).

In this case, hermit crab weight and shell size were correlated (the slope of the line relating the 2 variables differs significantly from zero), even though variation in hermit crab weight accounted for only 47.7% of the variation in the sizes of the shells occupied (this is the meaning of the r^2 term).

Note carefully how the word "significant" was used in the above examples, **and that the writers put the focus clearly on biology**; they said very little about the statistics themselves. Statistics are used only to support any claims you wish to make about your results, as in examples 1–3; resist the temptation to ramble on about how the statistics were calculated, how brilliant you are to have figured out which calculations to make, or how awful it was to make them.

Compare the first 3 examples with the following 2 examples.

EXAMPLE 4

Wrong:

A chi-square value of 6.25, with a P of 0.0124 revealed that the physical condition of the shell had a significant influence on shell choice by the 15 hermit crabs used in our study.

Corrected:

The physical condition of the shell had a significant influence on shell choice by the hermit crabs (χ^2 = 6.25, d.f. = 1, N = 15 hermit crabs, P = 0.0124).

EXAMPLE 5

Wrong:

A Student's *t*-test was used to determine the significance of the difference in mean interaction times. The data were not significant (i.e., we found no significant results in our experiment), and there was no difference in the mean contact

```
time between hermit crabs in the presence or ab-
sence of predators.
```

Analysis:

The first sentence, of course, should not be there at all. With the second sentence, the student has fallen into the very common trap of confusing the results of a significance test with the value of the data, or of the study itself ("the data were not significant . . ."). There is nothing wrong with the data. **Don't apologize for results that support H_0. Failure to discredit H_0 does not mean that your experiment was a failure**. If your sample size was small and the amount of natural variability was high, then it is very hard to discredit null hypotheses even when H_0 is wrong.

The student in this example then uses the results of a significance test to make a definitive pronouncement ("there was no difference in . . ."), by omitting the word "significant" from the sentence. As discussed earlier, statistics do not prove things, they only indicate degrees of likelihood. "No significant difference" is not the same thing as "No difference." And, of course, the student provides no statistical support for the final statement made.

Corrected:

```
The presence of a predator did not significantly
affect the amount of time that hermit crabs spent
interacting with each other (t = 1.012, d.f. = 12,
P = 0.332).
```

For more detailed advice about discussing "negative" results (i.e., those that fail to reject H_0) see Chapter 8, on Writing a Discussion section.

4

CITING SOURCES AND LISTING REFERENCES

As described briefly in Chapter 1, all statements of fact and opinion require support to be convincing to the thoughtful, critical reader. The firmer the statement, and the more important it is to your argument, the greater the need for support. In laboratory and other research reports, term papers, and theses, factual statements are supported by reference to the source (or sources) of the facts presented. Therefore, in a separate section, at the end of your presentation, you must list the books, research articles, and Web sites referred to so that they can be located by the interested (or skeptical) reader.

CITING SOURCES

Here are a few general rules to follow when citing sources to back up factual statements. These rules apply to term papers, theses, and research reports, and to all parts of the research report:

1. **Don't footnote: cite by author and year of publication**. In most papers published in biological journals, references are cited directly in the text, by author and year of publication, as in the following example:

   ```
   A variety of organic molecules are commonly used
   to maintain or adjust the osmotic concentration
   of  intracellular  fluids  (Hochachka  and  Somero,
   1984; Schmidt-Nielsen, 1990).
   ```

   When more than 2 authors have collaborated on a single publication, a shortcut is standard practice:

   ```
   A mutation is defined as any change occurring in
   the nitrogenous base sequence of DNA (Tortora et
   al., 1982).
   ```

The *et al.* is an abbreviation for *et alii*, meaning "and others." The words are underlined or italicized, even when abbreviated, because they are in a foreign language, Latin; underlining tells a printer to set the designated words or letters in italics. Note that in each of the examples given, **the period follows the closing parenthesis, since the reference, including the publication date, is part of the sentence.** Where appropriate, you may incorporate the authors' names directly into a sentence:

```
Kim (1976) demonstrated that magnetic fields es-
tablished by direct current can alter the rates of
enzyme-mediated reactions in cell-free systems.
```

or:

```
The ability of magnetic fields established by di-
rect current to alter the activity of certain
liver enzymes was first demonstrated by Kim
(1976).
```

If you cite 2 papers published in a single year by the same author, use letters to distinguish between them: (Asmodeus and Li, 1998 a, b) or (Asmodeus *et al.*, 1999 a, b).

Try to make the relevance of the cited reference clear to the reader. For example, rather than writing:

```
Temperature tolerances have been determined for
gastropods,   bivalves,   annelids,   and   insects
(Merz, 1988; Heibert Burch, 1998; Merz and Heib-
ert Burch, 1993 a, b).
```

it would be clearer to write:

```
Temperature tolerances have been determined for
gastropods (Merz, 1988), bivalves and annelids
(Heibert Burch, 1998), and insects (Merz and
Heibert Burch, 1993 a, b).
```

You can cite your laboratory manual by its author (for example, Professor S. Heibert Burch, 1999) or as follows:

```
Preparation of buffers and other solutions is de-
scribed elsewhere (Biology 1 Laboratory Manual,
Swarthmore College, 1999).
```

If your information comes from a lecture or from a conversation with a particular individual, support your statement as follows:

```
California gray whales migrate up to 18,000 km
yearly (Professor William Morgan, personal commu-
nication, September 2002).
```

In some biological journals, the "author–year" format for citing references has been replaced by a more compact "number–sequence" format. In the number–sequence format, each reference cited in the paper is represented by a unique number. The first paper to be cited is assigned the number 1, the second paper to be cited is assigned the number 2, and so forth, as in the following example:

```
Substantial declines in amphibian populations
have been documented from numerous locations
around the world over the past 40 years (3,5,
8-12).
```

The numerals 3 and 5 represent the 3rd and 5th references to have been cited in the student's paper. Earlier in the paper the author must have cited references 1–7. References 3 and 5, although cited earlier in the paper, are relevant here and so are cited again using the same numbers.

    Unless your instructor asks you to adopt this format in your own work, use the author–year format discussed earlier. For one thing, it is a nuisance for the reader to have to keep turning to the back of a paper to see whose work is being cited. Moreover, biologists commonly refer to particular papers by their author(s) and year of publication ("Have you read Wolcott and Wolcott, 2002, yet?"), and using the author–year format of citing references helps you remember who did what, and when. But perhaps most importantly, research papers are written by real people, and as you become more familiar with the literature in any particular field, you will find yourself coming across many of the same names repeatedly. Using the author–year format is a good way to learn which people are best associated with your field of interest. Perhaps you will decide to do graduate work with one of these people in the future.

2. **Be concise in citing references**. Avoid writing:

```
In his classic work, The Biology of Marine Ani-
mals, published in 1967, Colin Nicol reviewed the
literature on invertebrate bioluminescence.
```

Instead, write:

```
The phenomenon of invertebrate bioluminescence
has been carefully reviewed by Nicol (1967).
```

Again, the period follows the parenthesis.

3. **Cite only those sources you have actually read and would feel confident discussing with your instructor**. Don't list references simply to add bulk to this section of your report; your instructor is perfectly justified in expecting you to be able to discuss any material you cite. Listing a few references you have thoughtfully incorporated into your paper should do more for your grade than any attempt to create the illusion that you have read everything in the library.

   You may occasionally have to cite a source that you have not actually read. For example, results reported by Hendler (1999) may be cited in a book or article written by Dufus (2003), and you have read only the work by Dufus. Your citation should then read, "(Hendler, 1999, as cited by Dufus, 2003)." Let Dufus take the blame if he or she has misinterpreted something. In the Literature Cited section of your report, you would include both sources.

4. **Avoid citation overkill**. When discussing a series of facts from a single source or group of sources, it is not necessary to cite the same source(s) in every sentence. There are many ways of informing the reader that a series of sentences is based on a single source of information, as in the following example:

```
Hochachka and Somero (1984) discuss the physio-
logical adaptations in diving mammals in consid-
erable detail. In particular they note that div-
ing Weddell seals exhibit a pronounced decline in
both rate of metabolism and ATP turnover rate. In
one experiment, ATP turnover rates were reduced
by as much as 50% during a 20-minute dive.
```

SUMMARY OF CITATION FORMAT RULES

- Use the author–year format for citing references unless told otherwise by your instructor, or unless you are submitting a manuscript to a journal using a different (number-citation) format.
- Cite authors only by their last names, unless you include in your paper citations by 2 authors sharing a last name, e.g., Bilbo Baggins and Frodo Baggins. In such a case, distinguish between the

2 authors by using the first letter of the first name; e.g., B. Baggins, 1946.

- Cite work by 2 authors using the last names of both (e.g., Fraga and Iyengar, 2000).
- Cite work by 3 or more authors using only the last name of the first author, followed by *et al.* (meaning, "and others").
- If you must cite a reference that you have not read, do it as follows: (Tankersly, 1995, as cited by Rittschof, 1999).
- Cite information provided directly by your instructor (orally or through e-mail) as follows: (J. Bolker, personal communication, Oct. 2003).

PREPARING THE LITERATURE CITED SECTION

Whenever you cite sources to support statements, you must provide a separate Literature Cited section, giving the full citations for each source cited. This presentation enables the interested reader, including, perhaps, you, at a later date, to locate and examine the basis for factual statements made in your report. It occasionally happens that a reference is used incorrectly; your interpretation or recollection of what was said in a textbook, lecture, or journal article may be wrong. By giving the source of your information, the reader can more easily recognize such errors. If the reader is your instructor, this list of references may provide an opportunity for him or her to correct any misconceptions you may have acquired. If you fail to provide the source of your information, your instructor will have more difficulty in determining where you went wrong. Proper referencing is even more crucial in scientific publications. Misstatements of fact are readily propagated in the literature by others; the Literature Cited section of a report enables a reader to verify all factual statements made, and the careful scientist consults the listed references before accepting statements made by other authors.

Listing the References

Include only those references that you have actually read (see p. 69 for one exception to this rule) **and that you specifically mention in your report or paper**, and include all of the references that you cite. Unless you are told otherwise by your instructor, list references in alphabetical order according to the last name of the first author of each publication. If you cite several papers written by the same author, list them chronologically. If one author has published 2 papers in the same year, list them as, for example, Hentschel, B. 1995a, and Hentschel, B. 1995b.

Each listing must include the names of all authors, the year of publication, and the full title of the paper, article, or book.

In addition, **when citing books**, you must report the publisher, the place of publication, and the pages referred to, or the total number of pages in the book.

When citing journal articles, you must include the name of the journal, the volume number of the journal, and the page numbers of the article consulted.

When citing Internet sources, you must include the date that the material was posted (or the most recent revision date), the date you accessed the material, and the full URL for the Web site.

Unfortunately, there is no single acceptable format for preparing this section of a report; formats differ from journal to journal, despite the best efforts of the Council of Science Editors (CSE). A few rules, however, do apply to most journals:

Spell out only the last names of authors; initials are used for first and middle names.

Include the names of all authors, even though the names of only one or at most 2 authors (for example, Woodin *et al.*, 1995; Svane and Havenhand, 1994) are cited in the text of the report.

Latin names, including species names, are italicized, or underlined to indicate italics.

Titles of journal articles are not enclosed within quotation marks.

Journal names are usually abbreviated. In particular, the word *Journal* is abbreviated as *J.*, and words ending in *-ology* are usually abbreviated as *-ol*. The *Journal of Zoology* thus becomes *J. Zool.* Do not abbreviate the names of journals whose titles are single words (for example, *Science* or *Evolution*). Acceptable abbreviations for the titles of journals can usually be found within the journals themselves.

The most important rule in preparing the Literature Cited section is to **provide all the information required and to be consistent in the manner in which you present it**. When preparing a paper for publication, you should religiously follow the format used by the journal to which your entry will be submitted.

TECHNOLOGY TIP   2
Producing Hanging Indents

To produce the "hanging indent" format shown in the examples below, open the Format menu in the Word tool bar, and then click on "Paragraph" and then on the arrow associated with the term "Special" toward the right side of the layout. Then select "hanging indent" and specify how much you would like to indent (0.3" works well). Click OK to leave the menu and you're ready to roll—I mean indent. Alternatively, you can type all the references first, and then highlight them. Next open the Format menu, select Paragraph, open Special, and then choose the hanging indent option and specify the amount of indenting that you want.

The following examples should be helpful in preparing the Literature Cited section of your report. Note that the citation begins at the far left, and that subsequent lines are indented several spaces to the right. This format is called a "hanging indent" (see Technology Tip 2, above, to learn how to do this automatically in Microsoft Word).

LISTING JOURNAL REFERENCES

Biernbaum, C. K. 1996. Biogeography of coastal and anchialine amphipods of Ascension Island, South Atlantic Ocean. *J. Nat. Hist.* 30: 1597–1615.

Jarrett, J. N. 1997. Temporal variation in substratum specificity of *Semibalanus balanoides* (Linnaeus) cyprids. *J. Exp. Mar. Biol. Ecol.* 211: 103–114.

Twombly, S., Burns, C.W. 1996. Effects of food quality on individual growth and development in the freshwater copepod *Boeckella triarticulata. J. Plankton Res.* 18: 75–82.

Woodin, S. A., Lindsay, S.M., Wethey, D.S. 1995. Process-specific recruitment cues in marine sedimentary systems. *Biol. Bull.* 189: 49–58.

LISTING BOOK REFERENCES

Campbell, N. A. 1999. *Biology*, 4th ed. Addison-Wesley, NY, pp. 136–142.

LISTING AN ARTICLE FROM A BOOK

Thompson, S. N. 1997. Physiology and biochemistry of snail-larval trematode relationships. In: *Advances in Trematode Biology* (Fried, B., Graczyk, T.K., eds.). CRC Press, NY, pp. 149–195.

LISTING A LABORATORY MANUAL OR HANDOUT

Biology 13 Laboratory Manual. 2000. Exercise in enzyme kinetics, pp. 16–23. Tufts University, Medford, MA.

Bernheim, H. 2002. Principles of physiology, using insects as models. II. Excretion of organic compounds by Malpighian tubules. Biology 50 Laboratory Handout. Tufts University, Medford, MA.

LISTING ITEMS FROM THE WORLD WIDE WEB

As explained in Chapter 2 (pp. 43, 46–47), information posted on Web sites is ephemeral and has usually not been peer-reviewed: avoid using Web pages as sources of information unless you are fully confident of the accuracy of the material presented. In general, this means relying only on peer-reviewed electronic journals or Web sites maintained by recognized scientific authorities, such as those associated with major museums and research institutions, or government organizations such as the U.S. Department of Agriculture (USDA), the National Oceanic and Atmospheric Administration (NOAA), and the World Health Organization (WHO).

World Health Organization. Malarial mortality in Africa. 3 July 2001. *<http://www.who.int/rbm/Presentations>*. [accessed 2003 May 5]

If you know the author of the information, you should cite the author's name rather than the institutional name. For the latest information on citing Web sources, see *http://www.councilscienceeditors.org/pubs_citing_internet.shtml* and *www.bedfordstmartins.com/online/cite8.html*

SAMPLE LITERATURE CITED SECTION

A sample Literature Cited section follows, with items arranged alphabetically and chronologically. Your instructor may specify a different format for this section of your report, so check first if you are uncertain.

Literature Cited

Bayne, B. L., Livingstone, D. R., Moore, M. N., Widdows, J. 1976. A cytochemical and biochemical index of stress in *Mytilus edulis* L. *Mar. Poll. Bull.* 7: 221–224.

Biology 220 Laboratory Manual. 2002. Exercise in enzyme kinetics, pp. 16–23. College of Wooster, OH.

Eyster, L. S., Morse, M. P. 1984. Early shell formation during molluscan embryogenesis, with new studies on the surf clam, *Spisula solidissima. Amer. Zool.* 24: 871–882.

Finch, C. E., Rose, M. R. 1995. Hormones and the physiological architecture of life history evolution. *Q. Rev. Biol.* 70: 1–52.

Fox, D. S., Heitman, J. 2002. Good fungi gone bad: the corruption of calcineurin. BioEssays 24 (10): 894–903. TDNet database. [accessed 1 Jan. 2003]

Haas, W., Haberl, B. 1997. Host recognition by trematode miracidia and cercariae. In: *Advances in Trematode Biology* (B. Fried and T. L. Graczyk, eds.), CRC Press, NY, pp. 197–227.

Havenhand, J. H. 1993. Egg to juvenile period, generation time, and the evolution of larval type in marine invertebrates. *Mar. Ecol. Progr. Ser.* 97: 247–260.

Lima, G. M., Lutz, R. A. 1990. The relationship of larval shell morphology to mode of development in marine prosobranch gastropods. *J. Mar. Biol. Ass. U.K.* 70: 611–637.

Purves, W. K., Sadava, D., Orians, G. H., Heller, H. C. 2000. *Life: The Science of Biology*, 6th ed. Sinauer Assoc., Sunderland, MA, pp. 374–379.

Quinn, G. P., Keough, M. J. 2002. *Experimental design and data analysis for biologists.* Cambridge University Press, NY, 537 pp.

Wray, G. A. Echinodermata. 14 Dec. 1999. *<http://tolweb.org/tree?group=Echinodermata&contgroup=Metazoa>.* [accessed 1 Jan. 2003]

5

REVISING

Something that looks like a bad sentence can be the germ of a good one.
                                                        Ludwig Wittgenstein

What a very difficult thing it is to write correctly.
                                                        Charles Darwin, 1837

Much of this book concerns the reading, note-taking, thinking, synthesizing, and organizing that permit you to capture your thoughts and your evidence in a first draft. This chapter concerns the revising that must follow, in which you examine the first draft critically and diagnose and treat the patient as necessary. I typically revise my own writing 4 or 5 times before letting anyone else see it and several more times after it has been reviewed by others, so don't feel inadequate for not producing flawless prose on your first or second draft. Successful writers aren't necessarily more gifted than you are; most of them just revise more often.

Writing a first draft gives you the opportunity to get facts, ideas, and phrasings on paper, where they won't escape. Once you have captured your thoughts, you can concentrate on reorganizing and rephrasing them in the clearest, most logical way. **All writing benefits from revision.** For one thing, the acts of writing and rereading what you have written typically clarify your thinking. Then, too, there is the universal difficulty in getting any point across (intact) to a reader, even when you finally know precisely what it is that you *want* to say. Revising your work improves communication and often leads you to a firmer understanding of what you are writing about.

It is difficult to revise your own work effectively unless you can examine it with a fresh eye. After all, you know what you wanted to say; without some distance from the work, you can't really tell whether or not you've actually said it. For this reason, **plan to complete your first draft at least 3 days before the final product is due, to allow time for careful revision**. Reading your paper aloud—and listening to yourself as you read—often reveals weaknesses that you would otherwise miss. It also helps to have one or more fellow students carefully read and comment on your draft at this stage of its development; it is always easier to identify writing problems—wordiness, ambiguity, faulty logic, faulty organization, spelling and grammatical errors—in the work of others, so forming a peer-editing group is a clear step toward more effective writing. Be sure to tell readers of your work that you sincerely want constructive criticism, not a pat on the back. Remember, **your goal as a writer is to communicate**, clearly and succinctly, making it as easy as possible for readers to follow your argument. Your goal as a reader of someone else's draft is to help its author do the same. At the end of this chapter, you will find advice on how to be an effective reviewer.

Choose whatever system works best for you, but always revise your papers before submitting them. No matter how sound, or even brilliant, your thoughts and arguments are, it is the manner in which you express them that will determine whether or not they are understood and appreciated (or, in later life, whether they are even read). With pencil or pen at the ready (and scissors and tape, too, if you are not using a computer), the time has come to edit your first draft: for content, for clarity, for conciseness, for flow (coherence), and for spelling and grammar. If you are writing with a word processor, make at least your first set of revisions on printed copy rather than on-screen; to edit effectively, you must see more than one screen of text at a time. Continue editing and revising—printout by printout—until your work is ready for the eyes of the instructor, admissions committee, or potential employer. This chapter should help you know when you have arrived at that point.

PREPARING THE DRAFT FOR SURGERY: PLOTTING IDEA MAPS

First drafts are often disorganized messes. Almost always they contain at least a few good ideas, and sometimes they are full of them. But often the ideas are not connected to each other in ways that will seem logical to readers. In reorganizing the material, some ideas can be interconnected simply by presenting them in a different order. Others can be connected by adding new ideas that will act as bridges between existing ideas. Some ideas cannot be readily connected to the other ideas, so they do not belong in the same paper, or, at least, in the same section of the paper. One way to determine which ideas fall into which category is to sketch out an idea map.[*]

---

[*]The approach described here is based on a paper by Flower, L. S., Hayes, J.R. 1977. Problem-solving strategies and the writing process. *College English* 39: 449–461.

For the following example, students were asked to write a newspaper article (see Chapter 12) based on a research paper from the primary literature.°° Here is what one student's first draft looked like:

With their feathers bound by sticky tar, many seabirds could neither fly nor swim. An otter, washed up on the shore, was an unrecoverable black mess. A sudden oil spill killed these animals directly and swiftly. But it doesn't take a catastrophic spill of millions of gallons to cause such devastation.

Crude oil from boat engines, factory effluent, and runoff from city gutters enters the ocean, and takes a toll on some of the least suspected of animals exposed over a period of weeks to the deadly aromatic hydrocarbons that the oil delivers to water.

Using a carnivorous marine snail, *Thais lima*, scientists have developed a faster, more sensitive method for assessing toxicity of aromatic hydrocarbons. By measuring growth rates, this method identifies sublethal effects of the toxin, predicting concentrations that will cause eventual death of the animal. A snail with negative growth rate loses more energy than it consumes, so it has none left over to convert to new body tissue. In fact, it starts to burn its own mass to pay the debt.

The traditional method used to determine the toxicity of a pollutant is to expose organisms to various concentrations of the pollutant. The concentration that kills half the organisms in a certain amount of time is called the LC-50, which stands for "lethal concentration causing 50% mortality." This has long served as a benchmark for determining toxicity of different compounds in the environment. The lower the LC-50, the more toxic the compound.

°°Stickle, W. B., Rice, S.D., Moles, A. 1984. Bioenergetics and survival of the marine snail *Thais lima* during long-term oil exposure. *Marine Biol.* 80: 281–289.

Scientists typically have exposed invertebrates to aromatic hydrocarbons for 3 days to determine LC-50. In this study by Dr. Bill Stickle and colleagues at Louisiana State University, snails were exposed for up to 28 days. Concentrations of greater than 3000 parts per billion (ppb) were required to kill half the snails in 3 days; concentrations of only about 800 ppb killed half the snails in 28 days. LC-50s declined with duration of exposure. This means that LC-50s measured after only 3 days give a false picture of animals being more tolerant than they are in the field, where pollutants can persist over much longer periods of time.

While better than short-term assays for predicting effects of pollutants such as aromatic hydrocarbons that persist for a long time in the environment, long-term assays are costly and time consuming.

Growth rates, on the other hand, offer a quicker test for organism health in the presence of a pollutant. In this study, growth rate was determined indirectly by measuring energy intake by the snail (calories from mussel prey) and subtracting energy lost to respiration, feces, and metabolic waste. Growth rates are negative when energy lost is more than energy gained. In *Thais lima*, growth rates were negative when hydrocarbon concentrations exceeded 200 ppb. This concentration is considerably less than the 800 ppb determined to kill half the snails in 28 days. This finding suggests greater sensitivity of the growth rate assay than the LC-50 method to find negative effects of aromatic hydrocarbons.

This important study shows how determination of growth rates improves upon traditional measures of toxicity. Use of this technique could refine our knowledge of pollutant effects on marine fauna.

This draft isn't a complete disaster, but it certainly isn't easy to read. The ideas are there, but they aren't well organized. The first 2 paragraphs concern the devastation caused by fuel oils and their components, while the third paragraph discusses ways of measuring toxicity; the beginning of the third paragraph does not follow logically from the previous paragraph. Moreover, the third paragraph raises the issue of developing a faster method for assessing toxicity, while 2 paragraphs later we learn that the "breakthrough" methodology requires 28 days instead of the normal 3 days. That's not faster! Then we're back to LC-50 measurements and how the results vary with length of the study. Finally, in the next-to-last paragraph, we get to the point of the article: growth rates provide a faster way to judge snail health, by allowing us to predict whether the snails will eventually die or not. But it isn't a faster way to assess ecosystem health at all; it's a more sensitive method!

The student's seventh paragraph is confusing! The first sentence implies that growth rates *were* determined, the second sentence tells us that growth rates were *not* determined directly, and the fourth sentence implies that growth rates *were* determined ("growth rates were negative")! In fact, the researchers did not determine growth rates directly; instead, they measured feeding, respiration, and assimilation rates over a short time and were then able to estimate the extent to which growth rates would be affected. The final sentence of the draft is a give-away: the vague wording clearly indicates that the author has not yet come to grips with what this paper is about. Writing effective newspaper articles is not as easy as it might appear. Indeed, the clearer you try to be, the harder the task.

A sentence-by-sentence revision of this piece would be pointless. Massive reorganization is called for. This draft would benefit immensely from Idea Mapping.

What are the major components of the student's draft?

1. Effects of pollutants
2. LC-50s: what are they?
3. Lethal versus sublethal responses
4. This study was done using the marine snail, *Thais lima*
5. LC-50 results: 3-day versus 28-day experiments
6. Growth rate measurements: importance; how long does it take to make them?
7. Researchers measured respiration rate, feeding rate, assimilation.

To construct an idea map, scatter the main ideas on a piece of paper as in Figure 11a. Now we need to find a good entry point. I have suggested (Fig. 11b) that we begin by discussing the general issue of pollutant input into marine environments. From there we might discuss lethal versus

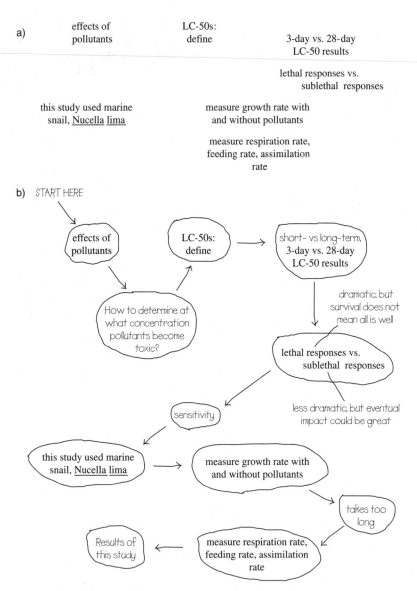

Figure 11. Organizing thoughts by creating Idea Maps.
        a) The main ideas scattered at random, based on a student draft (pp. 77–78).
        b) The ideas connected in one of several possible logical sequences.

sublethal responses—but how can we move smoothly between these 2 topics? One possibility would be to note the difficulty of determining the concentration at which any pollutant becomes toxic; this appears as a "bridge" topic in Figure 11b. At first I thought this might lead directly to a discussion of "lethal responses versus sublethal responses," but on further reflection it seems to lead more logically to a discussion of LC-50s. How to determine toxic pollutant concentrations? Determine the time it takes to cause something to happen in 50% of the animals tested. But that depends on how long the experiment runs. So, we add an arrow from "LC-50s" to the next topic, "short-term versus long-term LC-50 results" (Fig. 11b). From there we can discuss the relative merits of measuring either time to death or some sublethal response, which should be measurable at a lower pollutant concentration (thus increasing the sensitivity of the test). Increased sensitivity is an important point that wasn't in our original list, so I have added it in Figure 11b. Proceeding in this fashion, I have managed to connect all of the ideas presented in Figure 11b to produce a coherent story. It isn't the only way to link the ideas, but it's one way that works. What we end up with is a simple flowchart that can be used to write the next draft of the paper with little additional effort; all of the hard thinking work has been done before we begin the actual rewriting.

Idea maps can also be used before starting a first draft, but for most people they seem to work best as preparation for the next draft. Once you have a coherent story to tell your readers, you can begin to fine-tune the presentation, to make it clear, concise, and fully convincing. The rest of this chapter concerns that fine-tuning process.

REVISING FOR CONTENT

1. **Make sure every sentence says something**. Consider the following opening sentence for an essay on the tolerance of estuarine fish to changes in salinity:

   ```
   Salinity is a very important factor in marine
   environments.
   ```

   What does this sentence say? Does the author really think readers need to be told that the ocean is salty? What *is* important about salinity? The sentence is not substantive; it is really just a "running jump," a sentence that may be on the way to something of substance. A careful editor will delete the sentence and begin anew with a sentence that says something worth reading. For example:

```
Estuarine  fish  may  be  subjected  to  enormous
changes in salinity within only a few hours.
```

Similarly, a sentence like:

```
There are many physical and biological factors
that affect the growth of insect populations.
```

could profitably be revised to read:

```
Growth rates of insect populations are influenced
by such environmental factors as temperature,
food supply, buildup of metabolic wastes, avail-
ability of mates, and magnitude of predation.
```

The authors of the revised opening sentences know where their essays are headed, and so does the reader. The original versions got the writers started; the revision process focused the writers' attention on a destination.

Take a careful look at the first sentence of each paragraph that you write for a first draft. You will often find "running jumps," with the substance of the paragraph beginning with your second sentence. Consider the following example:

```
    The  damage  associated  with  UV  irradiation
(280-400 nm wavelengths) on plant and animal pop-
ulations is well documented. The UV irradiation
in sunlight severely damages DNA and other bio-
logical molecules in a variety of marine plant
and animal species (Gleason and Wellington, 1995;
Bingham  and  Reitzel,  2000;  Adams  and  Shick,
2001).
```

That first sentence is a running jump if ever I saw one. Cross it out, and get the paragraph off to a much stronger start with a slightly modified form of the second sentence:

```
    The UV irradiation (280-400 nm wavelengths) in
sunlight severely damages DNA and other biologi-
cal molecules in a variety of marine plant and
animal  species  (Gleason  and  Wellington,  1995;
```

Bingham and Reitzel, 2000; Adams and Shick, 2001).

2. **Use the word *relatively* only when making an explicit comparison**. Consider this example: "Many of the animals living near deep-sea hydrothermal vents are relatively large." The thoughtful reader wonders, "Relative to what?" Either delete the word and replace it with something of substance (for example, "Animals living near deep-sea hydrothermal vents can exceed lengths of 3 meters") or make a real comparison (for example, "Many of the animals living near deep-sea hydrothermal vents are large relative to their shallow-water counterparts," or "Some animals living near deep-sea hydrothermal vents are many times larger than their shallow-water counterparts").

3. **Never tell a reader that something is interesting**. Let the reader be the judge. Consider this rather uninformative sentence:

   ```
   Cell death is a particularly interesting phenome-
   non.
   ```

   Is the phenomenon interesting? If so, ask yourself *why* you find it interesting, and then make a statement that will interest the reader. This example could, for instance, be rewritten as follows:

   ```
   During the development of all animals, certain
   cells are genetically programmed for an early
   death.
   ```

4. **Be cautious in drawing conclusions, but not overly so**. It is always wise to be careful when interpreting biological data, particularly with access to only a few experiments or small data sets. For instance, write "These data suggest that . . ." rather than "These data demonstrate, or prove that. . . ." But don't get carried away, as in the following example:

   ```
   This suggests the possibility that inductive in-
   teractions between cells may be required for the
   differentiation of nerve tissue.
   ```

   Here, the author hedges 3 times in 1 sentence, using the words *suggests, possibility*, and *may*. Limit yourself to one hedge per sentence, as in the following rewrite:

   ```
   This suggests that inductive interactions are re-
   quired for the differentiation of nerve tissue.
   ```

If you are too unsure of your opinion to write such a sentence, reex-
amine your opinion.

5. **While revising for content, keep in mind an audience of your
   peers, not your instructor**. In particular, be sure to define all scientific terms and abbreviations; it is not enough simply to use them
   properly. Brief definitions will help keep the attention of readers
   who may not know or may not remember the meaning of some terms
   and will also demonstrate to your instructor that you know the meaning of the specialized terminology you are using. Try to make your
   writing self-sufficient; the reader should not have to consult textbooks or other sources in order to understand what you are saying.
   For example:

> The advantages of outbreeding include reduced ex-
> posure of deleterious recessive alleles and in-
> creased heterosis, the increased fitness commonly
> associated with increased heterozygosity.

would be a better sentence than:

> The advantages of outbreeding include reduced ex-
> posure of deleterious recessive alleles and in-
> creased heterosis.

Note that the author of the good example has cleverly defined the
term "heterosis" within the sentence rather than devoting a separate
sentence to its definition.

As always, if you write so that you will understand your work
years in the future, or so that your classmates will understand the
work now, your papers and reports will generally have greater impact
and will usually earn a higher grade.

REVISING FOR CLARITY

Taming Disobedient Sentences—Sentences That Don't Say What the Author Means

Be sure each sentence says what it's supposed to say; you want the
reader's head to be nodding up and down, not side to side. Which way is
the reader's head going in the following example?

```
These methods have different resorption rates and
tail shapes.
```

Do methods have tails? Can methods be resorbed? This sentence fails to communicate what its author had in mind. Indeed, it is difficult to tell *what* the author had in mind. Here is another sentence that does not reflect the intentions of its author:

```
From observations made in aquaria, feeding rates
of the fish were highest at night.
```

How many observers do you suppose can fit into an aquarium? Aquaria usually contain fish, not authors; is the author of our example all wet? A revised sentence might read:

```
Feeding rates of fish held in aquaria were highest
at night.
```

Similarly, let me introduce you to the remarkable Measuring Crab:

```
They measured the change in algal mass of each
sample with a crab.
```

In the experiment under discussion, the researchers determined feeding rates of crabs by measuring the rate at which the crabs' food (seaweed) lost weight (through consumption), but that certainly is not what the sentence says.

Some biologists are clearly more dedicated to their research than most of us are:

```
Ferguson (1963) examined autoradiographs of sea
star digestive tissue after being fed radioactive
clams.
```

Perhaps we should feed the clams not to Ferguson but to the sea stars?

```
Ferguson (1963) fed radioactive clams to sea
stars and then examined autoradiographs of the
sea star digestive tissue.
```

In the preceding example, note the advantages of summarizing a study in the order in which steps were undertaken; grammatical difficulties typically vanish, and the sentence automatically becomes clearer.

Here is another sentence that simply is not doing its author's bidding:

```
To keep the size of the samples constant, the
sampling pipet was calibrated so that the volume
of a single drop was known.
```

It is difficult to see how calibrating a pipet will keep sample sizes constant. Presumably, the author means that the same pipet was used for each sample (which would keep sample sizes constant). That the size of each sample was known is really a separate, independent thought.

Sometimes sentences are confusing because the author tries to stuff too much into them, as in the following example:

```
The Coomassie blue stain, a nonspecific dye that
binds to all proteins, was used to show all the
proteins in the samples allowing analysis of in-
duction of the appearance of a band after induc-
tion that is not found in the uninduced sample.
```

Whew! The goal of the experiment was to induce certain bacteria to express a cloned gene. The bacteria were then homogenized and their proteins separated on an electrophoretic gel. The gel was then stained with Coomassie blue to visualize the proteins present. If a new protein was present (the induced protein), it would show up as a new, separate band. Now that's just too much work for any one sentence to accomplish!

Confusing sentences also inevitably arise when 3 or more nouns are lined up in a row. Consider this example:

```
Sleep study results show that tryptophan signifi-
cantly decreases the time needed to fall asleep
(Miller and Brown, 1991).
```

At the first reading, the reader probably expects "results" to be a verb, but instead it is a noun, preceded by 2 other nouns. The reader must stop and decode the sentence. Ah! The author is discussing the results of studies of people sleeping. We can rewrite the sentence to make this much clearer:

```
Recent studies show that tryptophan decreases the
time needed for people to fall asleep (Miller and
Brown, 1991).
```

In revising your work, think twice before leaving more than 2 nouns together; 2 is company, 3 is a crowd.

Here are 3 additional examples of unclear writing:

```
This determination was based on mannitol's rela-
tive toxicity to sodium chloride.
```

```
The surface area of mammalian small intestines is
3 to 7 times greater than reptiles.
```

```
The snails from the unpolluted habitat accumu-
lated 67% more vincristine in their gills than in
the gills of snails from the polluted habitat.
```

How can one chemical be toxic to another chemical? The author is probably trying to tell us that 2 chemicals differ in their toxicity to some organisms or cell types. With the second example, one wonders how an intestinal surface area can be greater than a reptile; again, the author is not making the comparison he or she intended. Similarly, in the third example our author has snails from an unpolluted habitat somehow accumulating a chemical in the gills of snails from another habitat, which is difficult to believe. The author probably wishes to compare accumulation of the chemical by the gills of snails in the 2 populations, but that is not what he or she has written.

Readers should never have to guess what the proper comparisons are; **readers will appreciate your writing more the less you make them work**. In any event, never invoke the "You know what I mean" defense. If a student writes, "A normal human fetus has 46 chromosomes," how can I assume the student understands that each *cell* of the fetus has 46 chromosomes? It is your job to inform the reader, never the reader's job to guess what you are trying to say.

Of course, it doesn't help that confusing sentences surround us in our everyday lives. Consider this example taken from the local newspaper:

```
Offer void where prohibited by law, or while sup-
plies last.
```

The meaning of this sentence is not immediately clear. It is apparently impossible for anyone to take advantage of this offer; the offer is either prohibited by law or, if permitted by law, is void while supplies last. Supplies can never run out since the advertiser apparently is unwilling to fill your order as long as the items are available. If stocks become depleted, perhaps by eventual disintegration of the product, the advertiser could then honor your request; but the company would no longer have anything to send you!

Then there is this unfortunate wording I noticed on the side of some paper cups: "Put litter in its place." Since the cup isn't litter until it's on the ground, this is an apparent order to litter, probably not what the restaurant management intended. And how about these gems: "It is illegal for school workers to say that children should take a psychiatric drug because they are not doctors." "Our nuclear reactors are as safe as they can possibly be. And we are constantly working to make them safer."

With practice, you can find similarly confusing or absurd sentences almost anywhere you look; if they appear in your own writing, revise them. Make each sentence state its case unambiguously. Here is a sentence that does not do so:

```
Sea stars prey on a wide range of intertidal ani-
mals, depending on their size.
```

Is the author talking about the size of the sea stars that are preying or about the size of the intertidal animals that are preyed upon? Don't be embarrassed at finding sentences like this one in early drafts of your papers and reports. Be embarrassed only when you don't edit them out of your final draft.

The Dangers of "It"

Frequent use of the pronouns *it, they, these, their, this,* and *them* in your writing should sound an alarm: Probable ambiguity ahead. Consider the following example of the trouble *it* can cause:

```
The body is covered by a cuticle, but it is un-
waxed.
```

Which is unwaxed: the body or the cuticle? Similarly, *it* makes the second part of the following sentence equally ambiguous:

```
The chemical signal must then be transported to
the specific target tissue, but it is effective
only if it possesses appropriate receptors.
```

Are these receptors needed by the chemical signal or by the target tissue? I'm confused. In the next example, *these* causes similar problems for the reader:

```
Antigens   encounter   lymphocytes   in   the   spleen,
tonsils,   and   other   secondary   lymphoid   organs.
These   then   proliferate   and   differentiate   into
fully mature, antigen-specific effector cells.
```

Presumably the lymphocytes are proliferating, not the tonsils, although the author has certainly not made this clear. The problem is easily repaired by beginning the second sentence with "The lymphocytes. . . ." In the next example, *their* is guilty of a similar offense:

```
Like fanworms and earthworms, leeches have proven
very useful to neurophysiologists. Their neurons
are few and large, making them particularly easy
to study with electrodes.
```

Most readers are likely surprised to learn that neurophysiologists have so few neurons and are so easy to study. Now let us consider the difficulties *they* can cause:

```
Tropical   countries   are   home   to   both   venomous   and
nonvenomous snakes. They kill their prey by con-
striction or by biting and swallowing them.
```

How much clearer the last sentence could become by replacing *they* with a few words of substance and by deleting *them* entirely:

```
Tropical   countries   are   home   to   both   venomous   and
nonvenomous snakes. The nonvenomous snakes kill
their   prey   by   constriction   or   by   biting   and
swallowing.
```

And have you ever met researchers who glowed in the dark? One student apparently has:

```
Harper and Case (1999) found that the plainfish mid-
shipman, Porichthythys notatus, experienced twice
the rate of predation when they were not luminous.
```

If *they* have their way, the reader must guess who was glowing. Realizing that the sentence is in difficulty, we revise:

```
Harper and Case (1999) found that luminous plain-
fish midshipman (Porichthythys notatus) were twice
as likely to be eaten as nonluminous specimens.
```

Finally, look what can happen when a variety of these pronouns are scattered throughout a sentence:

```
Although they both saw the same things in their
observations of embryonic development, they had
different theories about how this came about.
```

A patient reader of the whole essay could probably figure out this sentence eventually, but its author has certainly violated one of our key rules, "Never make the reader back up," in a most extreme fashion.

In short, when editing your work, read it carefully and with skepticism, checking that you have said exactly what you mean. Never make the reader guess what you have in mind. Never give the reader cause to wonder whether, in fact, you have anything in mind. Everything you write must make sense—to yourself and to the reader. As you read each sentence you have written, think: What does this sentence say? What did I mean it to say? Make each sentence work on your behalf, leading the reader easily from fact to fact, from thought to thought.

Please note that you need not be a grammarian to write correctly and clearly. With a little practice, especially if you read your work aloud, you can quickly learn to recognize a sentence in difficulty and sense how to fix it without even knowing the name of the grammatical rule that was violated.

REVISING FOR COMPLETENESS

Make sure each thought is complete. Be specific in making assertions. The following statement is much too vague:

```
Many insect species have been described.
```

How many is "many"? After editing, the sentence might read:

```
Nearly one million insect species have been de-
scribed.
```

Similarly, the sentence

```
More caterpillars chose diet A than diet B when
given a choice of the 2 diets (Fig. 2).
```

would benefit from the following alteration:

```
Nearly 5 times as many caterpillars chose diet
A than diet B when given a choice between the
2 diets (Fig. 2).
```

Here is another kind of incompleteness:

```
If diffusion was entirely responsible for glucose
transport, then this would not have occurred.
```

This rears its ugly head again; the author avoids the responsibility of drawing a clear conclusion and forces the reader to back up and attempt to summarize the findings. Even the beginning of the sentence is unnecessarily vague because, it turns out, the discussion is concerned only with glucose transport in intestinal tissue. Try to make your sentences tell a more detailed story, as in this revision:

```
If diffusion was entirely responsible for glucose
transport into cells of the intestinal epithe-
lium, transport would have continued when I added
the inhibitors.
```

In the same way, "Cells exposed to copper chloride divided at normal rates" is a substantial improvement over "The copper chloride treatment was not affected."

Be especially careful to revise for completeness whenever you find that you have written *etc.*, an abbreviation for the Latin term *et cetera*, meaning "and others" or "and so forth." In writing a first draft, use *etc.* freely when you'd rather not interrupt the flow of your thoughts by thinking about exactly what "other things" you have in mind. When revising, however, replace each *etc.* with words of substance; in scientific writing, an *etc.* makes the reader suspect fuzzy thinking. Ask yourself, "What, exactly, *do* I have in mind here?" If you come up with additional items for your list, add them. If you find that you have nothing to add, simply replace the *etc.* with a period and you will have produced a shorter, clearer sentence.

Consider the following sentence and its 2 improvements:

ORIGINAL VERSION

```
Plant growth is influenced by a variety of envi-
ronmental factors, such as light intensity, nu-
trient availability, etc.
```

REVISION 1

```
Plant growth is influenced by a variety of envi-
ronmental factors, such as light intensity, day
length, nutrient availability, and temperature.
```

REVISION 2

```
Plant growth is influenced by such environmental
factors as light intensity, day length, nutrient
availability, and temperature.
```

In the original version, the author has dodged the responsibility of clear writing, forcing the reader to determine what is meant by *etc.* The sentence, although grammatically correct, is incomplete, waiting for the reader to fill in the missing information. The reader may justifiably wonder whether the writer knows what other factors affect plant growth. Both revised versions clearly indicate what the author had in mind. Revising for completeness often requires you to return to your notes or to the sources upon which your notes are based.

REVISING FOR CONCISENESS

Make every word count. Omitting unnecessary words will make your thoughts clearer and more convincing. I have already talked about entire sentences that are really nothing more than running jumps, particularly at the beginning of paragraphs (pp. 81–82). Often you can find running jumps at the start of sentences, too. In particular, such phrases as, "It should be noted that," "It is interesting to note that," "Evidence has shown that," "It has been documented that," "Analysis of the data indicated that," and "The fact of the matter is that" are common in first drafts, but should be ruthlessly eliminated in preparing the second.

Consider an example:

```
The data indicate that as hermit crabs gain in
size and weight, they tend to occupy larger
shells (Fig. 3).
```

To revise, we merely eradicate those first 4 words:

```
As hermit crabs gain in size and weight, they
tend to occupy larger shells (Fig. 3).
```

Here's an example of an even longer running jump:

> Evidence provided by Clarke and Faulkes (1999) has shown that reproductively mature female mole rats (*Heterocephalus glaber*) preferentially mate with unrelated males, reducing the frequency of inbreeding.

That sentence doesn't really become substantive until we get to the mature females, so let's remove the running jump to end up with

> Reproductively mature female mole rats (*Heterocephalus glaber*) preferentially mate with unrelated males, reducing the frequency of inbreeding (Clarke and Faulkes 1999).

Running jumps often find their way into sentences presenting the results of statistical analyses, as in this example:

> Chi-square analysis of the samples collected at Fanghorn Wood, Middle Earth, indicated that there was no significant difference in the proportion of occupied intact pine cones compared to the proportion of occupied damaged pine cones ($\chi^2 = 0.26$, d.f. $= 1$, $P = 0.61$).

Everything preceding and including the words "indicated that" constitutes a running jump. Let the reader dive right in:

> At Fanghorn Wood, Middle Earth, the proportion of pine cones occupied by weevils was not significantly affected by whether the pine cones were damaged ($\chi^2 = 0.26$, d.f. $= 1$, $P = 0.61$).

I discuss writing about statistics more fully in Chapter 3.

Verbal excess can also take less conspicuous forms. How might you shorten this next sentence?

> Dr. Smith's research investigated the effect of pesticides on the reproductive biology of birds.

Who did the work: Dr. Smith or his research? A reasonable revision would be:

> Dr. Smith investigated the effect of pesticides on the reproductive biology of birds.

We have eliminated one word, and the sentence has not suffered a bit. Working on the sentence further, we can replace "the reproductive biology of birds" with "avian reproduction," achieving a net reduction of 3 more words:

```
Dr. Smith investigated the effect of pesticides
on avian reproduction.
```

The next example requires similar attention:

```
It was found that the shell lengths of live
snails tended to be larger for individuals col-
lected closer to the low tide mark (Fig. 1).
```

A good editor would eliminate the first phrase of that sentence and prune further from there. In particular, what does the author mean by "tended to be larger"? Here are 2 improved versions of the sentence:

```
Live snails collected near the low tide mark had
greater average shell lengths (Fig. 1).
```

```
Snails found closer to the low tide mark typi-
cally had larger shells (Fig. 1).
```

These and most other wordy sentences suffer from one or several of four major ailments and can be brought to robust health by obeying the following Four Commandments of Concise Writing.

First Commandment:
Eliminate Unnecessary Prepositions

Consider this example:

```
The results indicated a role of hemal tissue in
moving nutritive substances to the gonads of the
animal.
```

Any sentence containing such a long string of prepositional phrases—"of . . . tissue," "in moving . . . substances," "to the gonads," "of the animal"—is automatically a candidate for the editor's operating table. This sentence actually contains a simple thought, buried amid a clutter of unnecessary words. After surgery, the thought emerges clearly:

```
The results indicated that hemal tissue moved nu-
trients to the animal's gonads.
```

Here is another example:

```
The cells respond to foreign proteins by rapidly
dividing and starting to produce antibodies reac-
tive to the protein groups that induced their
production.
```

The reader's head spins, an effect avoided by the following more concise incarnation of the same sentence:

```
In the presence of foreign proteins, the cells
divide rapidly and produce antibodies against
those proteins.
```

By eliminating prepositions, "Karlson arrives at the conclusion that . . ." becomes "Karlson concludes that. . . ." "Grazing may constitute a benefit to . . ." becomes "Grazing may benefit. . . ." "These data appear to be in support of the hypothesis that . . ." becomes "These data appear to support the hypothesis that. . . ." and "Schooling of fish is a well-documented phenomenon" becomes "Fish schooling is well documented."

Second Commandment: Avoid Weak Verbs

Formal scientific writing is often confusing—and boring—because the individual sentences contain no real action; commonly, the colorless verb *to be* is used where a more vivid verb would be more effective, as in this example:

```
The fidelity of DNA replication is dependent on
the fact that DNA is a double-stranded polymer
held together by weak chemical interactions be-
tween the nucleotides on opposite DNA strands.
```

This patient suffers from Wimpy Verb Syndrome, with a slight touch of Excess Prepositional Phrase. There is *potential* action in this sentence, but it is sound asleep in the verb "is dependent." Converting to the stronger verb "depends," we read:

```
The fidelity of DNA replication depends on the
fact that DNA is a double-stranded polymer. . . .
```

But why stop there? Let's eliminate some clutter ("on the fact that") and another weak verb ("is"):

```
The fidelity of DNA replication depends on DNA be-
ing a double-stranded polymer. . . .
```

Along the same lines, can you find a potentially stronger verb in this next sentence?

```
Activation of the immune response may be a trig-
ger for disease progression (Bernheim, 1980).
```

Why not replace "may be a trigger" [yawn] with "may trigger"? Then the sentence becomes

```
Activation of the immune response may trigger
disease progression (Bernheim, 1980).
```

Similarly:

```
Plant vascular tissues function in the transport
of food through xylem and phloem.
```

can be enlivened by converting the phrase "function in the transport of" to the more vigorous verb "transport":

```
Plant vascular tissues transport food through
xylem and phloem.
```

Note that by choosing a stronger verb, we have also eliminated 2 prepositional phrases ("in the transport of" and "of food"). Step by step, the sentence becomes shorter and clearer. As often happens during revision, fixing one problem reveals an additional problem, in this case a fundamental structural weakness that makes the reader wonder whether the student understands the relationship between "plant vascular tissues" and "xylem and phloem." Revising now for content, we might rewrite the sentence as:

```
Plant vascular tissues (the xylem and phloem)
transport nutrients throughout the plant.
```

or

```
Plants transport nutrients through their vascular
tissues, the xylem and phloem.
```

Third Commandment:
Do Not Overuse the Passive Voice

The passive voice is often a great enemy of concise writing, in part because the associated verbs are weak. If the subject ("Rats and mice," in the following example) is on the receiving end of the action, the voice is passive:

```
Rats and mice were experimented on by him.
```

If, on the other hand, the subject of a sentence ("He," in the coming example) is on the delivering end of the action, the voice is said to be active:

```
He experimented with rats and mice.
```

Note that the active sentence contains only 6 words, whereas its passive counterpart contains 8. In addition to creating excessively wordy sentences, the passive voice often makes the active agent anonymous, and a weaker, sometimes ambiguous sentence may result:

```
Once every month for 2 years, mussels were col-
lected from 5 intertidal sites in Barnstable
County, MA.
```

Whom should the reader contact if there is a question about where the mussels were collected? Were the mussels collected by the writer, by fellow students, by an instructor, or by a private company? Eliminating the passive voice clarifies the procedure:

```
Once every month for 2 years, members of the
class collected mussels from 5 intertidal sites
in Barnstable County, MA.
```

Similarly, "It was found that" becomes "I found," or "We found," or, perhaps, "Karlson (1996) found." Whenever it is important, or at least useful, that the reader know who the agent of the action is, and whenever the passive voice makes a sentence unnecessarily wordy, use the active voice:

Passive: Little is known of the nutritional requirements of these animals.

Active: We know little about the nutritional requirements of these animals.

Passive: The results were interpreted as indicative
of. . . .

Active: The results indicated. . . .

Passive: In the present study, the food value of 7
diets was compared, and the chemical composition
of each diet was correlated with its nutritional
value.

Active: In this study, I compared the food value of
7 diets and correlated the chemical composition
of each diet with its nutritional value.

Note in this last example that it is perfectly acceptable to use the pronoun
"I" in scientific writing; switching to the active voice expresses thoughts
more forcibly and clearly and often eliminates unnecessary words.

Fourth Commandment:
Make the Organism the Agent of the Action

Consider this example:

Studies on the rat show that the activity levels
vary predictably during the day (Hatter, 1976).

This is not a terrible sentence, but it can be improved by moving the action
from the studies ("Studies . . . show") to the organism involved, the rat:

Rats vary their activity levels predictably during the day (Hatter, 1976).

The revised sentence is shorter, clearer, and more interesting because
now an organism is *doing* something. Along the way, a prepositional
phrase ("on the rat") has vanished. Alternatively, one could include the
researcher in the action:

Hatter (1976) showed that rats vary their activity levels predictably during the day.

Similarly, redirecting the action transforms:

Increases in salinity increased larval growth
rates in Experiment I, but not in Experiment II.

into:

Larvae grew faster at higher salinities in Experiment I, but not in Experiment II.

and transforms:

The reaction rate increased as pH was increased
from 6.0 to about 8.0, and then declined between
a pH of 8.5 and 9.0 (Fig. 1).

to:

Trypsin was maximally effective at pHs between
about 8.0 and 8.5 (Fig. 1).

Note that in the original version of this last example the author redrew the graph in words: we can easily picture him or her staring at the graph and its axes while writing. In the revised version, the author makes the enzyme the agent of the action and the message comes through much more clearly.

Be a person of few words; your readers will be grateful.

REVISING FOR FLOW

A strong paragraph—indeed, a strong paper—takes the reader smoothly and inevitably from a point upstream to one downstream. Link your sentences and paragraphs using appropriate transitions so that the reader moves effortlessly and inevitably from one thought to the next, logically and unambiguously. Minimize turbulence. Always remind the reader of what has come before, and help the reader anticipate what is coming next. Consider the following example:

Since aquatic organisms are in no danger of
drying out, gas exchange can occur across the
general body surface. The body walls of aquatic
invertebrates are generally thin and water
permeable. Terrestrial species that rely on simple diffusion of gases through unspecialized body
surfaces must have some means of maintaining a
moist body surface, or must have an impermeable
outer body surface to prevent dehydration; gas
exchange must occur through specialized, internal
respiratory structures.

This example gives the reader a choppy ride indeed, and cries out for careful revision, not of the ideas themselves but of the way they are presented. In the following revision, note the effect of 2 important transitional expressions, *thus* and *in contrast to*. The first connects 2 thoughts; the second warns the reader of an approaching shift in direction:

> Since aquatic organisms are in no danger of drying out, gas exchange can occur across the general body surface. Thus, the body walls of aquatic invertebrates are generally thin and water permeable, facilitating such gas exchange. In contrast to the simplicity of gas exchange mechanisms among aquatic species, terrestrial species that rely on simple diffusion of gases through unspecialized body surfaces must either have some means of maintaining a moist body surface, or must have an impermeable outer body covering that prevents dehydration. If the outer body wall is impermeable to water and gases, respiratory structures must be specialized and internal.

In the first draft, the reader must struggle to find the connection between sentences. In the revised version, the writer has assisted the reader by connecting the thoughts, resulting in a more coherent paragraph.

Here is one more example of a stagnating paragraph that carries its reader nowhere:

> The energy needs of a resting sea otter are 3 times those of terrestrial animals of comparable size. The sea otter must eat about 25% of its body weight daily. Sea otters feed at night as well as during the day.

Revising for improved flow, or coherence, produces the following paragraph. Note that the writer has introduced no new ideas. The additions, here underlined, are simply clarifications that make the connections between each point explicit:

> The energy needs of a resting sea otter are 3 times those of terrestrial animals of comparable size. <u>To support such a high metabolic rate</u>, the sea otter must eat about 25% of its body weight

```
daily. Moreover, sea otters feed continually, at
night as well as during the day.
```

The following **transitional words and phrases are especially useful in linking thoughts to improve flow**: *in contrast, however, although, for example, thus, whereas, even so, nevertheless, moreover, despite, in addition to.* The use of such words can also help readers see connections between adjacent paragraphs, as in the following example (connecting words are underlined):

```
    Decreased fecundity due to inbreeding depres-
sion is well documented in plants. [The student
then gives several examples] . . . and in Trillium
erectum, self-pollinated plants produced 71%
fewer seeds than outcrossed plants (Irwin, 2001).
    Similar effects of inbreeding on fecundity
have been reported in a number of bird species.
For example, . . .
```

Repetition and summary are also highly effective ways to link thoughts. For instance, repetition was used to connect the first 2 sentences of the revised example about sea otters: "To support such a high metabolic rate" essentially repeats, in summary form, the information content of the first sentence. Repetition was also used to link paragraphs in the example about inbreeding; in reminding the reader of what has come before, the author consolidates his or her position and then moves on. Use these and similar transitions to move the reader smoothly from the beginning of your paper to the end. Be certain that each sentence—and each paragraph—sets the stage for the one that follows, and that each sentence—and each paragraph—builds on the one that came before.

A Short Exercise in Establishing Coherence

Your sentences should lead so logically and smoothly from one thought to the next that should the individual sentences of a paragraph become scattered by heavy winds, someone who collects all of those individual sentences should be able to reassemble the original paragraph. For example, I have deliberately disassembled a paragraph* into the following isolated sentences:

---

*From Lee, K.W., Webb, S.E., Miller, A.L. 1999. A wave of free cytosolic calcium traverses zebrafish eggs on activation. *Devel. Biol.* 214:168–180.

a. It is becoming clear, however, that although wave propagation is a common feature of activation, there are both subtle and significant differences in this response when comparing eggs from different species.
b. It appears that all vertebrate, invertebrate, and perhaps even some plant eggs are activated by the generation of calcium transients in their cytoplasm (Roberts *et al.*, 1994; Lawrence *et al.*, 1997).
c. In contrast, activation triggers a series of repetitive calcium waves or oscillations in annelids (Stricker, 1996), ascidians (Albrieux *et al.*, 1997), and mammals (Kline and Kline, 1992), including humans (Homa and Swann, 1994; Tesarik and Testart, 1994).
d. For example, in fish (Gilkey *et al.*, 1978), echinoderms (Stricker *et al.*, 1992), and frogs (Busa and Nuccitelli, 1985; Kubota *et al.*, 1987), a single calcium wave is propagated across the activating egg.
e. In most cases these transients take the form of propagating calcium waves (Jaffe, 1985; Epel, 1990; Whitaker and Swamm, 1993), which appear to be essential for activating the eggs.

Try reconstructing the original paragraph. Clearly, sentence "a" can't be the opening sentence of the paragraph. Why not? What sentence most likely proceeds sentence "a"? What sentence most likely follows sentence "a"? What words provide the clues that allow you to answer these questions? Which sentence provides the most general statement of the problem? I nominate that sentence as our best candidate for Opening Sentence of the Paragraph. The paragraph is shown in original form in Appendix A at the back of this book. Try to make your own paragraphs as easy to reconstruct, in part by using the tricks of repetition and summary, and by using appropriate transitional words and phrases.

Improving Flow Using Punctuation

Judicious use of the semicolon can also ease the reader's journey. In particular, when the second sentence of a pair explains or clarifies something contained in the first, you may wish to combine the 2 sentences into one with a semicolon. Consider the following 2 sentences:

```
This enlarged and modified bone, with its associ-
ated muscles, serves as a useful adaptation for
the panda. With its "thumb," the panda can easily
strip the bamboo on which it feeds.
```

The reader probably has to pause to consider the connection between the 2 sentences. Using a semicolon, the passage would read:

```
This enlarged and modified bone, with its associ-
ated muscles, serves as a useful adaptation for
the panda; with its "thumb," the panda can easily
strip the bamboo on which it feeds.
```

The semicolon links the 2 sentences and eliminates an obstruction in the reader's path. Similarly, a semicolon provides an effective connection between thoughts in the following 2 examples:

```
Recently we demonstrated the rapid germination of
radish seeds; nearly 80% of the seeds germinated
within 3 days of planting.
```

```
Recombinant DNA technology enables large-scale
production of particular gene products; specific
genes are transferred to rapidly dividing host or-
ganisms (yeast or bacteria), which then transcribe
and translate the introduced genetic templates.
```

REVISING FOR TELEOLOGY AND ANTHROPOMORPHISM

Remember, organisms do not act or evolve with intent (p. 12). Consider the following examples of teleological writing, and learn to recognize the trend in your own work:

```
Barnacles are incapable of moving from place to
place and therefore had to evolve a specialized
food-collecting apparatus in order to survive.
```

```
Squid and most other cephalopods lost their ex-
ternal shells in order to swim faster, and so
better compete with fish.
```

```
Many animals use antipredator behaviors to in-
crease their chance of survival.
```

Revise all teleology out of your writing. Don't have nonhuman animals thinking and planning.

Also beware of anthropomorphizing, in which you give human characteristics to nonhuman entities, as in this example:

```
The existence of sage in the harsh climate of the
American plains results from Nature's timeless
experimentation.
```

Again, this conveys a rather fuzzy picture about how natural selection operates. The author would be on firmer ground by writing something like:

```
Sage is one of the few plants capable of with-
standing the harsh, dry climate of the American
plains.
```

REVISING FOR SPELLING ERRORS

Misspellings convey the impression of carelessness, laziness, or perhaps even stupidity. These are not advisable images to present to instructors, prospective employers, or the admissions officers of graduate or professional programs. Using a spelling-checker computer program will save you from misspelling many nontechnical words, but it won't catch such spelling errors as "is" versus "if," or "nothing" versus "noting," and it is unlikely to be of much help in screening technical terms for you. Use the computer for a first pass, but use your own eyes for the second.

It helps to keep a list of words that you find yourself using often and consistently misspelling. *Desiccation* and *argument* were on my list for quite some time; *proceed* and *precede* are still on it. When in doubt, use a dictionary. And if you add technical terms to your computer program's dictionary, be careful to enter the correct spellings.

A few peculiarities of the English language are worth pointing out:

1. *Mucus* is a noun; as an adjective, the same slime becomes *mucous*. Thus, many marine animals produce mucus, and mucous trails are produced by many marine animals.
2. *Seawater* is always a single word. *Fresh water*, however, is usually 2 words as a noun and 1 word as an adjective. Thus, freshwater animals live in fresh water. The Council of Science Editors no longer insists on this usage, however, and different publishers are setting their own rules.
3. *Species* is both singular and plural: 1 species, 2 species. But the plural of *genus* is *genera*: 1 genus, 2 genera.

Here are 2 more spelling tips:

4. The plural forms of alga, bacterium, and hypothesis are algae, bacteria, and hypotheses.
5. When writing about insect larvae, "worm" is never written as a separate word, because insect larvae are not true worms (i.e., they are not annelids). One studies silkworms, for example, not silk worms. Similarly, for 2-part insect names the second part (e.g., fly or bug) is never written as a separate word when it is not correct systematically, but otherwise is written as a separate word. We write, for example, about butterflies (which do not belong to the order Diptera, containing the true flies) on the one hand, and about house flies (which *are* true flies) and bed bugs (which *are* true bugs, members of the order Hemiptera).

And don't forget to underline or italicize scientific names: *Littorina littorea* (the periwinkle snail), *Chrysemys picta* (the eastern painted turtle), *Taraxacum officinale* (the common dandelion), *Caenorhabditis elegans* (a nematode worm, the first animal to have its entire genome sequenced), *Homo sapiens* (the only animal that writes laboratory reports).

REVISING FOR GRAMMAR AND PROPER WORD USAGE

Appendix E lists a number of books that include excellent sections on grammar and proper word usage (see also Appendix H for some excellent Web sites). While on the lookout for sentence fragments, run-on sentences, faulty use of commas, faulty parallelism, incorrect agreement between subjects and verbs, and other grammatical blunders, you should also be on the lookout for violations of 11 especially troublesome rules of usage when revising your work.

1. *between* and *among. Between* (from *by twain*) usually refers to only 2 things:

   ```
   The 20 caterpillars were randomly distributed be-
   tween the 2 dishes.
   ```

   Among usually refers to more than 2 things:

   ```
   The 20 caterpillars were randomly distributed
   among the 8 dishes.
   ```

2. *which* and *that*. Most of your *which*s should be *that*s:

```
This fish, which lives at depths up to 1000 m, ex-
periences up to 101 atmospheres of pressure.
```

```
A fish that lives at a depth of 1000 m is exposed
to 101 atmospheres of pressure.
```

In the first example, "which" introduces a nondefining, or nonrestrictive clause. The introduced phrase is, in effect, an aside, adding extra information about the fish in question; the sentence would survive without it. On the other hand, the "that" of the second example introduces a defining, or restrictive clause; we are being told about a particular fish, or type of fish, one that lives at a depth of 1000 m.

Improper use of *that* and *which* can occasionally lead to ambiguity or falsehood. Consider the following sentence about the production of proteins from messenger RNA (mRNA) transcripts:

```
This difference in protein production is due to
different amounts of mRNA that translate and pro-
duce each particular protein.
```

Here, "that" correctly introduces a restrictive clause. Which mRNA molecules? The ones coding for these particular proteins. The writer is telling us that proteins are produced in proportion to the number of mRNA molecules coding for them within the cell. Replacing "that" with "which" drastically changes the meaning of the sentence:

```
The difference in protein production is due to
different amounts of mRNA, which translates and
produces each particular protein.
```

The sentence has lost clarity because "which" now introduces a nondefining clause that should be explaining only what mRNA does, in general. In the following sentence, using the word *which* conveys information that is actually wrong:

```
In squid and other cephalopods, which lack exter-
nal shells, locomotion is accomplished by con-
tracting the muscular mantle.
```

Here, the writer asserts that no cephalopods have external shells, which is not the case; some species *do* have external shells. The correct word is *that*:

```
In squid and other cephalopods that lack external
shells. . .
```

Now the writer correctly refers specifically to those cephalopods without external shells.

As in the examples given, *which* is commonly preceded by a comma. When deciding between *which* and *that* in your own writing, read your sentence aloud. If the word doesn't need a comma before it for the sentence to make sense, the correct word is probably *that*. If you hear a pause when you read, signifying the need for a comma, the correct word is probably *which*.

3. *its* and *it's*. *It's* is always an abbreviated form of *it is*. If *it is* does not belong in your sentence, use the possessive pronoun *its*:

```
When treated with the chemical, the protozoan
lost its cilia and died.
```

```
It's clear that the loss of cilia was caused by
treatment with the chemical.
```

While we're at it, let's revise that last sentence to eliminate the passive voice:

```
It's clear that treatment with the chemical
caused the loss of cilia.
```

In general, contractions are not welcome in formal scientific writing. Thus, you can avoid the problem entirely by writing *it is* when appropriate:

```
It is clear that treatment with the chemical
caused the loss of cilia.
```

4. *effect* and *affect*. *Effect* as a noun means a "result" or "outcome":

```
What is the effect of fuel oil on the feeding be-
havior of sea birds?
```

Effect as a verb means "to bring about":

```
What changes in feeding behavior will fuel oil
effect in sea birds?
```

Affect as a verb means "to influence" or "to produce an effect upon":

```
How will the fuel oil affect the feeding behavior
of sea birds?
```

Used as a verb, "effect" can indeed be replaced in the preceding example by *bring about*, but not by *influence*; and "affect" can indeed be replaced by *influence*, but not by *bring about*. Even so, memorizing the definitions of the 2 words may be of little help in deciding which word to use in your own writing because, as verbs, *affect* and *effect* are so similar in meaning. You may be more successful in choosing the correct word by memorizing each of the examples and then comparing the memorized examples with your own sentences.

5. *rate*. "Rates" have units of "something per time": moles of substrate degraded per minute, numbers of centimeters (cm) moved per second, numbers of births per year, and so forth. If you are writing about something that does *not* have units of "per time," then do not use the word "rate."

6. *i.e.* and *e.g.* These 2 abbreviations are not interchangeable. *I.e.* is an abbreviation for *id est*, which, in Latin, means "that is" or "that is to say." For example:

```
Data  on  sex  determination  suggest  that  this
species  has  only  two  sexual  genotypes,  i.e.,  fe-
male  (XX)  and  male  (XY).
```

```
The  embryos  were  undifferentiated  at  this  stage
of  development;  i.e.,  they  lacked  external  cilia
and  the  gut  had  not  yet  formed.
```

In contrast, *e.g.* stands for *exempli gratia*, which means "for example." I will give 2 examples of its use:

```
During  the  precompetent  period  of  development,
the  larvae  cannot  be  induced  to  metamorphose
(e.g.,  Crisp,  1974;  Bonar,  1978;  Chia,  1978;
Pires,  2000).
```

```
However,  the  larvae  of  several  butterfly  species
(e.g.,  Papilio demodocus  Esper,  P. eurymedon,  and
Pieris napi)  are  able  to  feed  and  grow  on  plants
that  the  adults  never  lay  eggs  on.
```

In the first case, the writer uses *e.g.* to indicate that what follows is only a partial listing of references supporting the statement: "for example, see these references," in other words. In the second case, the writer uses it to indicate only a partial list of butterfly species that don't lay eggs on all suitable plants.

7. *However, therefore,* and *moreover.* These words are often incorrectly used as conjunctions, as in the following examples:

```
The brain of a toothed whale is larger than the
human brain, however the ratio of brain to body
weight is greater in humans.
```

```
The resistance of mosquito fish (Gambusia affi-
nis) to the pesticide DDT persisted into the
next generation bred in the laboratory, there-
fore the resistance was probably genetically
based.
```

```
Protein synthesis in frog eggs will take place
even if the nucleus is surgically removed, more-
over the pattern of protein synthesis in such
enucleated eggs is apparently normal.
```

These examples all demonstrate the infamous comma splice, in which a comma is mistakenly used to join what are really 2 separate sentences. Reading aloud, you should hear the material come to a complete stop before the words "however," "therefore," and "moreover." Thus, you must replace the commas with either a semicolon or a period, as in these revisions of the first example:

```
The brain of a toothed whale is larger than the
human brain; however, the ratio of brain to body
weight is greater in humans.
```

```
The brain of a toothed whale is larger than the
human brain. However, the ratio of brain to body
weight is greater in humans.
```

8. *concentration* and *density.* People often use *density* when they mean *concentration*, as in the following example:

```
Larvae were more active at the highest of the 3
food densities.
```

Although "density" *can* refer to the number of things per unit volume (e.g., cells per milliliter (ml), as in this example, or moles per liter), it can also mean mass per unit volume. To avoid ambiguity, it would be better to write about the 3 food "concentrations."

9. *varying* and *various*. "Varying" means "changing over time" or with changing circumstances, while "various" means "different."

Consider the following example:

```
We  also  examined  feeding  rates  among  animals
maintained at varying temperatures.
```

It is certainly possible that temperature was caused to change over time during the study, but in reality the authors simply maintained animals at each of 4 different constant temperatures. A revised version of the sentence might read

```
    We  also  examined  feeding  rates  among  animals
maintained  at  4  different  temperatures  over  the
range 15-29°C.
```

Misuse of the word "varying" sometimes adds a bit of amusement to an otherwise dreary day:

```
Five  shells  of  varying  sizes  were  then  selected
for each hermit crab.
```

You can almost visualize each shell pulsating and undulating as it waits to be inspected by the hermit crabs. What the student meant to write, of course, was "various" or "different."

10. Proper use of commas in writing species names. Use commas to set off formal species names only when the formal names are preceded by specific common names. For example, you would use a comma before the species name here:

```
Genomic  DNA  was  extracted  from  embryos  of  the
common blue mussel, Mytilus edulis.
```

But not here:

```
Genomic  DNA  was  extracted  bryos  of  the  mussel
Mytilus edulis.
```

Or here:

```
. . . extracted from embryos of the marine bivalve
Mytilus edulis.
```

11. And don't forget: The data *are* . . . (see p. 14).

BECOMING A GOOD EDITOR

The best way to become an effective reviser of your own writing is to become a critical reader of other people's writing. Whenever you read a newspaper, magazine, or textbook, be on the lookout for ambiguity and wordiness, and think about how the sentence or paragraph might best be rewritten. You will gradually come to recognize the same problems, and the solutions to these problems, in your own writing. But don't try to fix everything at once. Whether you are editing an early draft of your own work or a fellow student's work, be concerned first with content. Until you are convinced that the author has something to say, it makes little sense to be overly concerned with how he or she has said it, for the same reason it would make little sense to wash and wax a car that was headed for the auto salvage.

Take an especially careful look at the title and the first few paragraphs. Does the title indicate exactly what the paper or laboratory report is about? Do the title and first paragraph seem closely related? In the first 1 or 2 paragraphs, does one sentence lead logically to the next, establishing a clear direction for what follows? Can you tell from the first paragraph or two exactly what this paper, proposal, or report is about, and why the issue is of interest? Or are you reading a series of apparently unrelated facts that seem to lead nowhere or in many different directions? Does the first paragraph head in one direction, the second in another, and the third in yet another? If so, there is serious work to be done.

Second drafts commonly arise from only a small portion of the first—perhaps a few sentences buried somewhere in the last third of the original. In such a case, you must abandon most of the first draft and begin afresh, but this time you are writing from a stronger base. Always leave at least several days to make revisions, and insist that your fellow students give you drafts of their work to look over at least several days before the final piece is due.

Once the piece has a clear direction, you can revise for flow and clarity. Does each sentence make sense, and does each lead in logical fashion to the next? Does each paragraph follow logically from the previous paragraph? Does the concluding paragraph address the issue raised in the first paragraph?

If you are examining a laboratory report, study the Results section first. Does it conform to the requirements outlined in Chapter 8? Does the Materials and Methods section answer all procedural questions that were not addressed in the figure captions and table legends? Should some of those questions (for example, experimental temperature) be addressed in the captions and legends, or directly on the graphs or in the tables? Does the Introduction state a clear question and provide the background information needed to understand why that question is worth asking? Does the Discussion section interpret the data or does it simply apologize, and does the Discussion clearly address the specific issue raised in the Introduction?

Only when you can answer yes to these questions should you worry about fine-tuning the paper—editing for conciseness, completeness, grammar, and spelling.

Giving Criticism

> You don't always have to chop with the sword of truth. You can point with it, too.
>
> Anne Lamott, 1994 (*Bird by Bird*)

Look at someone else's paper the same way you should look at your own, concerning yourself first with content. Avoid the temptation to smother the paper with notations about prepositional phrases and spelling errors; as already discussed, it is worth commenting on such things only when you feel the piece is a draft or two away from perfection. When examining a first draft, it may be most useful to write a few paragraphs of commentary to the author and not write on the paper at all. Don't feel compelled to rewrite the paper for the author; your role is simply to point out strengths and perceived weaknesses and to offer the best advice you can about potential fixes. Here is an example of how this might be done; the student is making comments about the first draft of a research proposal written by a fellow student.

Jim, I think you have a good idea for a project here, but it's not reflected in your introduction (or the title, but that can wait). The question you finally state in the middle of p. 4 caught me completely by surprise; at least until the bottom of p. 2 I thought you were interested in the effects of electromagnetic fields on human development, and by the end of p. 3, I wasn't sure *what* you were planning to study! On pp. 2-3 especially, I couldn't see how the indicated paragraphs (see my comments on your paper) related to the question you ended up asking. Or perhaps they *are* relevant, and you just haven't made the connections clear to me? The entire introduction seems to be in the "book report" format we discussed in class, rather than a piece of writing with a point to make (I'm having this trouble, too). The information you present is *interesting*, but a lot of it seems irrelevant. Try to make clearer connections between the paragraphs, perhaps by leaving some things out. As the Pechenik book says, "Be sure each paragraph sets the stage for the one that follows" etc.—isn't that a great book? Here is a possible reorganization plan: Introduce the concept of electromagnetic fields in the first few sentences (what they are, what produces them); then mention potential damaging effects on physiology and development (at present it's not clear why the question is so important until one gets to p. 6!); then state your question and note why sea urchins are especially good animals to study. Will that work?

Also in the Introduction, I would expand the paragraph on gene expression effects; discuss one or two of the key experiments in some detail, rather than just tell us the results. I think this is important, since your experiments are a follow-up on these.

Your experimental design seems sound, although I'm not sure the experiments really address the

exact question you pose in your introduction (see
my comments on the draft; probably you just need
to rephrase the question?). But I didn't see any
mention of a control; without the control, how
will you be sure that any effects you see are due
to the electromagnetic field? Also, won't your
treatment raise the water temperature? If so, you
will need to control for that as well.

Finally, you might want to ask Professor Cor-
nell about this, but I think you should write for
a more scientifically advanced audience. Your tone
seems a bit too chatty and informal. And watch
those prepositions—you use them almost as freely
as I do! I enjoyed reading your paper and look
forward to seeing the next draft!

Notice that this reviewer points out the strengths of the piece without over-
looking the weaknesses and deals with the major problems first. **Be firm
but kind in your criticism; your goal is to help your colleague, not
to crush his or her ego**. Be especially careful to avoid sarcasm. Write a
page of constructive criticism that you would feel comfortable receiving.

To help you give your classmates helpful criticism on drafts of their
assignments, your instructor may provide you with, or ask you to develop,
a peer review sheet (see Appendix G for an example). You can also use
such forms to self-criticize your own writing. For advice on preparing
peer review forms, see *http://mwp01.mwp.hawaii.edu/peer_review.htm*.

Receiving Criticism

Be pleased to receive suggestions for improving your work. A colleague
who returns your paper with only a smile and a pat on the back does you
no favors. It is good to receive *some* positive feedback, of course, but what
you are really hoping for is constructive criticism. On the other hand,
don't feel you must accept every suggestion offered. Examine each one
honestly and with distance, and decide for yourself if the reader is on target or not; these reviews of your work are advisory only, giving you a
chance to see how another person interprets what you have written.
Sometimes the reader will misinterpret your writing, and you may therefore disagree with the specific criticisms and suggestions leveled at you;
however, if something was unclear to one reader, it may be equally un-

TECHNOLOGY TIP   3
Tracking Changes Made to Documents

When co-authoring a paper with other students, one person generally writes the first draft and the other authors then suggest modifications. For group work, you might draft the Materials and Methods section, for example, while another student drafts the Results section. The Track Changes feature of Word allows you to e-mail a draft of your section or paper (as an attachment) to another student and then to receive comments and suggested changes from that student directly on the document, and in ways that distinguish the reviewer's comments from the original text that you sent. You can then decide whether or not to accept the suggested changes.

To use this feature, open your document, click Tools on the menu bar, then select Track Changes, and finally select "Track changes while editing," and "Highlight changes on screen." If you are reviewing someone else's manuscript, be sure that this feature is selected before you do any editing.

When you receive a document that has been reviewed by someone else, open it, and then access the Track Changes feature through the Tools item on the menu bar. Click on "Accept or Reject Changes," and you can then accept or reject each specific change that your reviewer suggested. Go through the comments one by one, using the Find arrow, and either Accept or Reject each one. Alternatively, you can consider the suggested changes by first clicking on View, then Toolbars, and then Reviewing, which brings a special tool bar into view. Just to be safe, before printing out the final version of your document, print out just the first page (or the first page with corrections), to be sure that it looks the way you want it to look.

Don't send your draft to other students until you have revised it a few times yourself. The closer the draft is to final form, the more useful reviewers can be in improving it.

clear to others. Try to figure out where the reader went astray, and modify your writing to prevent future readers from following the same path.

It is hard to read criticism of your writing without feeling defensive, but learning to value those comments puts you firmly on the path to becoming a more effective writer. After all, you *want* to communicate; if you are not communicating well, you need to know it, and you need to know why.

Fine-Tuning

Once the writing is blessed with a clear direction and solid logic, it is time to make 1 or 2 final passes to see that each sentence is doing its job in the clearest, most concise fashion. As a first step in developing your ability to fine-tune writing, read the following 25 sentences and try to verbalize the ailment afflicting each one. Then revise the sentences that need help. Pencil your suggested changes directly onto the sentences, using the guide to proofreader's notation presented in Table 2 and the following example:

Hermaphoditism is commonly encountered among
invertebrates. For example, the young East Coast oyster,
Crassostrea virginica, matures as a male, later becomes a
female and may change sex every few years there after.
sequential hermaphrodites generally change sex only once,
and usually change from male to female. In contrast to
species that change sex as they age, many invertebrates are
simultaneous hermaphrodites. Self-fertilization is rare among
simultaneous hermaphrodites, it can occur, as in the
                                although
tapeworms.

It is wise when editing someone else's work to use a different color pen or pencil to be sure the reader will see suggested changes.

Table 2. Proofreader's symbols used in revising copy.

Problem	Symbol	Example
1. Word has been omitted	∧ caret	Study describes *the* effect ∧
2. Letter has been omitted	∧ caret	that b͜ok
3. Letters are transposed	∿	fo͡rm the sea
4. Words are transposed	∿	was (only exposed)
5. Letter should be capitalized	≡ (three short underlines)	these data
6. Letter should be lowercase	/ (slash)	These Ⅾata
7. Word should be in italics	⎯⎯ (underline once)	Homo sapiens
8. Words are run together	| (draw vertical line in between)	edit|carefully
9. Word should be deleted	⎯⎯⎯ (draw line through)	the ~~nice~~ data
10. Space should not have been left	‿ (sideways parentheses)	the e‿nd
11. Wrong letter	/ (draw line through and add correct letter above)	ʄemale
12. Wrong word	⎯⎯ (draw line through and add correct word above)	*These* ~~This~~ data
13. Need to begin a new paragraph	¶ (paragraph symbol)	¶ female. In contrast
14. Restore original	(STET)	(STET) the ~~energy~~ needs

Sentences in Need of Revision

1. To perform this experiment there had to be a low tide. We conducted the study at Blissful Beach on September 23, 2001, at 2:30 PM.
2. In *Chlamydomonas reinhardi*, a single-celled green alga, there are two matine types, 1 and 2. The 1 and 2 cells mate with each other when starved of nitrogen and form a zygote.
3. Protruding form this carapace is the head, bearing a large pair of second antennae.
4. The order in which we think of things to write down is rarely the order we use when we explain what we did to a reader.
5. The purpose of Professor Wilson's book is the examination of questions of evolutionary significance.
6. Swimming in fish has been carefully studied in only a few species.
7. One example of this capacity is observed in the phenomenon of encystment exhibited by many fresh water and parasitic species.
8. In a sense, then, the typical protozoan may be regarded as being a single-celled organism.
9. An estuary is a body of water nearly surrounded by land whose salinity is influenced by freshwater drainage.
10. The résumé represents a summary of your educational background, research experience and goals.
11. In textbooks and many lectures, you are being presented with facts and interpretations.
12. The human genome contains at least 50,000 genes, however there is enough DNA in the genome to form nearly 2×10^6 genes.
13. It should be noted that analyses were done to determine whether the caterpillars chose the different diets at random.
14. These experiments were conducted to test whether the condition of the biological films on the substratum surface triggered settlement of the larvae.
15. Various species of sea anemones live throughout the world.
16. This data clearly demonstrates that growth rates of the blue mussel (mytilus Edulis) vary with temperature.
17. Hibernating mammals mate early in the spring so that their offspring can reach adulthood before the beginning of the next winter.
18. This study pertains to the investigation of the effect of this pesticide on the orientation behavior of honey bees.
19. The results reported here have lead the author to the conclusion that thirsty flies will show a positive response to all solutions, regardless of sugar concentration (see figure 2).

20. Numbers are difficult for listeners to keep track of when they are floating around in the air.
21. Those seedlings possessing a quickly growing phenotype will be selected for, whereas. . . .
22. Under a dissecting microscope, a slide with a drop of the culture was examined at 50×.
23. Measurements of respiration by the salamanders typically took one-half hour each.
24. The results suggest that some local enhancement of pathogen specific antibody production at the infection site exists.
25. Usually it has been found that higher temperatures (30°C) have resulted in the production of females, while lower temperatures (22–27°C) have resulted in the production of males. (e.g., Bull, 1980; Mrosousky, 1982)
26. Octopus have been successful trained to distinguish between red and white balls of varying size.

There are several ways to improve each of these sentences. For reference, my revisions are shown in Appendixes B and C, but you should make your own modifications before looking at mine. Be sure that you can identify the problem suffered by each original sentence, that you understand how that problem was solved by my revision, and that your revision also solves the problem (and does not introduce any new difficulties).

CHECKLIST

1. Allow adequate time for revision (pp. 75–76).

2. Read your paper aloud, slowly, and listen for problems as you read (pp. 75, 109).

3. Don't worry about problems within individual sentences until your paper or report has a beginning, middle, and ending, with each idea leading logically into the next. Use idea maps to help organize your thoughts (pp. 76–81).

4. Revise for content, clarity, and completeness:

   Make sure that each sentence says something of substance, and says what you intend it to say (pp. 81–84).

   Be cautious in drawing conclusions (pp. 83–84).

   Keep an audience of interested peers in mind as you revise (p. 84).

Use *it, they, their*, and other pronouns sparingly, and be sure they don't create ambiguity (pp. 88–90).

Make each statement as specific as possible (pp. 90–92).

5. Revise next for conciseness:

Delete "It is interesting to note that . . ." and other running jumps. Just dive right into the issue being presented (pp. 81–82, 92–94).

Eliminate unnecessary prepositions (pp. 94–95).

Replace weak verbs with stronger ones (pp. 95–99).

Try to have animals, enzymes, and molecules DOING something (pp. 98–99).

6. Revise next for flow (coherence): Improve the logical connections between sentences and paragraphs using appropriate transitional words, summary and repetition, and occasional semicolons (pp. 99–103).

7. Eliminate teleology and anthropomorphism (pp, 12 [Chapter 1], 103–104).

8. Proofread for spelling and grammatical errors (pp. 104–111).

9. Turn in work that you are proud to have completed.

10. Practice finding problems with other people's writing, including that in published papers (pp. 111–112).

11. Give criticism to others that is substantive and honest, but constructive and not insulting (pp. 112–114).

II

GUIDELINES FOR SPECIFIC TASKS

6

WRITING SUMMARIES AND CRITIQUES

For assignments in writing summaries and critiques, you are asked to read a paper from the original scientific literature (the "primary literature") and summarize or assess that paper, usually in fewer than 2 double-spaced, typewritten pages. *Brief* does not, in this case, mean *easy*. In fact, producing that 1- or 2-page summary or critique will probably require as much mental effort as that involved in preparing a full essay or term paper.

On the other hand, once you can write good summaries of individual papers you will have a much easier time writing introductions, discussions, and term papers incorporating multiple references. Indeed, **until you can write clear and convincing summaries of individual papers in your own words, synthesizing material effectively from different sources is virtually impossible**. To do well in these short assignments, you must fully understand what you have read, which usually means that you must read the paper many times, slowly and thoughtfully.

Follow the same procedures whether you are asked to write a summary or a critique; indeed, a critique begins as a summary, to which you then add your own evaluation of the paper.

To begin, read the paper once or twice without taking notes, following the advice given in Chapter 2. Fight the temptation to underline, highlight, or otherwise create the illusion that you are accomplishing something. It is often difficult to distinguish the important from the not-so-important points during the first reading of a scientific paper; skim the paper once for general orientation and overview. Don't try for detailed understanding in the first reading, but do jot down any unfamiliar terms or the names of unfamiliar techniques so that you can look these up in a textbook before you reread the paper.

After you have read the entire paper once, try writing down what you remember about the paper, what you don't understand about what you read, and any other questions that come to mind as you write. This will help to focus your attention on some of the major points for a second reading. It often helps to consult a textbook about the general biology of the organisms being studied or the specific topic being investigated before returning to the paper.

During the next, more careful, reading of the paper, pay special attention to the Materials and Methods and the Results sections; the essence of any scientific paper is contained here, as discussed in Chapter 8. The results obtained in a study depend on how the study was conducted. Were samples taken only at one particular time of year? Was the study replicated? How many individuals were examined? What techniques were used? In an experiment, what variables (for example, photoperiod, temperature, salinity, or food supply) were held constant? Were proper controls provided for each experiment? Which factors might affect the outcome of the study?

As you begin to study the Results section, scrutinize every graph, table, and illustration, developing your own interpretations of the data before rereading the author's verbal presentation, as discussed in Chapter 2. We are readily influenced by the opinions of others, especially when those opinions are well written. Keep an open mind when reading the author's words, but try to form your own opinions about the data first; you may see something that the author did not.

WRITING THE FIRST DRAFT

You will know that you are ready to write your first draft of the assignment when you can distill the essence of the paper into a single, intoxicating summary sentence, or, at most, 2 summary sentences, as discussed in Chapter 2 (pp. 28–29). These sentences should include *all* the key points, present an *accurate* summary of the study, be *fully comprehensible* to someone who has never read the original paper, and be in *your own words*. As a general rule, **do not begin to write your review until you can write such an abbreviated summary**; this exercise will help you discriminate between the essential points of the paper and the extra, complementary details. Several examples of good summary sentences are given later.

If you cannot write a satisfactory 1- or 2-sentence summary, reread the article; you'll get it eventually. Once your summary sentence is committed to paper, ask yourself these questions:

1. Why was the study undertaken? To answer this, draw especially from information given in the Introduction and Discussion sections of the paper.
2. What specific questions were addressed? Summarize each question in a single sentence.
3. How were these questions addressed? What specific approaches were taken to address each question on your list?
4. What assumptions were made by the author(s)? Might any of them be wrong? Are they testable? How might they be tested?

5. What were the major findings of the study?
6. What was particularly interesting about the paper? The questions asked? Some aspect of the methodology? Some particular result or set of results? Some particular conclusion?
7. What questions remain unanswered by the study? These may be questions addressed by the study but not answered conclusively, or they may be new questions arising from the findings of the study under consideration.

WRITING THE SUMMARY

When you can answer these questions without referring to the paper you have read, you can begin to write. Writing without looking at the original paper will help you avoid unintentional plagiarism (p. 30), and will self-test your understanding of the paper. You can (and should) always go back to the original paper later to double-check and fill in specific factual details.

At the top of the page—below your name, the course designation, and the date—give the complete citation for the paper being discussed, beginning at the left-hand margin: names of all authors, year of publication, title of the paper, title of the journal in which the paper was published, and volume and page numbers of the article. On a new line, indent 5 spaces and begin your summary with a few sentences of background information. Your introductory sentences must lead up to a statement of the specific questions the researchers set out to address. Next, tell (1) what approaches were used to investigate each question and (2) what major results were obtained. Be sure to state, as succinctly as possible, exactly what was learned from the study.

To cover so much ground within the limits of one typewritten page is no small feat, but it can be done if you first make certain that you fully understand what you have read. Consider the following example of a brief, successful summary. Before writing the summary, the student condensed the paper into these 2 sentences.

> The tolerance of a Norwegian beetle (*Phyllodecta laticollis*) to freezing temperatures varied seasonally, in association with changes in the blood concentration of glycerol, amino acids, and total dissolved solute. However, the concentration of nucleating agents in the blood did not vary seasonally.

Note that the 2-sentence distillation contains considerable detail despite its brevity, implying impressive mastery of the paper's contents; it is complete, accurate, and self-sufficient. When you can write such sentences, pat yourself on the back and proceed; the hardest work is over.

SAMPLE STUDENT SUMMARY

Minnie Leggs

Bio 101

September 30, 2002

Van der Laak, S. 1982. Physiological adaptations to low temperature in freezing-tolerant *Phyllodecta laticollis* beetles. *Comp. Biochem. Physiol.* 73A: 613–620.

Adult beetles (*Phyllodecta laticollis*), found in Norway, are exposed to sub-zero (°C) temperatures in the field throughout the year. In general, organisms that tolerate freezing conditions either produce extracellular nucleating agents that trigger ice formation outside the cells rather than within them or they produce biological antifreezes, such as glycerol, that lower the freezing point of the blood and tissues to below that of the environment, thereby preventing ice formation. This study (Van der Laak, 1982) documents the tolerance of *P. laticollis* to below-freezing temperatures and determines how seasonal shifts in the temperature tolerance of these beetles are mediated.

Beetles were collected throughout the year and frozen to temperatures as low as −50°C; post-thaw survivorship was then determined. Determinations were also made of the concentrations of solutes in the blood (that is, blood osmotic concentration), total water content, amino acid and glycerol concentrations in the blood, presence of nucleating agents in the blood, and the temperature to which blood could be super-cooled before it would freeze.

The temperature tolerance of *P. laticollis* varied from about −9°C in summer to about −42°C in winter; this shift in freezing tolerance was paralleled by a dramatic winter increase in glycerol concentration and in total blood osmotic concentration. Amino acid concentration also increased in winter, but the contribution to blood osmolarity was small compared to that of glycerol. Nucleating agents were present in the blood year-round, ensuring that ice formation will occur extracellularly rather than intracellularly, even in summer.

For beetles collected in midwinter and early spring, blood glycerol concentrations could be artificially reduced by warming beetles to 23°C (room temperature) for about 24–150 h. When glycerol concentrations of spring and winter beetles were reduced to identical levels by warming, the spring beetles tolerated freezing better than the winter beetles; these differences in tolerance could not be explained by differences in amino acid concentrations. This result indicates that some other factors, as yet unknown, are also involved in determining the freezing tolerance of these beetles.

Analysis of Student Summary

The student has, within one typed page, successfully distilled a 7-page technical report to its scientific essence. Note that the student used the first 3 sentences to introduce the topic and then summarized the purpose of the research in one sentence. The next short paragraph summarizes the experimental approach taken, and the main findings of the study are then stated. No superfluous information is given; the author of this assignment provided only enough detail to make the summary comprehensible. The product glistens with understanding. Rereading the student's 2-sentence encapsulation of the paper (p. 124), you can see that the student was indeed ready to write the report.

As a challenge to yourself, try writing a one-paragraph summary of the above example, cutting the length of the original summary by about 75%. Summary is the ultimate test of understanding.

WRITING THE CRITIQUE

A critique is much like a summary, except that you get to add your own assessment of the paper you have read. This does not mean you should set out to tear the paper to shreds; a critical review is a thoughtful summary and analysis, not an exercise in character assassination. Most biological studies have shortcomings, most of which become obvious only in hindsight. Yet every piece of research contributes some information, even when the original goals of the study are not attained. Emphasize the positive—**focus on what was learned from the study**. Although you should not dwell on the limitations of the study, you should point out these limitations toward the end of your critique. Were the conclusions reached by the authors out of line with the data presented? Do the authors generalize far beyond the populations or species studied? Which questions remain unanswered? How might these questions be addressed? How might the study be improved or expanded in the future? Keep this in mind as you write: you wish to demonstrate to your instructor (and to yourself) that you understand what you have read. Do not comment on whether or not you enjoyed the paper, or found it to be well written; stick to the science unless told to do otherwise.

The Critique

Before writing the critique, the student produced this one-sentence summary of the paper.

> The egg capsules of the marine snails *Nucella lamellosa* and *N. lima* protect developing embryos against low-salinity stress, even though the solute concentration within the capsules falls to near that of the surrounding water within about 1 h.

Again, note that this one-sentence summary satisfies the criterion of self-sufficiency: it can be fully understood without reference to the paper it summarizes. The critique follows.

Saul Tee

Bio 101

April 2, 2001

Kĭnehcép, N.A. 1982. Ability of some gastropod egg capsules to protect against low-salinity stress. *J. Exp. Marine Biol. Ecol.* 63: 195–208.

The fertilized eggs of marine snails are often enclosed in complex, leathery egg capsules with 30 or more embryos being confined within each capsule. The embryos develop for 1 or more weeks before leaving the capsules. The egg capsules of intertidal species potentially expose the developing embryos to thermal stress, osmotic stress, and desiccation stress. This paper (Kînehcép, 1982) describes the ability of such egg capsules to protect developing embryos from low-salinity stress, such as might be experienced at low tide during a rainstorm.

Two snail species were studied: *Nucella lamellosa* and *N. lima*. Embryos were exposed, at 10–12°C, either to full-strength seawater (control conditions) or to 10–12% seawater solutions (seawater diluted with distilled water). The ability of egg capsules to protect the enclosed embryos from low-salinity stress was assessed by placing intact egg capsules into the test solutions for up to 9 h, returning the capsules to full-strength seawater, and comparing subsequent embryonic mortality with that shown by embryos removed from capsules and exposed to the low-salinity stress directly.

Encapsulated embryos exposed to the low salinities suffered less than 2% mortality, even after low-salinity exposures of 9 h duration. In contrast, embryos exposed directly to the same test conditions for as little as 5 h suffered 100% mortality. All embryos survived exposure to control conditions for the full 9 h, showing that removal from the capsules was not the stress killing the embryos in the other treatments. Sampling capsular fluid at various times after capsules were transferred to the diluted seawater, Kînehcép found that the concentration of solutes within capsules fell to near that of the surrounding water within about 1 h after transfer.

This study clearly demonstrates the protective value of the egg capsules of 2 snail species faced with low-salinity stress. However, Kînehcép was unable to explain how egg capsules of these 2 species protect the enclosed embryos since the capsules did not prevent decreases in the solute concentration of the capsular fluid. Although Kînehcép plotted the rate at which the solute concentration falls within the capsules (his Fig. 1), he sampled only at 0, 60, and 90 min after the capsules were transferred to water of reduced salinity. I think he should have sampled at frequent intervals during the first 60 min to discover how rapidly the solute concentration of the capsule fluid falls. As Kînehcép himself suggests, perhaps the embryos are less stressed if the concentration inside the capsule falls slowly. These experiments were all performed at a single temperature even though encapsulated embryos are likely to experience fluctuation in both temperature and salinity as the tide rises and falls during the day; the study should be repeated using a range of temperatures likely to be experienced in the field. In addition, I suggest repeating these experiments using deep-water species whose egg capsules are never exposed to salinity fluctuations of the magnitude used in this study.

Analysis of Student Critique

As before, this student begins with just enough introductory information to make the point of the study clear and ends the first paragraph with a succinct statement of the researcher's goal. The methods and results of the study are then briefly reviewed, as in a summary. Whereas a summary would probably end at this point, the critique continues with thought-provoking assessments by the student. Note that the student was careful to distinguish his thoughts from those of the paper's author (see pp. 30–33, on plagiarism).

CONCLUDING THOUGHTS

Clearly, successfully completing either type of assignment is no trivial matter. But preparing good summaries and critiques is an excellent way to push yourself toward true understanding of what you read—and of the nature of scientific inquiry.

7

WRITING ESSAYS AND TERM PAPERS

A term paper is really just a long essay, its greater length reflecting more extensive treatment of a broader issue. Both assignments ask you to present critical evaluations of what you have read. In preparing an essay, you synthesize information, explore relationships, analyze, compare, contrast, evaluate, and organize your own arguments clearly, logically, and persuasively, gradually leading up to an assessment of your own. A good term paper or short essay is a creative work; **you must interpret thoughtfully what you have read and come up with something that goes beyond what is presented in any single article or book consulted**. Your goal is to come up with new thoughts based on what others have already done.

Essays and term papers are based mostly on readings from the primary scientific literature—that is, the original research papers published in scientific journals such as *Biological Bulletin, Cell, Developmental Biology, Ecology*, and *Journal of Comparative Biochemistry and Physiology*. Textbooks and review articles (such as those in *Scientific American* or *Quarterly Review of Biology*) compose the secondary literature, which gives someone else's interpretation and evaluation of the primary literature. In preparing an essay or term paper, you will go through the same processes that the writers of textbooks and review articles go through in presenting and discussing the primary research literature.

WHY BOTHER?

Every time you are asked to write an essay or term paper, your instructor is committing himself or herself to many hours of reading and grading. There must be a good reason to require such assignments; most instructors are not masochists.

In fact, writing essays or term papers benefits you in several important ways. For one thing, you end up teaching yourself something relevant to the course you are taking. **The ability to self-teach is essential for success in graduate programs and academic careers, and it is a skill worth cultivating for success in almost any profession**. In addition, you gain experience in reading the primary scientific literature. Textbooks and many lectures present you with facts and interpretations. By reading the papers on which these facts and interpretations are based, you come face to face with the sorts of data, and interpretations of data, on which the so-called facts of biology are based, and you gain insight into the true nature of scientific inquiry. The data collected in an experiment are always real; interpretations, however, are always subject to change. Preparing thoughtful essays and term papers will help you move away from the unscientific, blind acceptance of stated facts toward the scientific, critical evaluation of data. These assignments are also superb exercises in the logical organization, effective presentation, and discussion of information, skills that can only ease your career progress in the future. How fortunate you are that your instructor cares enough about your future to give such assignments!

There is one last reason that instructors often ask their students to prepare essays and larger papers. One can simply summarize a dozen papers in succession without understanding the contents of any of them. I call this the "book report" format, in which the writer merely presents facts uncritically: this happened, that happened; the authors suggested this; the authors found that. By evaluating and synthesizing, rather than simply paraphrasing and listing what others have already done, you can show your instructor that you really understand what you have read, that you have really learned something rather than simply memorized or mimicked the information presented to you.

GETTING STARTED

You must first decide on a general subject of interest. Often your instructor will suggest topics that have been successfully explored by former students. Use these suggestions as guides, but do not feel compelled to select one of these topics unless so instructed. Be sure to choose or develop a subject that interests you. It is much easier to write successfully about something of interest than about something that bores you.

All you need for getting started is a general subject, not a specific topic. Stay flexible. As you research your selected subject, you will usually find that you must narrow your focus to a particular topic because you encounter an unmanageable number of references pertinent to your original idea. You cannot, for instance, write about the entire field of primate behavior, because the field has many different facets, each associated with a large and growing literature. In such a case, you will find a smaller topic, such as the social significance of primate grooming behavior, to be more appropriate; as you continue your literature search, you may even find it necessary to restrict your attention to one or a few primate species.

Alternatively, you may find that the topic originally selected is too narrow and that you cannot find enough information on which to base a substantial paper. You must then broaden your topic, or switch topics entirely, so that you will end up with something to discuss. Don't be afraid to discard a topic on which you can find too little information.

Choose a topic you can understand fully. You can't possibly write clearly and convincingly on something beyond your grasp. Don't set out to impress your instructor with complexity; instead, dazzle your instructor with clarity and understanding. Simple topics often make the best ones for essays and papers.

RESEARCHING YOUR TOPIC

Reread Chapter 2 carefully on the subjects of reading and note-taking before you begin your research. You are not setting out to mindlessly regurgitate what others have done and found, and you will not be reading to memorize anything. Instead, **you will be aiming to evaluate and synthesize information from a number of sources in order to come up with a new way of looking at the field**. You are setting out to make a specific point (called a thesis statement) and to convince readers that the point is valid. To accomplish this you will need to read your sources selectively and slowly, and think, think, think as you read. You will also need to start researching your general topic (e.g., the use of snails as intermediate hosts in the life cycles of parasitic flatworms) many weeks before the first draft is due, to give yourself time to read carefully and especially to digest the material that you read.

Begin by carefully reading the appropriate section of your textbook to get an overview of the general subject of which your topic is a part, and then consult at least one more specialized book before tackling the primary literature. Now you are ready to locate and read research reports on your topic, following the advice presented in Chapter 2. The goal is to select a number of interrelated papers and to read these with considerable care and patience, not simply to accumulate a huge number of references that then receive cursory attention.

Be sure you understand thoroughly what you have read. One of the best ways to self-assess your understanding is to summarize the material in your own words as you read along, paragraph by paragraph, section by section. When you have completed the entire paper, try writing a 1-paragraph summary of what you have read, and then a 1- or 2-sentence summary. You cannot evaluate or synthesize information until you can first write a clear, accurate, and specific summary of that information in your own words, as discussed more fully in Chapters 2 and 6.

DEVELOPING A THESIS STATEMENT

It takes a fair amount of mental effort to come up with a useful thesis statement. Continually ask yourself while taking notes,

- Why am I writing this down?
- What is especially interesting about this particular information?
- What puzzles me about what I have read?
- Can I see any relationship between this information and what I have already read, written, or learned?
- What assumptions did the authors make, and does each assumption seem reasonable and well supported?

Look also for apparent contradictions in the results of different studies, and in the interpretations of different authors. And look for patterns, and for exceptions to those patterns.

As you finish each paper, jot down some ideas about what you would like to know more about. As you start developing opinions about what you have read, jot those thoughts down, too, and ask yourself what those opinions are based on. Writing down such thoughts will help self-provoke intellectual engagement with the material, an essential ingredient in the recipe for success.

Eventually you will begin coming up with original ideas, interesting things you hadn't thought about before, and then you will be ready to draft a thesis statement that both you and the reader will find interesting.

A thesis statement needs support to be convincing. You might, for example, suggest that while many authors assume that all snail species serve as intermediate hosts for parasitic flatworms, there are good reasons to question this assumption. Or you might suggest that the remarkable diversity of reproductive patterns among marine animals is made possible by the chemical and physical properties of seawater. Or you might argue that frog tadpoles rely more on chemical cues than on visual cues to distinguish relatives from nonrelatives.

Or, you may not reach any definitive conclusion at all. Your argument might be just that we don't seem to understand as much about some particular topic as some people think we do, and that there are specific issues that need to be studied further.

Refine your draft thesis statement as you keep reading and as you keep writing, until you have a statement that you find interesting, that is not self-evident, and that requires support. This statement will fuel the entire project. You will present this statement near the beginning of your paper, and devote the rest of the paper to supporting it.

There's something magical about thesis statements and where they come from. As you continue to read and think and write, they just mysteriously appear. If you start your assignment well in advance of when it is due, and spend several hours a week reading and thinking about your topic—following the methods advocated in Chapter 2—I can almost guarantee that it will happen for you. If you wait to begin reading and thinking until a week or so before your report is due, I can almost guarantee that it will not.

WRITING THE PAPER

Getting Underway

Some instructors add considerable work to their lives by monitoring your progress [e.g., asking to see your notes, lists of papers read, summaries of those papers (Chapter 6), and partial drafts]. This is splendid for you because it puts you on a schedule. Otherwise you must schedule yourself. Start on the project as early as possible, and allocate at least a few hours a week to it, every week until it's done.

Once you have at least a draft of a thesis statement, begin the formal writing process by reading all of your notes, preferably without pen or pencil in hand. Having completed a reading of your notes to get an overview of what you have accomplished, reread them, this time with the intention of sorting your ideas into categories. Notes taken on index cards are particularly easy to sort, provided that you have not written many different ideas on a single card; one idea per card is a good rule to follow. To arrange notes written on full-sized sheets of paper, some people suggest annotating the notes with pens of different colors or using a variety of symbols, with each color or symbol representing a particular aspect of the topic. Still other people simply use scissors to snip out sections of the notes, and then group the resulting scraps of paper into piles of related ideas. And of course if you have entered notes directly into a computer, you can cut and paste to group together notes on related issues. You should experiment to find a system that works well for you.

At this point, you must eliminate any notes that are irrelevant to the specific topic you have decided to write about. No matter how interesting a fact or idea is, it has no place in your paper unless it clearly relates to your thesis statement and therefore helps you develop your argument. Some of the notes you took early on in your exploration of the literature are especially likely to be irrelevant to your essay because these notes were taken before you had developed a firm focus. Put these irrelevant notes in a safe place for later use; don't let them coax their way into your paper.

You must next decide how best to arrange your categorized notes so that your essay or term paper progresses toward some conclusion. Again, ask yourself whether a particular section of your notes seems especially interesting to you, and why it does, and look for connections among the various items as you sort. Idea mapping (Chapter 5, pp. 75–81) can be a great help in organizing your material.

The Crucial First Paragraph

The direction your paper will take must be clearly and specifically indicated in the opening paragraph, as in the following example written by student A:

> Most lamellibranch bivalves are sedentary, living either in soft-substrate burrows (e.g., soft-shell clams, *Mya arenaria*) or attached to hard substrate (e.g., the blue mussel, *Mytilus edulis*) (Barnes, 1980). However, individuals of a few bivalve species live on the surface of substrates, unattached, and are capable of locomoting through the water. One such species is the

```
scallop Pecten maximus. In this essay, I will ar-
gue that swimming is made possible in P. maximus
by a combination of unique morphological and
physiological adaptations, and will then consider
some of the evolutionary pressures that may have
selected for these adaptations.
```

The nature of the problem being addressed is clearly indicated in this first paragraph, and student *A* tells us clearly why the problem is of interest: (1) the typical bivalve doesn't move and certainly doesn't swim, (2) a few bivalves can swim, (3) so what is there about these exceptional species that enables them to do what other species can't? and (4) why might this swimming ability have evolved? Note that use of the pronoun "I" is now perfectly acceptable in scientific writing.

In contrast to the previous example, consider the following weaker (although not horrible) first paragraph written by student *B* on the same subject:

```
Most bivalved molluscs either burrow into, or
attach themselves to, a substrate. In a few
species, however, the individuals lie on the sub-
strate unattached and are able to swim by ex-
pelling water from their mantle cavities. One
such lamellibranch is the scallop Pecten maximus.
The feature that allows bivalves like P. maximus
to swim is a special formation of the shell
valves on their dorsal sides. This formation and
its function will be described.
```

In this example, the second sentence weakens the opening paragraph considerably by prematurely referring to the mechanism of swimming. The main function of the sentence should be to emphasize that some species are not sedentary; the reader, not yet in a position to understand the mechanism of swimming, becomes a bit baffled. The next-to-last sentence of the paragraph ("The feature that allows. . . .") also hinders the flow of the argument. Indeed, there doesn't seem to *be* any argument. This sentence summarizes the essay before it has even been launched, and again, the reader is not yet in a position to appreciate the information presented; what is this "special formation," and how does it have anything to do with swimming? The first paragraph of a paper should be an introduction, not a summary. It must set the stage for all that follows.

The last sentence of student *B*'s paragraph does clearly state the objective of the paper, but the reader must ask, "Toward what end?" The author has set the reader up for a book report, not a critical evaluation or a persuasive argument. Reread the paragraph written by student *A*, and notice how the same information has been used so much more effectively, introducing a thoughtful essay rather than a tedious recitation of facts. Student *A*'s first paragraph was written with a clear sense of purpose, with each sentence carrying the reader forward to the final statement of intent, the argument on which the rest of the paper will be based. You might guess (correctly, as it turns out) from reading student *B*'s first paragraph that the rest of the paper was somewhat unfocused and rambling. In contrast, student *A*'s first paragraph clearly signals that what follows will be well focused and tightly organized. It might take 3–4 revisions, but be sure to get your papers off to an equally strong start.

Another example of a typical, but not especially effective, first paragraph will be helpful:

```
The crustaceans have an exceptional capability
for changing the intensity and pattern of their
coloring (Russell-Hunter, 1979). Many species
seem able to change their color at will. The
cells responsible for producing the characteris-
tic color changes of crustaceans are the chro-
matophores. The function of these cells will be
discussed in this essay.
```

What is wrong with this introductory paragraph? The author is certainly off to a strong start with the first sentence. The second sentence, however, begins by repeating information already given in the first sentence (crustaceans can change color), and ends by saying nothing at all (what does "at will" mean for a crustacean?). The last sentence sets up a book report, even though the author calls it an essay. *Why* will the function of these cells be discussed? More to the point, why should the reader be interested in such a discussion? The reader will be more readily drawn into your intellectual net if you indicate not only where you are heading but also why you are undertaking the journey.

The first paragraph of your paper must state clearly what you are setting out to accomplish and why. Every paragraph that follows the first paragraph should advance your argument clearly and logically toward the stated goal.

Supporting Your Argument

State your case, and build it carefully. Use your information and ideas to build an argument, to develop a point, to synthesize. **Sketching an**

"idea map" (Chapter 5, pp. 76–81) is an excellent way to organize your thoughts into a powerful and logical progression of ideas. If you are writing an extensive term paper, you can (and should) use many of your idea map topics as headings or subheadings to help guide readers through the issues covered. *The Quarterly Review of Biology* and *Biological Reviews* provide particularly good examples of the effective use of headings and subheadings in structuring lengthy literature reviews.

Avoid the tendency to simply summarize papers one by one: the authors did this, then they did that, and then they suggested the following explanation. Instead, set out to compare, to contrast, to illustrate, to discuss. As described more fully in Chapter 4, you must back up all statements of fact or opinion with supporting documentation; this documentation may be an example drawn from the literature you have read or a reference (author and date of publication) to a paper or group of papers that support your statement, as in the following examples:

> Schistosomiasis is one of the most serious parasitic diseases of mankind, afflicting hundreds of millions of people and causing hundreds of millions of dollars in economic losses yearly through livestock infestations (Roberts and Janovy, 1996).

> The ability of an organism to recognize "self" from "non-self" is found in both vertebrates and invertebrates. Even the most primitive invertebrates show some form of this immune response. For example, Wilson (1907) found that disassociated cells from 2 different sponge species would regroup according to species; cells of one species never reaggregated with those of the second species.

In referring to experiments, don't simply state that a particular experiment supports some particular hypothesis, or that a researcher reached a particular conclusion; *describe* the relevant parts of the experiment, and explain how the results relate to the hypothesis in question. For example, how potent are the following sentences?

> Dudash and Carr (1998) presented evidence that deleterious recessive alleles were responsible for

inbreeding depression in 2 closely related plants in the genus *Mumulus*. In contrast, Karkkainen (1999) showed that deleterious recessive alleles could not account for inbreeding depression in the self-incompatible herb *Arabis petraea*.

There is nothing in these sentences to convince readers of anything, not even that their author has read more than the title and abstract of the papers cited. In contrast, look at how much more convincing the following 2 examples are:

EXAMPLE 1

Foreign organisms or particles that are too large to be ingested by a single leukocyte are often isolated by encapsulation, with the encapsulation response demonstrating clear species-specificity. For example, Cheng and Galloway (1970) inserted pieces of tissue taken from several species into an incision made in the body wall of the gastropod *Helisoma duryi*. Tissue transplanted from other species was completely encapsulated within 48 hours of the transplant. Tissue obtained from individuals of the same species as the host was also encapsulated, but encapsulation was not completed for at least 192 hours.

EXAMPLE 2

Above a certain temperature, further temperature increases often have a depressing effect on larval growth rates (Kingston, 1974; Leighton, 1974). This break point can be very sharply defined. For instance, larvae of the bivalve *Cardium glaucum* were healthy and grew rapidly at 31°C, grew abnormally and less rapidly at 32–33°C, and grew hardly at all at 34°C (Kingston, 1974).

In all of your writing, avoid quotations unless they are absolutely necessary; rely on your own words and your own understanding of what you have read.

The Closing Paragraph

At the end of your essay, summarize the problem addressed and the major points you have made, as in the following example:

> Clearly, the basic molluscan plan for respiration that had been successfully adapted to terrestrial life in one group of gastropods, the terrestrial pulmonates, has been successfully readapted to life in water by the freshwater pulmonates. Having lost the typical molluscan gills during the evolutionary transition from salt water to land, the freshwater pulmonates have evolved new respiratory mechanisms involving either the storage of an air supply (using the mantle cavity) or a means of extracting oxygen while under water, using a gas bubble or direct cutaneous respiration. Further studies are required to fully understand how the gas bubble functions in pulmonate respiration.

Never introduce any new information in your summary paragraph.

CITING SOURCES

Cite only sources that you have actually read and would feel confident discussing with your instructor. Unless told otherwise, cite sources directly in the text by author and date of publication rather than by using footnotes. For example:

> Kim (1976) demonstrated that magnetic fields established by direct current can alter the rates of enzyme-mediated reactions in cell-free systems. Similarly, magnetic fields established by alternating current can affect the activity of certain liver enzymes (Yashina, 1974) and mitochondrial enzymes (Kholodau, 1973).

More detailed information about citing sources is given in Chapter 4 (pp. 66–70).

At the end of your paper, include a Literature Cited section, listing all the publications referred to in your paper. Your instructor may specify a particular format for preparing this section of your paper. For specific information about preparing the Literature Cited section, see pp. 70–74.

CREATING A TITLE

By the time you have finished writing, you should be ready to title your creation. Give the essay or term paper a title that is appropriate and interesting, one that conveys significant information about the specific topic of your paper (see also pp. 206–208):

> **No:** Factors controlling sex determination in turtles
>
> **Yes:** The roles of nest site selection and temperature in determining sex ratio in loggerhead sea turtles
>
> **No:** Biochemical changes during hibernation
>
> **Yes:** Adaptations to environmental stress: the biochemical basis for depressed metabolic rate in hibernating mammals
>
> **No:** Reproductive diversity in marine animals
>
> **Yes:** The role played by the chemical and physical properties of seawater in the evolution of reproductive patterns in marine animals

In your enthusiasm to make your title specific and informative, don't also make it unnecessarily wordy. How would you improve the following title?

> Does adaptation to copper result in a decrease in glutathione S-transferase activity over time in the marine mussel *Mytilus galloprovincialis*?

Following the Second Commandment of concise writing (Chapter 5, p. 95), let's strengthen the verb by replacing "result in a decrease" with simply "decrease." Also, doesn't "decrease" imply the passage of time? By eliminating the redundancy, the title then becomes:

Does adaptation to copper decrease glutathione S-transferase activity in the marine mussel *Mytilus galloprovincialis*?

REVISING

Once you have a working draft of your paper, you must revise it, clarifying your presentation, removing ambiguity, eliminating excess words, and improving the logic and flow of ideas. Revising is discussed in Chapter 5. If you are having difficulty organizing your ideas, I urge you to try Idea Mapping (pp. 76–81). You may also have to edit for grammar and spelling. Always leave time for at least 1–2 revisions of your work.

8

WRITING LABORATORY AND OTHER RESEARCH REPORTS

Inside every practical scientist the same pleasure in competing against nature lurks below the surface, the same enthusiasm for experiment, the same satisfaction in dreaming up new gambits and thrusts that can trick or tease the natural world into revealing its secrets.

Janet Browne (2002. *Charles Darwin—The Power of Place*)

WHY ARE YOU DOING THIS?

It is no accident that most biology courses include laboratory components in addition to lecture sessions. Doing biology involves making observations, asking questions, formulating hypotheses, devising experiments to test the hypotheses, presenting data, evaluating data, interpreting data, and formulating new questions and hypotheses. Those so-called facts you learn from lectures and textbooks are primarily interpretations of data. By participating in the acquisition and interpretation of data, you glimpse the true nature of the scientific process.

If you are contemplating a career in research, be assured that learning to write effective research reports now is an investment in your future. As a laboratory technician or research assistant, you will often be asked to analyze, summarize, and graph data so that the future path of the research can be decided. If you eventually pursue a research M.S. or Ph.D., you will find that a graduate thesis is essentially a large lab report. Writing up your research for publication, as a graduate student or as a researcher with a laboratory of your own, you will quickly find that you are again following exactly the procedures you used in preparing good laboratory reports in college biology courses; it can't hurt to learn the tools of your trade now.

You can also benefit from writing good laboratory reports even if you do not expect to go on in biology. Preparing laboratory reports develops the ability to organize ideas logically, think clearly, and express yourself accurately and concisely. It is difficult to imagine a career in which the mastery of such skills is not a great asset.

THE PURPOSE OF LABORATORY AND FIELD NOTEBOOKS

The first step in preparing a good research report is to keep a detailed notebook. Research notebooks function to:

1. Record the design and goals of your experiments and observations.
2. Record and organize your thoughts and questions about the work you are doing or planning to do.
3. Record your observations and numerical data.
4. Help you organize your activities in the laboratory so that you can work quickly and accurately.

Keeping a detailed notebook will make the task of writing your report much easier, and you will end up producing a better report; after all, all products benefit from the use of quality materials. Moreover, the skills you learn in keeping the notebook could really pay off later in life. The Nobel Prize for the isolation of insulin would probably have gone to J. B. Collip instead of to Frederick Banting and C. H. Best had Dr. Collip learned to keep a more careful record of his work as a student; Collip was apparently the first to purify the hormone, but his notes were incomplete and he was therefore unable to repeat the procedure successfully in subsequent studies.

Similarly, Charles Darwin neglected to make careful field notes about the birds he collected among the Galapagos Islands. Not realizing at the time that the birds collected on the different islands represented different species of finch, all new to science, Darwin didn't even keep the specimens from different islands in separate packages. Fortunately for him, Captain FitzRoy and some of the crew members aboard the *Beagle* (including his much underacknowledged servant Syms Covington) made their own bird collections during the voyage and *did* keep track of which birds came from which islands. Without their help, he would never have been able to put the now-famous finch story together at all.

You might not be so lucky: Take notes carefully and in detail.

Taking Notes and Making Drawings

In keeping your research notebook, assume that you are doing something worthwhile, that you might well discover something remarkable (it does happen), and that you will suffer complete amnesia while you sleep that night. In other words, take the time to write down—in your own words— everything you are about to do, everything you actually do, and why you do it. You can't always tell what will turn out to be important later on.

Record your data clearly, with each number identified by the appropriate units. Many of the details that seem too obvious to write down (today's date [including the year], the name and location of your field site, the name of the species you are working with, or the units of measurements, for example) are forgotten surprisingly quickly upon leaving the laboratory or field; you *can* write down too little, but it's difficult to write down too much.

Write so legibly and clearly that, should you be run over by a truck on your way to class the next day, other students in the course would have no difficulty reconstructing your study and following your results. Similarly, if you use abbreviations in your notebook, be sure to indicate what each stands for. These procedures will greatly facilitate the writing of your laboratory report. They are in fact crucial in any functioning research laboratory because anyone in the lab must be able to pick up your work or interpret your work where you left off if you are unable to come in one day or if you leave that laboratory permanently.

Some of this writing can be done before the laboratory session. Whenever possible, read about the day's study ahead of time, being sure (through writing in your notebook) that you understand its goals, and plan exactly how you will record your data. You will get more out of the exercise and will undoubtedly finish your work in the lab or field sooner if you arrive prepared. **It often helps to sketch a simple flowchart of your planned activities ahead of time**, as in Figure 12. (You can use this flowchart again later, in writing the Materials and Methods section of your report.)

Your research notebook should contain any thoughts, observations, or questions you have about what you are doing, along with the actual protocol and data. A sample page from a model notebook is shown in Figure 13. Note that the notebook entry begins by stating the date and a specific goal. With such clear, well-organized, and well-thought-out notes, this student is well on his or her way to preparing a fine report.

A notebook recording field observations (a "field notebook") would look similar to that shown in Figure 14, which records part of a study

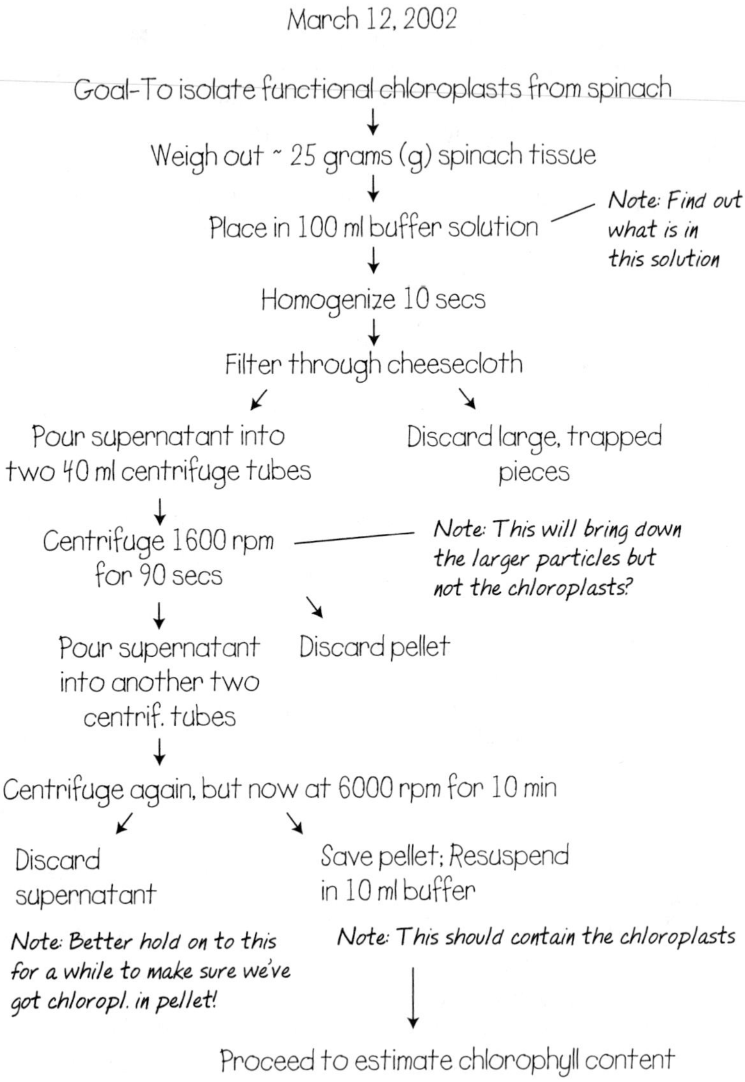

March 12, 2002

Goal–To isolate functional chloroplasts from spinach

↓

Weigh out ~ 25 grams (g) spinach tissue

↓

Place in 100 ml buffer solution ⟶ *Note: Find out what is in this solution*

↓

Homogenize 10 secs

↓

Filter through cheesecloth

↙   ↘

Pour supernatant into two 40 ml centrifuge tubes   Discard large, trapped pieces

↓

Centrifuge 1600 rpm for 90 secs ⟶ *Note: This will bring down the larger particles but not the chloroplasts?*

↓   ↘

Pour supernatant into another two centrif. tubes   Discard pellet

↓

Centrifuge again, but now at 6000 rpm for 10 min

↙   ↘

Discard supernatant   Save pellet; Resuspend in 10 ml buffer

Note: Better hold on to this for a while to make sure we've got chloropl. in pellet!   *Note: This should contain the chloroplasts*

↓

Proceed to estimate chlorophyll content

Figure 12. A page from a student's laboratory notebook. The flowchart is based on more-detailed information provided by the instructor.

October 4, 2002

  Goal-to determine rate at which the marine bivalve
Mercenaria mercenaria (hardshell clam) moves water across
its gills.

Approach--Use unicellular alga (phytoplankton) Dunaliella
tertiolecta.

Determine initial cells $\cdot$ ml $^{-1}$, final cells $\cdot$ ml $^{-1}$. If know elapsed time
and volume of seawater in container, can calculate cells eaten
per hour per clam. and ml of sea H_2O cleared of cells/h/clam.

  Weight of clam (incl. shell): 9.4g [Fisher/Ainsworth balance,
                                      Model MX-200]

Find initial concentration of algal cells:

  1. 1 ml of culture + drop of Lugol's iodine to kill cells.
  2. Load hemacytometer for cell counts--finally got it right on
     5th try!
     Helps to tilt pipet at about 45° angle.

                            ↗ because of dilution w/0.05ml Lugol's sol'n
Data: (multiply by 1.05 and then by 10^4 -----→ cells ml $^{-1}$)

                                                    Note: ask
             counts per section of hemacytom slide   *Prof. Scully*
         Sample 1   Sample 2   *why 10^4.*
            22   18
      2) 13   21
           18   20
      4) 22   20
           26   16
      6) 21   12
           20   18
      8) 16   22
           22   19
      $\overline{X}$ = 20.0 (x 1.05) ——→   18.4 (x 1.05) ——→
      ——→ 21.0 x 10^4 cells ml $^{-1}$ 19.4 x 10^4 cells ml $^{-1}$
                                                ↘
                                          good agreement!

Put clam in 150ml of this solution at 2:10 PM; H_2O = 21.4°C

Figure 13. A sample page from a student's laboratory notebook.

September 17, 2002. 1-3 PM. Sunny, 27° C air temp.; 17° C water.
Goal: investigate size distribution of L. littorea shells at different
distances from high tide line.
ME: might expect shells to get larger as get closer to water,
since these are marine snails and so should be able to feed more
hours per day if spend more time under water. (What do they
eat? Can they only eat in water?)

- - - -

Note: Many of the empty shells have large round holes made by a
drilling predator--probably Nucella lapillus or Lunatia heros,
which seem to be the only carnivorous gastropods living here.
——► Should calc. % of dead snails (empty shells) that have drill
holes. Drill holes seem to be in exact same location on each shell.
How is this possible?

- - - -

Note: Most of the rocks in this area are almost completely
covered by very tiny (young) barnacles. Covering = so dense in
some places can't even see the rock surface.
Question: Why no big, adult barnacles on these rocks?
Perhaps all die off during the summer for some reason.
There are many large barnacles on rocks much farther down the
beach. Same species? If so, why only die here? Would be
interesting to come back and monitor survival of young
barnacles here and down the beach a few times during the
summer and fall--perhaps once a month?
SAMPLING: 0.25m^2 around each transect point, every 2m from
high tide (HT) mark.
DATA: No snails found from 0-3 meters (m) below high tide mark.
D = DRILLED

Distance from high tide (m)	Shell lengths (cm)	
	Live snails	Empty shells
4m	1.6, 1.4, 0.5	1.4
	1.7, 0.9, 2.1	
6m	1.7, 1.9, 1.1	1.8D
	2.0, 1.8, 1.8	1.4
		1.4

etc.

Figure 14. A sample page from a student's field notebook.

investigating the size distributions of the common marine intertidal snail *Littorina littorea* along a Massachusetts beach. Again, the quality of the entries suggests that this student is not simply trying to "get it over with," or to simply write down textbook facts and paraphrases of lecture notes; the student is clearly looking around and thinking—every instructor's dream.

In both laboratory and field work, it is often necessary to draw what you are seeing, particularly when working with living organisms. Perhaps the most important benefit of such drawing is that, **done properly, the act of drawing forces you to look more carefully at the object or organism before you**. As you draw, pay special attention to the relative sizes, shapes, and textures of different parts. Is part *A* connected to part *B*, or are they only adjacent to each other? Are the widths of parts *A* and *B* similar, or is one wider than the other? How much wider? Is *A* twice as wide as *B*, or 3 times as wide? The closer you look, the more you will see.

Draw using hard lead pencil if possible, so that you can modify your drawings easily while you work. If you must use pen, be sure the ink does not smear when wet. Try to figure out what things are as you draw, and label them as you go along. Be sure to indicate the approximate size of what you are drawing, and include a scale bar if appropriate. Most important, make your drawings *big* so that they can accommodate plenty of detail. Most beginning students make their drawings much too small; think big. Even if you are looking at something through a microscope, your drawing of that something should fill a 4-by-6-inch space. Remember, the goal is not to become a great artist, but to learn how to observe closely and how to record those observations accurately and in sufficient detail.

COMPONENTS OF THE RESEARCH REPORT

A research report is typically divided into 6 major sections:

1. *Abstract*. In the Abstract, you summarize the problem addressed, why the problem was addressed, your approach to the problem, and the major findings and conclusions of your study. This is probably the most difficult part of the report to write well.
2. *Introduction*. The introductory section, usually only 1 or 2 paragraphs long, tells why the study was undertaken; a brief summary of relevant background facts leads to a statement of the specific problem that is being addressed. If appropriate, also describe the specific hypotheses that you set out to test.

3. *Materials and Methods.* This section is *your* reminder of what you did, and it also serves as a set of instructions for anyone wishing to repeat your study in the future.

4. *Results.* This is the centerpiece of your report. What were the major findings of the study? Present the data or summarize your observations using graphs and tables to reveal any trends you found. Point out these trends to the reader. If you make good use of your tables and graphs, the results can commonly be presented in only 1 or 2 paragraphs of text; one picture is worth quite a few words. Avoid interpreting the data in this section.

5. *Discussion.* How do your results relate to the goals of the study, as stated in your Introduction, and how do they relate to the results that might have been expected from background information obtained in lectures, textbooks, or outside reading? Do your results argue against one or more of the hypotheses presented in your Introduction? What new hypotheses might now be formulated, and how might these hypotheses be tested? This section is typically the longest part of the report.

6. *Literature Cited.* This section includes the full citations for any references (including textbooks and laboratory handouts) you have cited in your report. Double-check your sources to be certain they are listed correctly because this list of citations will permit the interested reader to check the accuracy of any factual statements you make, and often, to understand the basis for your interpretations of the data. With only one exception (p. 69), cite only material you have actually read. The proper formats for citing literature and presenting citations are described in Chapter 4.

You may also be asked to include one additional section in your reports: an Acknowledgments section, in which you formally thank people for their contributions to the project. And, of course, your report will need a revealing title.

Before writing your report, first study a few short papers in a major biological journal, such as *Biological Bulletin, Developmental Biology,* or *Ecology.* Your instructor may provide you with a few especially good models. Reading these journal articles for content is unnecessary; you don't need to understand the topic of a paper to appreciate how the article is crafted. But do pay attention to the way the Introduction is constructed, the amount of detail included in the Materials and Methods section, and the material that is and is not included in the Results section.

In studying an article or two, note that figures and tables are always accompanied by explanatory captions (for figures) and legends (for tables), and that the axes of graphs and the columns and rows of tables are clearly labeled. Note the location of figure captions and table legends. Study the captions and legends carefully and imitate them in crafting your own.

WHERE TO START

> Beginnings are hardest. . . . How can you write the beginning of something till you know what it's the beginning of?
>   Peter Elbow (1973. *Writing Without Teachers*)

Strangely enough, you should begin writing your report with neither the Title, the Abstract, nor the Introduction. It is far easier to write the Introduction—and the title—toward the end of the job, after you have fully digested what it is that you have done. And since the Abstract is a tight summary of the entire report, this would be the worst section to begin with: How can you summarize something you haven't yet written? **Start work with either the Materials and Methods section or the Results section.** Better still, you may profitably work on the two in tandem; working on the Results section sometimes helps clarify what should be included in the Methods section, and working on the Methods section sometimes clarifies the order in which results should be presented in the Results section.

Because the Materials and Methods section requires the least mental effort, completing it is a good way to overcome inertia. You may not know why you did the experiment or what you found out by doing the experiment, but you can probably reconstruct what you did without much difficulty. Moreover, reminiscing carefully about what you did puts you in the right frame of mind to consider *why* you did it.

WRITING THE MATERIALS AND METHODS SECTION

Results are meaningful in science only if they can be obtained over and over again, whenever the experiment is repeated. Unfortunately, the results of any study depend to a large extent on the way the study was done.

It is therefore essential that you describe your methods in detail sufficient to permit your experiment to be repeated exactly as originally performed. Perhaps the best reason for writing a detailed Materials and Methods section is that it helps you review what you have done in an organized way and starts you thinking about why you've done it. Developing a good Materials and Methods section puts you in the right frame of mind to do an equally good job on the other sections of the report.

The difficulty in writing this section of a research report (or journal manuscript) is in selecting the right level of detail. Students commonly give too little information; when informed of this defect, they may then give too much information. It's hard to hit it just right, but keeping your audience in mind (yourself and your fellow students) will help.

Determining the Correct Level of Detail

Many students begin with a one-sentence Materials and Methods section: "Methods were as described in the lab manual." Although this sentence meets the criterion of brevity, it is generally unacceptable as a stand-alone Methods section. For one thing, studies are rarely performed exactly as described in a laboratory manual or handout. Your instructions may call for the use of 15 animals, for example, but only 12 animals might be available for use on the day of your experiment. In addition, many details of a study will vary from year to year, week to week, or place to place, and must therefore be omitted from your set of instructions.

But don't get carried away. Consider the following overly detailed description of a study involving the growth of radish seedlings:

```
On January 5, I obtained 4 paper cups, 400 g of
potting soil, and 12 radish seeds. I labeled the
cups A, B, C, D and planted 3 seeds per cup, us-
ing a plastic spoon to cover each seed with about
1/4 inch of soil.
```

The author has used the first sentence simply to list the materials; whenever possible, it is far better to mention each new material as you discuss what you did with it. Furthermore, why do we need to know the weight of the soil obtained, or that the cups were labeled A–D rather than 1–4, or that a plastic spoon was used to add soil? Omitting the excess details and starting right in with what was done, we obtain:

```
On January 5, I planted 3 radish seeds in each of
4 individually marked paper cups, covering the
seeds with about 1 cm of potting soil.
```

Note that the essential details—individually marked cups, 3 seeds per cup, 1 cm of soil—not only survive in the edited version, but now stand out clearly. The trick, then, is to determine which details are essential and which are not. Happily, I've come up with a can't-fail method for getting this right.

Begin by listing all the factors that might have influenced your results. If, for example, you measured the feeding rates of caterpillars on several different diets, your list might look something like this:

    Species of caterpillar used

    Diets used

    Amount of food provided per caterpillar

    Time of year

    Time of day

    Air temperature in room

    Manufacturer and model number of any specialized
    equipment used (such as balances, centrifuges, or
    spectrophotometers)

    Size and age of caterpillars

    Duration of the experiment

    Container size or volume

    Number of animals per container

    Total number of individuals in the study

    Precision of measurements made

This list, which you do not turn in with your report, contains the bricks with which you will construct the Materials and Methods section. Each of the listed details must find its way into your report (not necessarily in the order in which you jotted them down) because each gives information essential for later replication of the experiment. Some of this information may also help you explain why your results differed from those of others who have gone before you, a topic that will deserve some attention later, in the Discussion section of your report. Details that do not merit inclusion in the list are superfluous and should not appear in your Materials and Methods section.

In describing the procedures followed, you must say what you did, but you should freely refer to your laboratory manual or handouts in describing how you did it. For example, you might write:

```
The 3 different diets were distributed to the
caterpillars in random fashion, as described in
the laboratory manual (Lynch, 2001).
```

The important point here is that the diets were distributed at random; the outcome might be quite different if the largest caterpillars were to receive one diet and the smallest caterpillars another. The interested reader, including you, perhaps, at some later date, can refer to the stated source (Lynch, 2001) for detailed instruction in the method of randomization. You might want to append the relevant portion of your handout or manual at the end of your report as an appendix; this is a fine way to keep everything together for later use.

Mention, for your own benefit as well as that of your reader, why particular steps were taken whenever you think it might not be obvious. Imagine yourself explaining things to a classmate who has not yet performed the experiment. We might, for example, profitably rewrite the sentence given in the preceding example to read:

```
To avoid prejudicing the results by distributing
food according to size of caterpillar, the 3 dif-
ferent diets were distributed to the caterpillars
in random fashion as described by Lynch (2001).
```

It is also usually appropriate to include any formulas used in analyzing your data. The following sentences, for example, would belong in a Materials and Methods section:

```
The data were analyzed by a series of chi-square
tests. The rate at which food was eaten was cal-
culated by dividing the weight loss of the food
by 3 hours, according to the following formula:
Feeding rate = (Initial food weight − final food
weight) ÷ 3 h.
```

Often this information is presented in a separate subsection at the end of the Materials and Methods section (see below).

Note in this example that **"rates" always have units of "per time."** If it doesn't have units of "per time," it is not a rate (p. 108).

Be sure to note any departures from the given instructions. Suppose you were told to weigh the caterpillars individually but found that your balance was not sensitive enough to record the weight of a single animal. Your laboratory instructor, never at a loss for good ideas, probably suggested that you weigh the individuals in each container as a group. Your report might then include the following information:

Determining the weight gained by each caterpillar over the 3-hour period of the experiment
required that both initial and final weights be determined. The caterpillars were too small to be
weighed individually. Therefore, similarly sized
caterpillars were weighed in groups of 3 at a
time, to the nearest 0.1 g. The average weight of
each caterpillar in the group was then calculated.

Use of Subheadings

Unless your Materials and Methods section is very short (e.g., a single
paragraph), use informative subheadings to help organize and present
your material by topic. The emphasis here is on the word "informative."
Here are some uninformative subheadings, relating to a study of shell
choice by hermit crabs, followed by more substantive revisions on the
same topic:

Uninformative: Field experiment

Informative: Occupancy of damaged and intact shells
in the field

Uninformative: Shell choice

Informative: Effect of shell condition on shell
choice in the laboratory

Two subsections commonly included at the end of the Materials and Methods section are "Data analysis" and a description of your study system or organism. An example of a Data Analysis subsection is given on p. 157. Here is
a sample subsection describing the study organism, from a paper° reporting
the role of environmental cues in stimulating larval metamorphosis:

Study Organism

Hydroides dianthus is a tube-dwelling serpulid
polychaete found from New England through the
West Indies, commonly on the underside of rocks
(Hartman, 1969). Individuals are gonochoristic

°Modified from Toonen, R., Pawlik, J.R., 2001. *Mar. Ecol. Progr. Ser.* 224: 103–114.

(i.e., they have separate sexes) and release gametes into seawater every 2-4 wk at 23°C (Zuraw
and Leone, 1968). The larvae begin feeding 18-24 h
after eggs are fertilized, and become capable of
metamorphosing after about 5 d at 23°C (Scheltema
et al., 1981; Bryan and Qian, 1997). The larvae
undergo rapid and substantial morphological
changes during metamorphosis that readily distinguish metamorphosed individuals from attached
larvae (Scheltema et al., 1981).

Alternatively, particularly if the organism or study site was chosen for specific attributes related to the nature of the research question, you could include this sort of information at the end of the Introduction (see p. 149).

A Model Materials and Methods Section

The Materials and Methods section of your report should be brief but informative. The following example completely describes an experiment
designed to test the influence of decreased salinity on the body weight of
a marine worm:

Obtaining and Maintaining Worms

The polychaete worms used in this study were
Nereis virens, freshly collected from Nahant, MA,
and ranging in length between 10 and 12 cm. All
treatments were performed at room temperature,
approximately 21°C, on April 15, 2002. One hundred ml of full-strength seawater was added to
each of six 200-ml glass jars; these jars served
as controls, to monitor worm weight in the absence of any salinity change. Another 6 jars were
filled with 100 ml of seawater diluted by 50% with
distilled water.

Monitoring Water Gain and Loss

Twelve polychaetes were quickly blotted with
paper towels to remove adhering water, and were
then weighed to the nearest 0.1 g using a Model
MX-200 Fisher/Ainsworth balance. Each worm was
then added to one of the jars of seawater. Blot-

ted worm weights were later determined at 30, 60, and 120 minutes after the initial weights were taken.

Determining Osmotic Concentration

The initial and final osmotic concentrations of all test solutions were determined using a Wescor VAPRO vapor pressure osmometer, following instructions provided in the handout (Gaudette, 1998).

Data Analysis

The rate of weight gain over time was examined by linear regression analysis, after log-transforming the independent variable (time). A series of Student's t-tests were used to assess the effect of salinity on rate of weight gain, by comparing mean weights of worms in the 2 treatment groups at 30, 60, and 120 minutes.

Note that all essential details have been included: temperature, species used, size of animals used, number of animals used per treatment, number of animals per container, volume of fluid in the containers, type and size of containers, time of year, equipment used, and how the data were analyzed. After reading this Materials and Methods section, you could repeat the study if you wanted to (or had to). Note, too, that the **writer has made clear why certain steps were taken**; 3 jars of full-strength seawater served as controls, for example, and worms were blotted dry to remove external water. The fact that worms were blotted dry before they were weighed was mentioned because this is a procedural detail that would obviously influence the results. On the other hand, the author does not describe how the balance or osmometer were operated since these techniques are standard. The author has written a report that might be useful to someone in the future—and ends up with a top grade.

On to the Results!

WRITING THE RESULTS SECTION

The Results section is the most important part of any research report. Other parts of the report reflect the author's *interpretation* of the data. Interpretations necessarily reflect the author's biases, hopes, and opinions, and are always subject to change, particularly as new information becomes available. In contrast, as long as a study was conducted carefully, and as long as the data were collected carefully, analyzed correctly, and presented accurately, the results are valid regardless of how interpretations change over time. Our understanding about how immune systems work has changed remarkably quickly in the past decade, for example, and the current interpretation of older data differs considerably from the original interpretation. But the older data are still valid. The *results* of any study are real; interpretations change. That's why the Results section is indeed the centerpiece of your report.

In this section, you summarize your findings, using tables, graphs, and words. The Results section is:

1. Not the place to discuss why the experiment was performed.
2. Not the place to discuss how the experiment was performed.
3. Not the place to discuss whether the results were expected, unexpected, disappointing, or interesting.

Simply present the results, drawing the reader's attention to the major observations and key trends in the data. Don't interpret them here. Most of the work in constructing this section of the report involves data presentation.

Summarizing Data Using Tables and Graphs

Before you even think about doing the writing part of your Results section, you must work with your data. The observations you've made and the data you've collected most likely contain a story that is crying out for recognition. Contrary to popular opinion, the purpose of showing data in tables and graphs is not to add bulk to laboratory reports. Rather, you wish to manipulate the data in tables and graphs to reveal trends, not only to your instructor but, more importantly, to yourself. The trick now is to organize the data so that (1) the underlying story is revealed and (2) the task of revealing the story to your reader is simplified.

There is no single right way to present data summaries; use any system that illustrates the trends clearly. First decide what relationships might be worth examining. Then experiment with different ways of tabulating and graphing the data to best explore and demonstrate those relationships. Suppose we return to the experiment in which caterpillars fed for 3 hours on 3 different diets. We determined both the initial weight of food provided and the weight of food remaining after the

3-hour period so that we can calculate the weight of food eaten per cater-pillar per hour. In your report, you should provide a sample calculation so that if you make a mistake your instructor can see where you went wrong. We also know the initial and final weights of the caterpillars for each diet, and the initial and final weights of dishes of food in the absence of cater-pillars; these control dishes will tell us the amount of water that the food lost by evaporation.

What relationships in the data might be especially worth examining? The first step in answering this question is to **make a list of specific questions that might be worth asking**, as follows:

1. Did the caterpillars feed at different rates on the different diets? That is, did feeding rate vary with diet?
2. Did larger caterpillars eat faster than smaller caterpillars? That is, did feeding rate vary with size of caterpillar?
3. How does the weight gained by a caterpillar relate to the weight lost by the food?
4. Did the weight of the control dishes change, and, if so, by how much?

The first question on this list was inspired by the null hypothesis estab-lished at the start of the study (in this case, H_0 = diet has no effect on feeding rate, see Chapter 3). But the other issues arose only after the data were col-lected and examined. **In scrutinizing your data, do not limit yourself to the questions and hypotheses posed at the start of your study.**

As in preparing the Materials and Methods section, this list of ques-tions is for your own use and is not to be included in your report. Don't take any shortcuts here. Write these questions in complete sentences. Once you have this list of questions, it is easy to list the relationships that must be examined in your Results section:

1. Feeding rate as a function of diet
2. Feeding rate as a function of caterpillar size
3. Caterpillar weight gain versus food weight loss for each caterpillar
4. Food weight loss in the presence of caterpillars versus food weight loss in controls

Constructing a Summary Table

Now you must organize your data into a table in a way that will let you ex-amine each of these relationships. Consider Table 3. This rough draft lists all the data obtained in the experiment. This table is for your own use,

Table 3. Summary of raw data.

Diet	Initial Caterpillar Wt. (g)	Final Caterpillar Wt. (g)	Caterpillar Weight Change (g)	Wt. of Food Lost (g) over 3 h	Feeding Rate (g food lost/h) of Caterpillar
A (Wheatgerm)	8.05	9.55	+1.55	3.65	15.2×10^{-2}
A	4.80	5.80	+1.00	1.74	7.2×10^{-2}
A	5.50	7.00	+1.50	3.33	13.9×10^{-2}
A	5.50	4.70	~~-0.80~~	~~0.00~~	0
A	5.90	6.95	+1.05	1.35	5.6×10^{-2}
Average	5.95	6.80	+1.28	2.52	8.4×10^{-2}
B (sinigrin 10^{-5} M)	4.40	5.11	+0.71	2.19	9.1×10^{-2}
B	5.20	5.60	+0.40	1.25	5.2×10^{-2}
.	.	.	.	.	.
.	.	.	.	.	.
.	.	.	.	.	.
Control 1	—	—	—	0.22	—
2 (no. caterpill.'s)	—	—	—	0.10	—
3	—	—	—	0.16	—

not something to be submitted as a formal part of your report; it tidies up your data so you can work with it more easily.

For the first relationship in our list (feeding rate as a function of diet), a simple table will tell the entire story. For your report, you can simply present a summary table, with explanatory caption, as in Table 4. Note that one of the caterpillars offered diet A ate no food and lost weight during the experiment. This individual died during the study, and the associated data were therefore omitted from Table 4. (The weight loss for this caterpillar probably reflects evaporation of body water.)

To Graph or Not to Graph

Finally, the time has come to reveal more subtle trends that may be lurking in the data. These trends may not be readily apparent from the summary table (Table 4); the trends may be made visible, however, to you and your reader, through graphing. A word of caution: **do not automatically assume that your data must be graphed**. If you can tell your story clearly using only a table—for example, if you are not interested in visualizing trends—a graph is superfluous. In other cases, you may be able to summarize some aspects of the data without using any graphs or tables. You might write, for example, "No animals ate at temperatures below 15°C," and then present data only for animals held at higher temperatures.

See Technology Tip 5 at the end of this chapter if you will be using Excel to plot graphs.

Graphs in biology generally take one of two basic forms: scatter plots (point graphs) or histograms and bar graphs. For the second relationship we wish to examine using the caterpillar data—feeding rate versus caterpillar size—a scatter graph, like Figure 15, will be especially appropriate.

Table 4. The effect of sinigrin (allyl glucosinolate) added to a basic wheatgerm diet, on food consumption of *Manduca sexta* caterpillars over 24 hours.

Diet	No. Caterpillars	(mean g food eaten/ caterpillar/h)
Wheatgerm control	4°	8.4×10^{-2}
Sinigrin (10^{-5} M)	5	7.9×10^{-2}
Sinigrin (10^{-3} M)	5	3.8×10^{-2}

°One individual died during the study without eating any food.

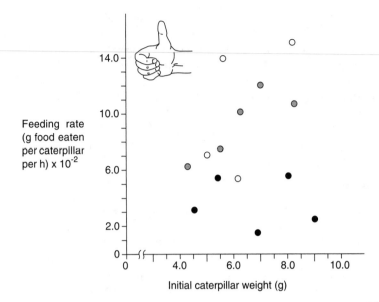

Initial caterpillar weight (g)

Figure 15. The relationship between initial caterpillar weight and rates of food consumption for *Manduca sexta* feeding for 3 hours on 1 of 3 different diets at 24°C. Each point represents data from a different individual. Feeding rates varied from about 0.01 to 0.15 g eaten per caterpillar^{-1} h^{-1}. $\circ$ = wheatgerm control diet; $\bullet$ = 10^{-5} M sinigrin; $\bullet$ = 10^{-3} M sinigrin).

In examining Figure 15, note that:

1. Each axis of the graph is clearly labeled, including units of measurement.
2. Tick marks on both axes are at intervals frequent enough to allow readers to estimate the value of each data point.
3. The meaning of each symbol is clearly indicated.
4. The symbols chosen facilitate interpretation of the graph: darker symbols represent increasing concentrations of sinigrin in the diet.
5. A detailed explanatory caption (figure legend) is below the figure.

All of your graphs should exhibit these 5 characteristics. In Figure 15, it would be insufficient to simply label the y-axis "Feeding Rate." Feeding rates can be expressed as per minute, per hour, per day, or per year, and can be expressed as per animal, per group of animals, or per gram of body weight. Similarly, it is unacceptable to label the *x*-axis as "Weight," or even as "Caterpillar Weight." Don't make readers guess what you have done. From the figure caption, the axis labels, and the graph itself, the reader should be able to determine the question being asked, get a good idea of how the study was done, and be able to interpret the figure without referring to the text. Never make the reader back up; **a good graph is self-contained**.

In this chapter a "thumbs up" symbol indicates a well-constructed, model graph, whereas a "thumbs down" symbol indicates a graph that suffers one or more major defects.

The third relationship (animal weight gain versus food weight loss) might well be left in table form since in this case the trend is readily discernible; caterpillars always gained less weight than that lost by the food (Table 3). The same trend could be revealed more dramatically (or, let us say, more graphically) with a scatter plot, as shown in Figure 16, but a graph is not essential here. Again, note the steps taken to

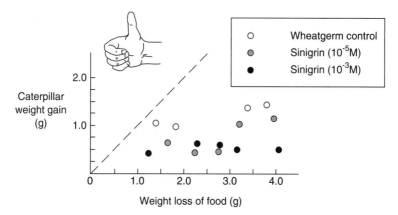

Figure 16. Caterpillar weight gain as a function of food consumption for *Manduca sexta* fed for 3 hours on 1 of 3 diets at 24°C. Points falling on the dotted line would indicate equality between weight gained and food eaten. Each point represents data from a different individual.

avoid ambiguity: the axes are labeled, units of measurement are indicated, symbols are interpreted on the graph, and the figure is accompanied by an informative figure legend. Note also that the symbols used in the student's Figure 16 are consistent with their usage in Figure 15. **Always use the same system of symbols throughout a report** so as not to confuse your reader; if filled circles are used to represent data obtained on diet *A* in one graph, filled circles should be used to represent data obtained on diet *A* in all other graphs. And, as mentioned earlier, **try to use symbols that make sense whenever possible**. In Figures 15 and 16, increasing concentrations of sinigrin are represented by increasingly dark symbols. Similarly, if you were comparing metabolic rates at different times of day, you could help readers interpret your data, for example, by representing daytime measurements with open symbols and nighttime measurements with solid symbols.

The fourth relationship in our list considers food weight loss in control dishes (no caterpillars). No graphs or tables are needed here; 2 sentences will do:

```
Control  containers  exhibited  less  than  a  3%
weight  loss  (N = 3 containers)  during  the  24-h
period.  In  contrast,  food  in  containers  with
caterpillars lost at least 23% of initial weight.
```

If the weight loss had been substantial, perhaps 5 to 10% or more of initial weight, you might wish to adjust all the data in your tables accordingly before making other calculations:

```
Control  containers  lost  7.6%  of  their  initial
weight  (N = 3 containers)  over  the  24-h  period.
We  therefore  adjusted  weight  loss  in  other  con-
tainers  for  this  7.6%  evaporative  loss  before
calculating feeding rates.
```

You would then provide a sample calculation so that your instructor could see how this was done and so that you will remember what you did if you consult your report again at a later date. A less desirable but nevertheless acceptable alternative would be to state the magnitude of the evaporative weight loss in your Results section and bring this point up again in interpreting your results in the Discussion section. In this case, you would label appropriate portions of graphs and tables as "Apparent Feeding Rates" rather than "Feeding Rates." Again, although there are many

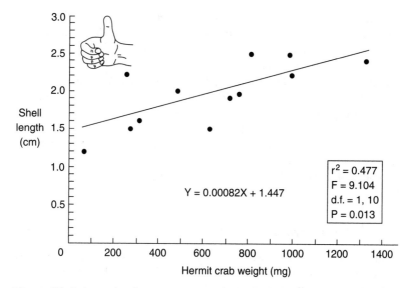

Figure 17. Relationship between wet weight (mg) of the hermit crab *Pagurus longicarpus* and the size of the periwinkle shells (*Littorina littorea*) occupied at Nahant, MA, on September 23, 2002 (N = 12). Each point represents a measurement on a single individual.

wrong ways to present the data, there is no single right way; you must simply be complete, logical, consistent, and clear.

Note that in Figure 16 the student has defined the symbols directly in the graph, rather than in the figure caption (compare with Fig. 15). When appropriate, you can also use empty space to report the results of statistical analyses, as in Figure 17, thus making the figure even more self-sufficient. Don't do this, however, if it will make the graph cluttered and difficult to read; instead put the information in the caption and/or in the text of the Results section.

If the slope of the regression line had not been significantly different from zero, by the way, the student would have included neither the line nor the equation of the line in the figure (or elsewhere in the report).

So far, we have looked only at examples of tables and point plots. If you were studying the differences in species composition of insect populations trapped in the light fixtures on 4 different floors of your biology building, a bar graph, as in Figure 18, might be more suitable. Note again that the axes are clearly labeled, including units of measurement, and that an explanatory legend accompanies the figure. Don't make the reader back up. Note also that the graph tells an interesting story; given that A is the fruit fly *Drosophila melanogaster*, it is not difficult to guess where the genetics laboratory is located!

Use tables and graphs only if they make your data work for you; if a table or graph fails to help you summarize some trend in your results, it contributes nothing to your report and should be left out. Be selective. Don't include a drawing, graph, or table unless you plan to discuss it, and include only those illustrations that best help you tell your story.

Preparing Graphs

Graphs may be constructed with the aid of a computer (see Technology Tip 5), but unless your instructor suggests otherwise, don't feel that you *must* submit computer-generated graphs to earn a top grade. Most instructors would rather see a carefully thought-out and neatly executed graph done by hand than a poorly thought-out, neatly executed piece of computer graphics. To emphasize the point, I have retained many hand-drawn graphs in this book. I have seen some gorgeous pieces of complete garbage prepared using computers and would rather see beginning students spend less time learning to use software and more time thinking about what they present, how they present it, and why they present it.

On the other hand, once you have mastered the key principles of graphing data, learning to use a good software package is certainly worthwhile, particularly since it allows you to quickly examine a variety of relationships in your data and determine which aspects of the data merit graphical presentation. But don't get carried away with all the bells and whistles; once the graphs are plotted, for example, it is sometimes faster to type or hand-print the axis labels or legends than to figure out how to have the computer execute these steps for you.

When preparing graphs by hand, always use graph paper, which can be purchased in your campus bookstore. The most useful sort of graph paper has heavier lines at uniform intervals—at every 4–5 divisions, for example, as shown in Figures 19–23. These heavy lines facilitate the plotting of data and reduce eyestrain considerably since every individual line need not be counted in locating data points.

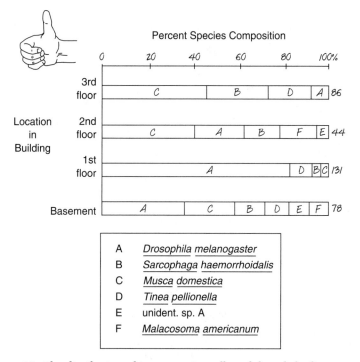

Figure 18. The distribution of insect species collected from light fixtures on 4 floors of the biology building on May 5, 1998. The number to the right of each bar gives the total number of insects collected on each floor.

By convention, the independent variable is plotted on the x-axis and the dependent variable is plotted on the y-axis: y is a function of x. For example, if you examined feeding rates as a function of temperature (Fig. 19), you would plot temperature on the x-axis and feeding rate on the y-axis; feeding rate *depends* on temperature. On the other hand, temperature is not controlled by feeding rate; that is, temperature varies independently of feeding rate. Temperature is the independent variable and is plotted on the x-axis. Note that each point in Figure 19 represents data averaged from 5 individuals so that each point is an average, or "mean" value. This is clearly indicated in the y-axis label and in the figure caption.

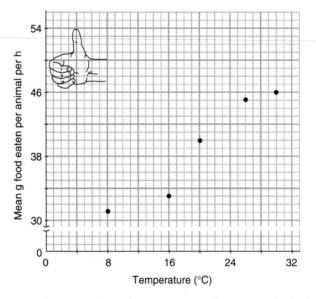

Figure 19. Feeding rate of *Manduca sexta* caterpillars on standard wheatgerm diet as a function of environmental temperature. Each point represents the mean feeding rate of 5 individuals measured over 24 hours.

It is good practice to label the axes of graphs beginning with zero. To avoid generating graphs with lots of empty, wasted space, breaks can be put in along one or both axes, as in Figure 19 (see also Fig. 15 and Figs. 22–24). If a break had not been inserted in the *y*-axis of Figure 19, for example, the graph would have been less compact, as in Figure 20.

(Not) Falsifying Data

You cannot move, add, or delete data points to improve or create trends in your data. Report the data you actually collected. **Falsifying data is, perhaps even more than plagiarism, an unforgivable offense**, and one that can get you into very serious trouble. Biologists build on the work of others, and that involves a lot of trust. Believe in the data that you collected and present it unaltered. Sometimes unusual or unexpected results lead to interesting new questions or discoveries.

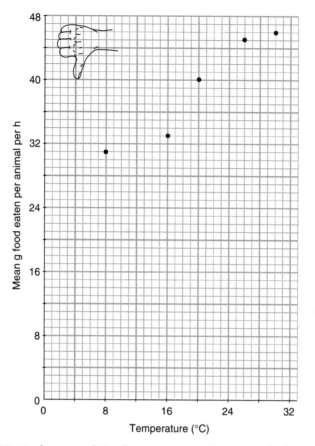

Figure 20. Feeding rate of *Manduca sexta* caterpillars on standard wheatgerm diet as a function of environmental temperature. Each point represents the mean feeding rate of 5 individuals measured over 24 hours.

The Question: To Connect or Not to Connect the Dots?

After plotting data points, lines are often added to graphs to clarify trends in the data. It is especially important to add such lines if data from several different treatments are plotted on a single graph, as in Figure 21. Note that this graph has been made easier to interpret by using different symbols for the data obtained at each temperature, and that the zero point on

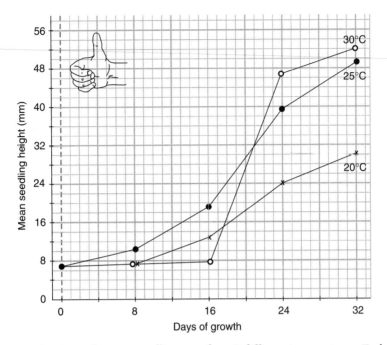

Figure 21. Rate of tomato seedling growth at 3 different temperatures. Each point represents the mean height of 15–17 individuals.

the *x*-axis has been displaced to the right, to prevent the first data point from lying on the *y*-axis, where it might be overlooked (compare with Figure 22, in which the first point does lie on the *y*-axis).

In some cases, it makes more sense to draw smooth curves than to simply connect the dots. For example, suppose we have monitored the increase in height of tomato seedlings over some period in the laboratory. Every week we randomly selected 15–20 seedlings to measure from the laboratory population of several hundred, so that different seedlings were usually measured at each sampling period. After about 2 months, the data were plotted as in Figure 22.

Connecting the dots would not be the most sensible way to reveal trends in the data of Figure 22 since we know that the seedlings did not really shrink between days 20 and 28, or between days 36 and 44; simply connecting the points would suggest that shrinkage had occurred. The

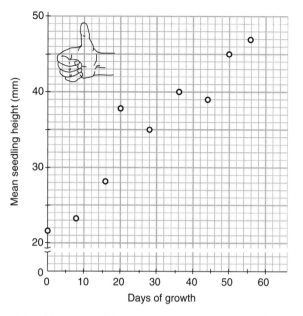

Figure 22. Rate of tomato seedling growth at 20°C. Fifteen to 20 seedlings were measured on each day of sampling, out of 205 seedlings in the population.

apparent decline in seedling height reflects the considerable variability in individual growth rates found within the same population, as well as the fact that we did not measure every seedling in the population on every sampling day. In this case, the trend in growth is best revealed by drawing a smooth curve, as in Figure 23.

When plotting average values (usually called arithmetic means) on a graph, **it is appropriate to include a visual summary of the amount of variation** present in the data by adding bars extending vertically from each point plotted (Figure 23). You may, for example, choose to simply illustrate the range of values obtained in a given sample. More commonly, you would plot "error bars" (typically the standard error or standard deviation about the mean), giving a visual impression of how much individual data points differed from the calculated mean values, as in Figure 23. The less overlap there is between error bars, the more likely it is that differences between mean values are statistically (and biologically) meaningful. Standard deviation and standard error calculations are reviewed in Chapter 3.

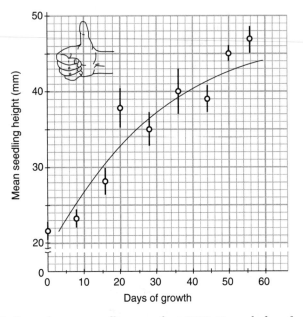

Figure 23. Rate of tomato seedling growth at 20°C. On each day of sampling, 15–20 seedlings were randomly sampled from a group of 205 seedlings and measured. Error bars represent one standard deviation about the mean.

Plots of standard deviations or standard errors are always symmetrical about the mean value and so convey only partial information about the range of values obtained. If more of your individual values are above the mean than below the mean, the error bars will give a misleading impression about how the data are actually distributed. If your graph is fairly simple, you may be able to achieve the best of both worlds, indicating both the range and standard deviation (or standard error), as in Figure 24. In Figure 24, the vertical bars extending from the point at day 30 indicate that although the average seedling height was about 37 millimeters (mm) on that day, at least one seedling in the sample was as small as 25 mm and at least one seedling was as large as 48 mm. Seedlings measured on day 50 also differed in height by somewhat more than 20 mm. But we also see that the error bars are much larger for day 30 than for day 50 even though the range of lengths measured was similar for both samples. This tells us that most seedlings were close to the mean

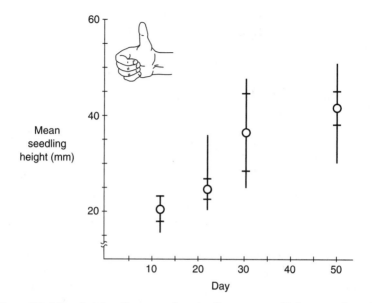

Figure 24. Mean height of tomato plant seedlings over a 50-day period. Each point represents the mean height of 18 seedlings raised at 20°C, with a photoperiod of 12L:12D. Vertical bars represent the range of heights; cross-bars represent one standard deviation about the mean.

length on day 50, about 42 mm long, but that many of the seedlings measured on day 30 were substantially larger or smaller than the mean value measured on that day.

Whether you choose to plot standard deviations, standard errors, ranges, or some other indicator of variation, **be sure to indicate in your figure caption what you have plotted, along with the number of measurements associated with each mean.**

Making Bar Graphs and Histograms

When the variable along the *x*-axis (the independent variable) is numerical and continuous, points can be plotted and trends can be indicated by lines or curves, as we have seen in Figures 15–24. In Figure 19, for example, the *x*-axis shows temperature rising continuously from 0°C to 32°C, with each centimeter (cm) along the *x*-axis corresponding to a 4°C rise in temperature. Similarly, the *x*-axes of Figures 22 and 23 reflect the march of time, from 0 to 60 days, with each cm along the *x*-axis reflecting 10 additional days.

When the independent variable is nonnumerical or discontinuous, or represents a range of measurements rather than a single measurement, the data are represented by bars, as shown in Figures 25 and 26. The *x*-axis of Figure 25 (a bar graph) is labeled with the names of different mammals. In contrast to the *x*-axes of Figures 15–24, the *x*-axis of Figure 25 does not represent a continuum; no particular quantity continually increases or decreases as one moves along the *x*-axis, and a line connecting the data for sea lion and Weddell seal would be meaningless. In Figure 26 (a histogram), the data for shell length are numerical, but are grouped together (for example, all shells 25.0–29.9 mm in length are treated as a single data point). Note also that the magnitude of the size categories represented by the different bars varies; the leftmost bar represents the percentage of shells found within a range of about 0.1 to 21 mm in length, whereas each of the next several bars to the right represents the percentage of shells found within a range of only about 5 mm in length. The size range of shells represented by the bar at the extreme right side of the

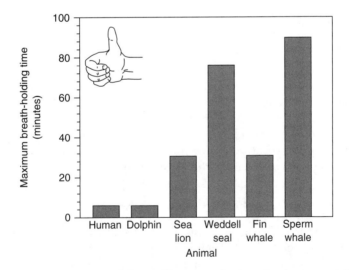

Figure 25.   Breath-holding abilities of humans and selected marine mammals.

Data from Sumich, J.L. 1999. An Introduction to the Biology of Marine Life, *7th ed. WCB/McGraw-Hill, Publishers.*

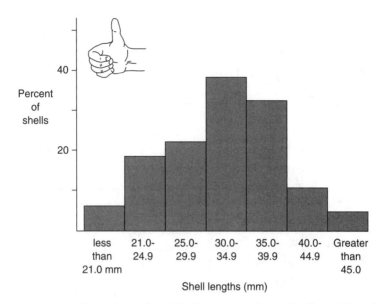

Figure 26. Size distribution of snail shells (*Littorina littorea*) collected from the low intertidal zone at Blissful Beach, Massachusetts, on August 15, 2000. Only living animals were measured. A total of 197 snails were included in the survey.

graph is unknown; we know that all shells found in this category exceeded 45 mm in length, but the graph does not indicate the size of the largest shell.

Use a single color or fill pattern for all bars unless there is a logical reason not to. In Figures 25 and 26, for example, all bars should be the same color or fill pattern.

Learning to Love Logarithms

Logarithmic scales make excellent sense when the data presented cover 2 or more powers of 10. Consider the following example: We wish to explore the relationship between the size of hermit crabs and the mass of the snail shells that they choose to live in. The relationship for the tropical hermit crab species *Clibanarius longitarsus* is presented using a standard linear scale in Figure 27a. The crabs measured ranged in mass from 0.3 g to nearly 40 g (2 powers of 10). Notice that data points for many quite small crabs are crowded together at the lower left side of the

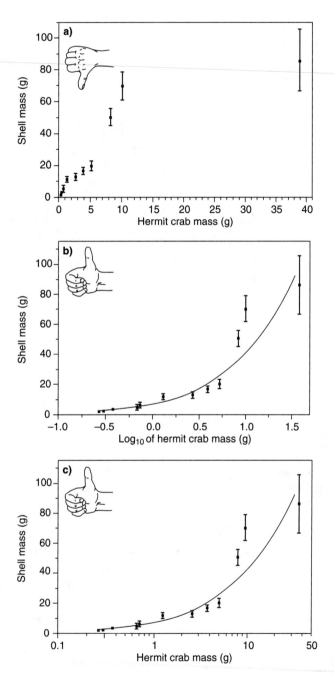

Table 5. Understanding logarithms. (a) In log base 10, each successive whole number is 10 times larger than the preceding whole number. Log base 10 scales are especially useful in presenting data that cover many powers of 10. (b) In log base 2, each successive whole number is twice as large as the preceding whole number. Log base 2 scales are especially useful for visualizing doublings of quantities. Note that in both systems, the log of a number is simply the exponent to which the base (10 in "a," 2 in "b") must be raised to obtain that number.

(a)		(b)	
Number	Log base 10	Number	Log base 2
$0.01 = 1/100 = 10^{-2}$ → (-2)		$1/4 = 2^{-2}$ → (-2)	
$0.1 = 1/10 = 10^{-1}$ → (-1)		$1/2 = 2^{-1}$ → (-1)	
$1 = 10^0$ → (0)		$1 = 2^0$ → (0)	
$10 = 10^1$ → (1)		$2 = 2^1$ → (1)	
$100 = 10^2$	2	$4 = 2^2$	2
$1,000 = 10^3$	3	$8 = 2^3$	3
$10,000 = 10^4$	4	$16 = 2^4$	4
$100,000 = 10^5$	5	$32 = 2^5$	5

graph so that it is difficult to tell the actual values for either crab mass or shell mass, or even to tell how many data points are represented. In addition, the data point for the largest (heaviest) crab is easily overlooked, since it is the only data point for any crab heavier than about 10 g (grams). Plotting logarithms (base 10) of the same data on the x-axis (Figure 27b) creates a more uniform distribution of data points. Individual data points are now much easier to see. However, this representation is still somewhat difficult to interpret, because it requires you to either know how to decode logarithms or to refer to Table 5. Alternatively, we

←——

Figure 27. The relationship between the mass of hermit crabs (*Clibanarius longitarsus*) from Mozambique and the mass of the shells they choose to occupy. (a) The data are plotted on a normal, linear scale. Note the large number of data points crowded together in the lower left corner of the graph. (b) The same data replotted after taking the log (base 10) of hermit crab mass. A value of "1" represents 10 g (grams) (see Table 5). (c) The same data plotted using a logarithmic scale (base 10) for the x-axis. Hermit crab mass increases 10-fold from one numbered tick mark to the next. In both (b) and (c), note the more even distribution of points.

Based on data of Barnes, D.K.A., 1999. Ecology of tropical hermit crabs at Quirimba Island, Mozambique: shell characteristics and utilisation. Mar. Ecol. Progr. Ser. 183: 241–251.

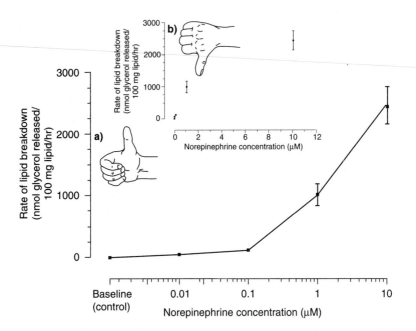

Figure 28. Influence of the neurotransmitter norepinephrine (= noradrenaline) on rate of lipid breakdown in the subcutaneous fatty tissue of hibernating marmots (*Marmota marmota*). Each point represents the mean of 11 determinations, and error bars represent one standard deviation about the mean. Note that the norepinephrine concentrations used in the study encompass 4 powers of 10, a situation that typically calls out for logarithmic data representation. (a) The data plotted using a log base 10 scale on the *x*-axis. (b) (inset) The same data plotted much less effectively, using a normal linear scale.

Based on data of N. *Cochet* et al., 1999. *Regional variation of white adipocyte lipolysis during the annual cycle of the alpine marmot.* Comp. Biochem. Physiol. C 123: 225–232.

can replot the data of Figure 27*a* using a log base 10 scale on the *x*-axis, with each major tick now representing 10 times the value of the preceding numbered tick. The value 0 on the *x*-axis of Figure 27*b* corresponds to the value 1 on the *x*-axis of Figure 27*c*, while the value 1.0 on the *x*-axis of Figure 27*b* corresponds to the value 10 on the *x*-axis of Figure 27*c* (see Table 5).

Similarly, compare the clarity of Figure 28*a* with that of the inset (Figure 28*b*). In this case the data extend through 4 powers of 10. Note

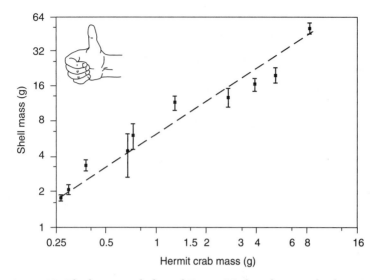

Figure 29. The hermit crab data of Figure 27 plotted using a log base 2 scale on each axis. Such scales are very helpful when you are interested in the effects of doublings, or in how much of a change in x is required to produce a doubling of y.

how most of the data form a difficult-to-decipher mess in the lower left-hand corner of the inset, but are spread out evenly using a scale of log base 10 on the x-axis.

Although logarithmic graphs are usually plotted using scales in base 10, base 2 scales can also be useful. The hermit crab data of Figure 27a are replotted using this log base 2 scale for both axes in Figure 29; now each numbered major tick represents a doubling of crab or shell mass. A quick visual inspection of this graph shows that as the mass of the hermit crab approximately doubles, the mass of the shell it prefers to inhabit also doubles, something not so obvious in the previous plots of the same data (Figure 27).

Logarithms can also be useful in forcing data into straight lines in some cases. Figure 30 shows the relationship between the basal diameter of barnacles (*Balanus amphitrite*) and the dry weight of their tissues. Plotted on a linear scale (Figure 30a), tissue weight increases exponentially with increases in barnacle length. Replotting the same data using a double-log scale (base 10), we have essentially bent the data into a

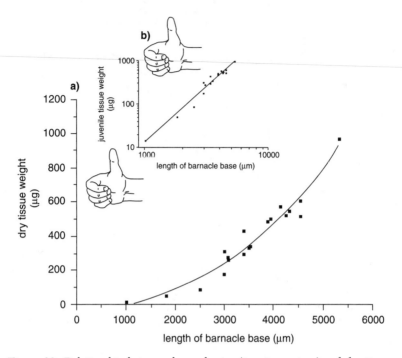

Figure 30. Relationship between barnacle size (in micrometers) and dry tissue weight (micrograms) for juveniles of *Balanus amphitrite*. Each point represents measurements on a single individual. (a) The data plotted on a normal linear scale. (b) The same data replotted using log base 10 scales for both axes. Notice that the exponential curve depicted in (a) becomes a straight line in (b).

Data from Pechenik et al., 1993. Influence of delayed metamorphosis on survival and growth of juvenile barnacles Balanus amphitrite. Mar. Biol. 115: 287–294.

straight line (inset), so that the relationship can be represented by a simple equation of the form $y = mx + b$.

Preparing Tables

Tables should always be organized with data related to a given characteristic being presented vertically rather than horizontally. Tables 6 and 7 present the same information, but in different formats. Table 6 correctly places all information about a single species in one row, so that readers can view the information for each species by scanning

Table 6. Characteristics of four snail populations sampled at Nahant, MA, on October 13, 1999. Data are means of 4 replicate samples ± 1 standard error.

Species	Average Shell Length (cm)	Sample Size	Average No. Animals per m^2
Crepidula fornicata	1.63 ± 0.21	122 indiv.	32.1 ± 4.7
C. plana	1.01 ± 0.34	116	20.8 ± 10.6
Littorina littorea	0.87 ± 0.11	447	113.6 ± 29.1
L. saxatilus	0.40 ± 0.10	60	8.2 ± 5.2

from left to right, and can compare data among different species by scanning up and down a single column. Note also that the independent variable ("species" in this case) is presented vertically in the first column.

Table 7 is incorrectly organized and more difficult to read. Like graphs, tables should be self-sufficient; note how much useful information the author has packed into the legend and column headings of Table 6. Note also that the table legend is placed above the table.

Making Your Graphs and Tables Self-Sufficient

A properly executed graph or table is largely self-sufficient: snipped out of your report along with its accompanying legend or caption, it should make perfectly good sense to any biology major you choose to hand it to. By examining only the axes of a graph and reading the figure caption, for example, the reader should be able to determine the specific question that was asked, how the study was done,

Table 7. Characteristics of four snail populations sampled at Nahant, MA, on October 13, 1999. Data are means of 4 replicate samples ± 1 standard error.

Species	*Crepidula fornicata*	*C. plana*	*Littorina littorea*	*L. saxatilus*
Av. shell length (cm)	1.63 ± 0.21	1.01 ± 0.34	0.87 ± 0.11	0.40 ± 0.10
Sample size	122 indiv.	116	447	60
Aver. no. animals per m^2	32.1 ± 4.7	20.8 ± 10.6	113.6 ± 29.1	8.2 ± 5.2

and what the main findings are, as discussed in Chapter 2 (pp. 23–25). Consider, for example, Figure 23 (p. 172); we can tell quite a lot about how and why this study was done just by carefully studying the figure and its caption. The study was apparently undertaken to determine how fast tomato seedlings grow at one particular temperature, 20°C. We know that the growth of 205 seedlings was followed over nearly 2 months, and that seedlings were measured 9 times over that period, approximately once each week. We also know that not all 205 seedlings were measured every time; instead, the researchers subsampled 15–20 each time so that different seedlings were probably measured each time. Finally, we see that each point represents a mean value and that the vertical bars represent 1 standard deviation about the mean.

Similarly, from Figure 19 (p. 168) we know what species was studied and for how long. We also know that caterpillars were maintained at 1 of 5 temperatures, and we know what those temperatures were; further, we know the number of caterpillars maintained at each temperature.

Try to make your graphs as self-sufficient as these examples are. The easier you make it for readers to understand your data, the more likely it is that your work will be read and that you will get your point across intact. Additional advice about constructing good graphs and tables is given in books by W.S. Cleveland; and J. Quinn and M.J. Keough (See Appendix E).

Putting Your Graphs and Tables in Order

Once you have your graphs (and other figures, such as drawings or photographs) prepared, you need to decide in what order to present them. Remember, all of these items are referred to as "figures." **Arrange them logically, in the order that you will discuss them.** The first figure that you refer to in the text of your report will be Figure 1, the second will be Figure 2, and so forth. Order your tables in the same way, with Table 1 the first table that you refer to, to facilitate a logical presentation of the data.

Incorporating Figures and Tables Into Your Report (or Not)

If you prepare your graphs on a computer, ask your instructor whether you should incorporate them into the text of the Results section, as they would appear in a published journal article, or whether you should print the figures on separate pages and include them at the end of your report.

To incorporate figures directly into your report, click on the figure to be inserted and then use the cut and paste function. Alternatively, you can use the Insert function in the Word menu.

Do not insert figures into the text unless your instructor asks you to. Many of us would prefer to see each figure on a separate page at the end of your report; larger figures are much easier to read and comment on.

Verbalizing Results: General Principles

One-sentence Results sections are common in student reports: "The results are shown in the following tables and graphs." However, *common* does not mean *acceptable*. **You must use words to draw the reader's attention to the key patterns in your data**. But do not simply redraw the graphs in words, as in this description of Figure 21:

> At 20°C, the seedlings showed negligible growth for the first 8 days of study. However, between days 8 and 16, the average seedling grew nearly 5 mm, from about 8 mm to about 13 mm. Growth continued over the next 16 days, with the seedlings reaching an average height of 24 mm by day 24, and 30 mm by day 32.

Let the graph do this work for you; **your task is to summarize** the most important trends displayed by the graph and then to indicate briefly the basis for the statements you make. Remember, in scientific writing every statement of fact or opinion must be backed up with evidence. For example, you might write:

> Temperature had a pronounced effect on seedling growth rates (Figure 21). In particular, seedlings at 25°C consistently grew more rapidly than those at 20°C. . . .

Here, a general statement is supported by reference to a figure, followed by a specific detail that illustrates the point particularly well. In some cases, only a single sentence is required:

> Caterpillars generally fed more slowly on the diet of 10^{-3} M sinigrin than on the wheatgerm controls (Fig. 15).

Readers can then look at Figure 15 (p. 162) and decide whether they see the same trend you saw; one sentence and a figure say it all.

Note the use of the past tense in the statement about caterpillar feeding rates:

```
Caterpillars  generally  fed  at  faster  rates  on
diet A.
```

This statement is quite different from the following one, which uses the present tense:

```
Caterpillars feed at faster rates on diet A.
```

By using the present tense, you would be making a broad generalization extending to all caterpillars, or at least to all caterpillars of the species tested. Before one can make such a broad statement, the experiment must be repeated many, many times, and similar results must be obtained each time; after all, the writer is making a statement about all caterpillars under all conditions. By sticking with the past tense here, you are clearly referring only to the results of your study. Be cautious: **Always present your results in the past tense**.

Note also that the authors of these examples **do not make the reader interpret the data**. You must tell your readers exactly what you want them to see when they look at your table or graph. Consider the following 2 examples. The data concern the shell lengths of a particular snail species collected along a rocky coastline, from 2 regions between the high-tide level and the low-tide level. I have not included any figures or tables from this survey, and so I refer to them only as "xx" in these examples:

```
Although individual specimens of Littorina lit-
torea  varied  considerably  in  shell  length  at
each tidal height (Figure xx), there was a sig-
nificant (t = 26.3; d.f. = 47; P < 0.05) distrib-
utional  effect  of  shore  position  on  mean  size
(Table xx).
```

```
Although  individual  specimens  of  Littorina  lit-
torea varied considerably in shell length at each
tidal  height  (Figure xx),  the  mean  shell  length
was  significantly  greater  (t = 26.3;  d.f. = 47;
P < 0.05) for snails collected higher up in the
intertidal zone (Table xx).
```

In the first of these examples, the author leaves it to the reader to figure out what specific information is important in the data. Sometimes this is because the author has not taken the time to think about the data carefully enough. The modified version conveys quite a different impression; we know exactly what the author wants us to see, and we can then decide whether we agree with the author's statements or not.

Note that in the example just presented, the lead factual statement was supported both by reference to a figure and by the results of statistical analyses. **Note also that the author provides not just the "p-value" associated with the result, to indicate how convincing the difference among means is, but also the name of the test statistic (a "t" statistic in this example, resulting from a "t-test") and the number of degrees of freedom associated with the analysis** (d.f., related to sample size as discussed in Chapter 3). The author correctly refers to the observed differences in shell length as being "significant." **Saying that differences are "significant" (or "not significant") implies that you have subjected your data to rigorous statistical testing.** If you have not conducted statistical analyses, it is perfectly fair to write that "Temperature had a pronounced effect on seedling growth rates," as in a previous example (p. 183), or that "Seedlings treated with nutrients appeared to grow at slightly faster rates than those treated with distilled water," referring readers to the appropriate table or figure. But if you cannot provide statistical support, you *cannot* say that seedlings in one treatment grew *significantly* faster than those in another treatment.

As discussed more fully in Chapter 3, even if you analyze your data statistically, you must nevertheless be cautious in drawing conclusions. Your data may support one hypothesis more than another, but they cannot *prove* that any hypothesis is true or false. Chapter 3 is worth reading even if you are not required to conduct statistical analyses of your data; as biologists in training, the *why* of statistical analysis is more important to you than the *how*.

In presenting your own data, first **decide exactly what you want your reader to see when looking at each graph or table, and then stick the reader's nose right in it**.

Verbalizing Results: Turning Principles into Action

Let us apply these principles to the caterpillar study discussed earlier in this chapter. First, is there anything about the general response of the animals worth drawing attention to? You might, for example, be able to write:

```
All   the   caterpillars   were   observed   to   eat
throughout the experiment.
```

More likely, living things behaving as they do, you will say something like:

```
One of the animals offered diet A and 2 of the an-
imals offered diet B were not observed to eat dur-
ing the 3 h experiment, and the results from these
animals were therefore excluded from analysis.
```

Such a decision to exclude data from further analysis is fine, by the way—it won't be considered data falsification—as long as you indicate the reason for the decision, and as long as the decision is made objectively; as discussed earlier, **you cannot exclude data simply because it violates a trend that would otherwise be apparent, or because the data contradict a favored hypothesis**.

Next, go back to your initial list and reword each question as a statement. For example, the first question posed on p. 159 ("Do the caterpillars feed at different rates on the different diets?"), might be reworded as:

```
Caterpillars generally fed at slower rates on the
10⁻³ M sinigrin diet than on the wheatgerm con-
trols (Fig. 15).
```

or:

```
Caterpillars fed at significantly slower rates on
the 10⁻³ M sinigrin diet than on either the lower-
concentration sinigrin diet or the wheatgerm con-
trols (Fig. 15) (F = 30.3, d.f. = 2,11, P <
0.0001).
```

If you follow this procedure for each question on your list, your Results section will be complete. The written part will generally be quite short.

Note that in all of the examples given in this chapter, data summaries are formally referred to as either tables or figures. "Figures" include graphs of all types; photographs of all types, whether of organisms or of electrophoretic gels; drawings; and flowcharts. **Anything and everything, in fact, that is not a "table" is a "figure."**

Writing about Negative Results

An experiment that was correctly performed always "works." The results may not be what you had expected, but this does not mean that the experiment has been a waste of time. If biologists threw away their data every time something unexpected happened, we would rarely learn anything new. The data you collect are real; it is only the interpretation that is open to question. Therefore, always treat your data with respect. The lack of a trend or the presence of a trend contrary to expectation is itself a story worth telling. See also pp. 63–65 for related advice about dealing with statistical analyses that fail to support a favored hypothesis or expected outcome.

Writing about Numbers

According to the Council of Biology Editors (*CBE Style Manual*, sixth edition), you should use numerals rather than words when writing about counted or measured items, percentages, decimals, magnifications, and abbreviated units of measurement (see pp. 286–287): 6 larvae, 18 seedlings, 25 drops, 25%, 1.5 times greater, 50× magnification, a 3:1 ratio, 0.7 g, 18 ml.

But all rules have exceptions. Use words rather than numerals if beginning a sentence with a number or percentage:

> Twenty grams of NaCl were added to each of 4 flasks.

> Thirty percent of the tadpoles metamorphosed by the end of the second week.

Note the difference in how quantities are presented if we rewrite the first example as, "To each of 4 flasks we added 20 g of NaCl."

When 2 numbers are written adjacent to each other without being separated by words or a comma, write one of the numbers in words: "The sample was divided into five 25-seedling groups." Better still, that sentence could easily be rewritten so that numerals are appropriate for both numbers: "The samples were divided into 5 groups of 25 seedlings each."

Zero and one present special problems: a "0" is easily mistaken for the letter "O," the numeral "1" is easily mistaken for the letters "l" (as in the abbreviation for "liters") or "I". Plus, it just looks odd to read, "I know that 1 day my prince will come." The CBE (now the CSE, Council of Science Editors) has recently clarified its position on these issues (see Appendix H). In most cases, unless the zero or one is followed by units of measure (e.g., "I added 1 mg of sucrose to the solution"), or is part of an equation (e.g., "$n = 1$"), or is part of a series that includes larger numbers ("1, 8, and 25 individuals . . ."), use words rather than numerals.

When writing about numbers smaller than zero, precede the decimal point with a zero:

> . . .and we then added 0.25 g NaCl to each flask.

When using ordinal numbers (e.g., first, fifth), the CSE suggests using words for the first 9 numbers and numerals for the others ("the 25th replicate . . ."). However, you should be consistent within a series ("first, fifth, ninth" and "13th, 14th, 15th"; but "5th, 9th, 15th," rather than "fifth, ninth, 15th").

When writing about very large or very small numbers, particularly in association with concentrations or rates, use scientific notation. It is preferable, for example, to write about solute concentrations of 5.6×10^{-3} g/ml rather than 0.0056 g/ml, and about cell concentrations being approximately 1.8×10^5 cells/ml rather than about 180,000 cells/ml. Note that I could have avoided both scientific notation and commas in the first example by describing the solute concentration as 5.6 mg/ml. By the way, the word *per*, as in "cells per ml" or "distance per second" may be indicated using either a slash or an exponent: "1.8×10^5 cells/ml" and "1.8×10^5 cells ml^{-1}" are equally acceptable forms of expression. See Technology Tip 1 (pp. 16–18) to learn about programming Word to produce such formatting automatically.

Finally, the CSE recommends using commas only when numerals contain more than 4 numbers, as in the following example:

```
Only 1073 of the original 12,450 frog tadpoles
died during the study.
```

In Anticipation—Preparing in Advance for Data Collection

Much of the work involved in putting together a good research report goes into preparing the Results section. You can save yourself considerable effort and frustration by planning ahead before you enter the laboratory to do the experiment. Be prepared to record your data in a format that will enable you to make your calculations easily. For the caterpillar experiment referred to previously, you would be well ahead by coming to the laboratory with a data sheet set up like the one in Figure 31. Using this data sheet, the data are recorded in the *x* areas during the laboratory period; the blank spaces will be filled in later, as you make your calculations. If possible, leave a few blank columns at the right to accommodate unanticipated needs discovered as you record or work up your data.

In introductory laboratory exercises, students are often provided with data sheets already set up in a useful format. Take a careful look at those data sheets to understand how they are organized and why they are

Date and time started: _____
Date and time ended: _____

Caterpillar No.	Diet	Caterpillar wt. (g) Initial	Caterpillar wt. (g) Final	Weight Change (g)	Food wt. (g) Initial	Food wt. (g) Final	Food wt. Change (g)	Feeding rate g eaten/caterp./h
X	X	X	X		X	X		

Figure 31. Sample format for a laboratory data sheet.

TECHNOLOGY TIP   4
Using Computer Spreadsheets for Data Collection

One advantage of entering data directly into a spreadsheet (such as Excel) is that you can preprogram automatic calculations into the spreadsheet. Consider, for example, Table 3 (p. 160). If we enter data into columns 2, 3, and 5 (Initial Caterpillar Weight, Final Caterpillar Weight, and Weight of Food Lost), we can enter formulas into columns 4 and 6 so that Caterpillar Weight Change and Feeding Rate will be calculated automatically. Before entering formulas in Excel, remember to first click on the appropriate box and then click "=" to indicate that a formula is on its way.

Whenever you enter formulas into a spreadsheet, make one sample calculation by hand or with a calculator, to be sure that the formula you entered is correct. Also check to be sure that the formula is correctly applied to all entries in each column.

as they appear; in more advanced laboratory courses you will be responsible for organizing your own data sheets. As mentioned earlier, always follow any number you write down with the appropriate units, such as mg (milligrams), cm (centimeters), or mm/min (millimeters per minute, often written as $mm \cdot min^{-1}$). This will avoid potential confusion later.

You can also enter data directly into a computer if you set up a data sheet in advance (See Technology Tip 4 above).

Following the advice of the previous paragraph can save you hours of work later. Even so, it takes time and care to put together an effective Results section. But this section is the heart of your report; craft it properly, and the remainder of the work will be relatively easy.

CITING SOURCES

The next sections to prepare are the Discussion section and the Introduction, in that order. In both sections, you will be making statements of fact that require support, often from written sources. As stated in Chapter 1

(Rule 8, p. 7) and discussed more fully in Chapter 4, every statement of fact or opinion must be supported with a reference to its source. Read Chapter 4 (pp. 66–70) for specific instructions on citing sources.

WRITING THE DISCUSSION SECTION

> The scientific method does not require researchers to be unbiased observers of nature. Scientists almost always have a theory in mind when they perform an experiment. But the method does require that scientists be willing to change their views about nature when the data demand it.
>
> R.M. Hazen and J. Trefil, 1991. *Science Matters*

In this section of the report, you must interpret your results in the context of the specific questions you set out to address in this experiment and in the context of any relevant broader issues that have been raised in lectures, textbook readings, previous coursework, and, possibly, library research. You will consider the following issues:

1. What did you expect to find, and why?
2. How did your results compare with those expected? If you set out to test specific hypotheses, do your data support one hypothesis more than another, or allow you to eliminate one or more of them?
3. How might you explain any unexpected results?
4. How might you test these potential explanations?
5. Based on your results, what question or questions might you logically want to ask next?

Clearly, if your results coincide exactly with those expected from prior knowledge, your Discussion section will be rather short. Such a high level of agreement is rarely obtained in 3- or 4-hour laboratory studies. Indeed, high degrees of variability characterize many aspects of research in biology, especially at the level of the whole organism. After all, genetically based variation in traits is the raw material of evolution: without such variation, evolution by natural selection would not be possible. Often a study will need to be repeated many times, with very large sample sizes, before clear trends emerge. This point is discussed further in Chapter 3, beginning on p. 55. A short paper in a biological journal may well represent years of work by several competent, hardworking individuals. Even the simplest of questions are often not easily answered.

Nevertheless, every experiment that was carried out properly tells you *something*, even if that something is not what you specifically intended to find out.

Expectations

State your expectations explicitly, and back your statements up with a reference. Scientific hypotheses are not simply random guesses. Your expectations must be based on facts, not opinions; these facts could come from lectures, laboratory manuals or handouts, textbooks, or any other traceable source. In discussing a study on the effectiveness of different wavelengths of light in promoting photosynthesis, for example, you might write something like:

> All wavelengths of light are not equally effective in promoting photosynthesis: green light is said to be especially ineffective (Ellmore and Feldberg, 2003). This is because green light tends to be reflected rather than absorbed by plant pigments, which is why most plants look green (Ellmore and Feldberg, 2003). Our results supported this expectation. In particular. . . .

Alternatively, a Discussion section might profitably begin:

> The results of our experiment failed to support the hypothesis (Freudenreich and Meller, 1991) that caterpillars of *Manduca sexta* reared on one uniquely flavored diet will prefer that diet when subsequently given a choice of foods.

Here we have managed to state our expectations and compare them with our results in a single sentence. In both cases, we have begun our discussion on firm ground—with facts rather than unsupported opinions.

Note that in this last example the expectations were based on previously published research. Your expectations might instead be based on a hypothesis stated in your Introduction and tested in the Results section.

Explaining Unexpected Results

When results refuse to meet expectations, students commonly blame the equipment, the laboratory instructor, their laboratory partners, or themselves. Generally, more scientifically interesting possibilities than experimenter incompetence are the culprits. A few years ago I did an experiment with 2 colleagues, testing to see if dopamine receptors were involved in the pathway that led to metamorphosis in a particular marine snail species. The idea was to add to seawater a chemical known to disable dopamine receptors and then see if the larvae could nevertheless be made to metamorphose. Every time we did the experiment we got a different result. Sometimes the chemical did block metamorphosis, but in other experiments it actually stimulated larvae to metamorphose! What on earth was going on? It turns out that the response of competent larvae to the chemical changes predictably as larvae age, something never reported before. The paper we ended up publishing[*] was very different from the paper we had originally envisioned. Yes, dopamine receptors are involved in the metamorphic pathway of this species, but that turned out to be, in my view, the least interesting aspect of the work.

Don't be too hard on yourself if your results don't fit your expectations or if they don't disprove your null hypothesis (Chapter 3) when you expected them to. Base your discussion on the data you obtain. And don't limit yourself to assessing *a priori* hypotheses: Probe your data thoroughly, expect the unexpected, and consider all potential aspects of, and reasonable explanations for, your data. Take another look at the list of factors you wrote when beginning to work on your Materials and Methods section. Could any of these factors be sufficiently different from the normal or standard conditions under which the experiment is performed to account for the difference in results? Look again at your laboratory manual or handout. Are any of the conditions under which your experiment was performed substantially different from those assumed in the instruction manual? If you discover no obvious differences in the experimental conditions, or if the differences cannot account for your results, include this point in your report, as in this example:

---

[*]Pechenik, J.A., Cochrane, D.E., Li, W. 2001. Timing is everything: The effects of putative dopamine antagonists on metamorphosis vary with larval age and experimental duration in the prosobranch gastropod *Crepidular fornicata. Biol. Bull.* 202:137–147.

> The discrepancy in results cannot be explained by
> the unusually low temperature in the laboratory
> on the day of the experiment, since the control
> animals were subjected to the same conditions and
> yet behaved as expected.

If potentially important differences are noted, put this ammunition to good use:

> In prior years, these experiments have been per-
> formed using species X (Professor E. Iyengar,
> personal communication). It is possible that
> species Y simply behaves differently under the
> same experimental conditions.

Note that the writer does not *conclude* that species X and species Y behave differently; the writer merely *suggests* this explanation as a possibility. **Always be careful to distinguish possibility from fact**. Suggesting a logical possibility won't get you into any trouble. Stating your idea as though it was an accepted fact, on the other hand, is sticking your neck out far enough to get your head chopped off.

Continue your discussion by indicating possible ways that the differences in behavioral responses might be tested. For example:

> This possibility can be examined by simultane-
> ously exposing individuals of both species to the
> same experimental conditions. If species X be-
> haves as expected, and species Y behaves as it did
> in the present experiment, then the hypothesis of
> species-specific behavioral differences will be
> supported. If species X and species Y both re-
> spond as species Y did in the present study, then
> some other explanation will be called for.

Continue in this vein, evaluating all the reasonable, testable possibilities you can think of. An instructor enjoys reading these sorts of analyses because they indicate that students are thinking about what they've done. Go ahead; make an instructor happy.

Notice that in the preceding example the writer did not say, "If species X behaves as expected, and species Y behaves as it did in the present experiment, then the hypothesis will be supported." This writer remembers rule number 13 (p. 10): Never make the reader back up. Notice, too, that the writer does not write, "then the hypothesis will be true" or "then the hypothesis will be proven." **Experiments cannot *prove* anything; they can only support or disagree with hypotheses**. As scientists, our interpretations of phenomena may make excellent sense based on what we know at the moment, but those interpretations are not necessarily correct. New information often changes our interpretations of previously acquired data.

Analysis of Specific Examples

EXAMPLE 1

In this study, tobacco hornworm caterpillars were raised for 4 days on one diet, and then tested over a 3-hour period to see if they preferred that food when given a choice of diets.

STUDENT PRESENTATION

The data indicate that the choice of food was not related to the food upon which the caterpillars had been reared. These data run counter to the hypothesis (Back and Reese, 1976) that hornworms are conditioned to respond to certain specific foods. Only one set of data out of the 4 gave any indication of a preference for the original diet, and that indication was rather weak.

There are many possible explanations for data that are so contrary to previous experimental results. Inexperience of the experimenters, combined with the fact that 3 different people were recording data about the worms, may account for part of the error. Keeping track of many worms and attempting to interpret their actions as having chosen a food or having merely been passing by may have proven to be too much for first-time worm watchers. The mere fact that each of 3 people will interpret actions differently and will have somewhat different methods of recording information introduces bias into the data.

ANALYSIS

This Discussion section starts out well, with a comparison between results expected and results obtained. The hypothesis being discussed is clearly stated, and a supporting reference is given. The student even recognizes that "data are" rather than "data is." (On the other hand, the student persists in calling the animals worms rather than caterpillars; the term *worms* usually refers to annelids, whereas these animals are arthropods). The next paragraph, however, betrays a total lack of confidence in the data obtained; the results could not possibly have turned out this way unless the researchers were incompetent, writes the student. Although inexperience can certainly contribute to suspicious results, are there no other possible explanations? Does it really take years of training to determine whether a caterpillar is eating food *A* or food *B*?

Compare this report with the one in the next example. This Discussion section deals with the same experiment. In fact, the 2 students were laboratory partners.

EXAMPLE 2

Contrary to expectation, the results suggest that caterpillars show no preference in the diet they touched first and the diet they spent the most time feeding on. This unexpected finding may be due to the fact that the caterpillars were not reared on the original diets for a long enough period of time to acquire a lasting preference. They ate only the diets they were reared on for 4 days, whereas the laboratory handout had suggested a pre-feeding period of 5-10 days (Orians and Starks, 2003). This possibility may be tested by performing the same experiment but varying the amount of time that the caterpillars are reared on the original diets. Such an experiment would determine whether there is a critical time that caterpillars should be reared on a particular diet before they will show a preference for that diet. Another possible explanation for our results may be that the caterpillars used were very young, weighing only 3-6 mg. Finally, this experiment lasted only 3 hours. Perhaps different results would have been obtained had the organisms

been given more time to adjust to the test conditions. It would be interesting to run the identical experiment for a longer period of time, such
as 10-12 hours.

The author of this report produced a paper that clearly indicates thought. Which report do you suppose received the higher grade?

EXAMPLE 3

In this experiment, several hundred milliliters (ml) of filtered pond water were inoculated with a small population of the ciliated protozoan *Paramecium multimicronucleatum* and then distributed among 3 small flasks. Over the next 5 days, changes in the numbers of individuals per ml of water in each flask were monitored.

STUDENT PRESENTATION

The large variation observed between the
groups of 3 replicate populations suggests that
the experimental technique was imperfect. The
sampling error was high because it was difficult
to be precise in counting the numbers of individuals. Some animals may have been missed while
others were counted repeatedly. More accurate
data may be obtained if the number of samples
taken is increased, especially at the higher population densities. In addition, more than 3
replicate populations of each treatment could be
established. Finally, extremely precise microscopes and pipets could be used by experienced
operators to reduce sampling error.

ANALYSIS

This writer, like the writer of Example 1, starts out by assuming that the experiment was a failure, and spends the rest of the report making excuses for this failure. The quality of the microscopes was certainly adequate to recognize moving objects, and *P. multimicronu-cleatum* was the only organism moving in the water; the author is grasping at straws. If the author had more confidence in his or her abilities, the paper might have been far different. Isn't there some chance that the experiment was performed correctly? Lacking confi-dence in the data, the student looked no further, even though he or she actually had access to data that would have allowed several of the stated hypotheses to be assessed. On each day, for example, several sets of samples were taken from each flask, and each set gave similar estimates for numbers of organisms per milliliter; this consistency of results suggests that the variation in population density from flask to flask was not due to experimenter incompetence. In addition, although the student stated correctly that larger sample sizes would have been helpful, he or she should have supported that statement with additional data analysis. Fifteen drops were sampled from each flask for each set of samples. The student could have calculated the mean number of individuals in the first 3 drops, the first 6 drops, the first 9 drops, the first 12 drops, and then the full 15 drops, to see how estimates of population size changed as the sample size was increased. If the student had done this, he or she would probably have found that larger sample sizes are especially important when population density is low. (Why might this be so?)

EXAMPLE 4

In this last study, a group of students went seining for fish in a local pond. Every fish was then identified to species. It turned out that 91% of the fish in the sample of 73 individuals belonged to a single species. The remaining fish were distributed among only 2 additional species.

STUDENT PRESENTATION

        I find the small number of species represented
in our sample surprising, since the pond is fed
by several streams that might be expected to introduce a variety of different species into it,
assuming that the streams are not polluted. The
lab manual states that 12 fish species have been
found in the adjacent streams. It appears that
the conditions in the pond at the time of our
sampling were especially suitable for one species
in particular of all those that most likely have
access to it. Perhaps the physical nature of the
pond is such that the number of niches is small,
in which case competition would become very keen;
only one species can occupy a given niche at any
one time (Smith, 1958). The reproductive pattern
of the fishes might also contribute to the ob-

served results. Possibly *Lepomis macrochirus*,
the dominant species, lays more eggs than the
others, or perhaps the juveniles of this species
survive better.

Another possible explanation for our findings
is that we sampled only the perimeter of the
pond, since our seining was limited to a depth
of water not exceeding the heights of the sein-
ers. The species distribution could be very different in the middle of the pond at a greater
depth.

ANALYSIS

I have not reproduced the entire Discussion section of the student's
paper, but even this excerpt demonstrates that a little thinking goes a
long way. Note that the student did not require much specialized knowledge to write this Discussion section, only a bit of confidence in the data.
Another student might well have written:

Most likely, the fish were incorrectly identified; more species were probably present than
could be recognized by our inexperienced team.
It is also possible that the net had a large
tear, which let most of the species escape. I
didn't notice this rip in the fabric, but my
glasses were probably dirty, and then again, I'm
not very observant.

WRITING THE INTRODUCTION SECTION

The Introduction section establishes the framework for the entire report.
In this section, you briefly present background information that leads to a
clear statement of the specific issue or issues that will be addressed in the
remainder of the report; by the time you have finished writing the Materials and Methods, Results, and Discussion sections of your laboratory report, you should be in a good position to know what these issues are. In 1
or 2 paragraphs, then, you must present an argument explaining why the
study was undertaken. More to the point, perhaps, the Introduction provides you with your first opportunity to convince your instructor that you
understand why you have been asked to do the exercise.

Every topic that appears in later sections of your report should be anticipated clearly in the Introduction. Conversely, the Introduction should contain only information that is directly relevant to the rest of the report.

Stating the Question

Even though the statement of questions posed, or issues addressed, generally concludes the Introduction section of a report, it is useful to deal with this issue first. What *was* the point of this study?

Write the following words: "In this study" or "In this experiment." Then complete the sentence as specifically as possible. Three examples follow:

```
In this study, the oxygen consumption of mice and
rats was measured in order to investigate the re-
lationships between metabolic rate, body weight,
and body surface area.

In this study, we collected fish from 2 local
ponds and classified each fish into its proper tax-
onomic category.

In this experiment, we asked the following ques-
tion: Do the larvae of Manduca sexta prefer the
diet upon which they have been reared when of-
fered a choice of diets?
```

Note that each statement of intent is phrased in the past tense since the students are describing studies that have now been completed.

The strong points of these statements are best revealed by examining a few unsatisfactory ways to complete sentences dealing with the same material:

```
In this study, we measured the metabolic rate of
rats and mice.

In this study, we made a variety of measurements
on fish.

In this experiment, the feeding habits of Manduca
sexta larvae were studied.
```

Each of these unsatisfactory statements is vague; the reader will assume, perhaps correctly, that you are as much in the dark about what you've done as your writing implies. Be specific. Here, in one sentence, you must come fully to grips with your experiment or study. There *was* some point to the time that you were asked to spend in the laboratory; find it.

If you go on to state specific expectations, or to present specific hypotheses that you set out to test, make the source of those hypotheses clear, as in the following example:

```
We expected larger mice to respire faster than
smaller mice, since larger mice support a greater
biomass. However, we also predicted that respira-
tion rates per gram of tissue would be similar in
large and small individuals, since dividing by
weight should adjust for size differences.
```

As mentioned earlier (p. 192), you must provide a rationale (e.g., results from prior studies) for any expectations or specific hypotheses that you state.

An Aside: Studies versus Experiments

An experiment always involves manipulating something, such as an organism, an enzyme, or the environment, in a way that will permit specific relationships to be examined or hypotheses to be tested. Containers of protozoans in pond water could be distributed among 3 different temperatures, for example, to test the influence of temperature on the reproductive rate of the particular species under study. As another example of an experiment, the ability of salivary amylase to function over a range of pHs might be examined to test the hypothesis that the activity of this enzyme is pH-sensitive. In the field, a population of marine snails from one location might be transplanted to another location and the subsequent survival and growth of the transplanted population studied so as to test the hypothesis that conditions in the new location are less hospitable for that species than in the location from which the original population was obtained. As a control, of course, the survival and growth of animals not transplanted would also have to be monitored over the same period. Note that an experiment may be conducted in the laboratory or in the field.

It is permissible to refer to experiments as "studies," but not all studies are "experiments." In contrast to the preceding experiments, some exercises require you to collect, observe, enumerate, or describe. You should avoid referring to such studies as experiments; where there are no manipulations, there are no experiments. You might, for example, collect insects from light fixtures located at several different locations within the biology building and identify them to species, enabling you to examine the distribution of insect species within the building. Or you might be asked to provide a detailed description of the feeding activities of an insect. Or you might spend an afternoon documenting the depth to which light penetrates in various areas of a lake, and then correlate that information with data on the distribution of aquatic plants in the different areas. In each case, you should refer to your work as a study, not as an experiment. For example:

```
In this study, insects were collected from all
light fixtures on floors 1, 3, and 5 of the Dana
building, and the distribution of species among
the different locations was determined.
```

Providing the Background

Having posed, in a single sentence, the question or issue that was addressed, it is relatively easy to fill in the background needed to understand why the question was asked. A few general rules should be kept in mind:

1. **Support all statements of fact with a reference to your textbook, laboratory manual, outside reading, or lecture notes.** Unless you are told otherwise by your instructor, do not use footnotes. Rather, refer to your reference within the text, giving the author of the source and the year of publication, as in the following example:

```
Many marine gastropods enclose their fertilized
eggs within structurally complex encapsulating
structures (Hunt, 1966; Tamarin and Carriker,
1968).
```

Note that the period concluding the sentence comes after the closing parenthesis.

2. **Define specialized terminology.** Most likely, your instructor already knows the meaning of the terms you will use, but by defining them in your own words in your report you can convince the instructor that you, too, know what these words mean. Write to illuminate, not to impress. As always, if you write with your future self in mind as the audience, you will usually come out on top; write an Introduction you will be able to understand 5 years from now. The following 2 examples obey this and the preceding rule:

A number of caterpillar species are known to exhibit induction of preference, a phenomenon in
which an organism develops a preference for the
particular flavor on which it has been reared
(Jones and Smith, 1983).

Molluscs are common inhabitants of the intertidal zone, that region of the ocean lying between the high- and low-tide marks (Lutz and
Turner, 1983).

The development of mature female gametes, a
process termed oogenesis, is regulated by changing hormonal levels in the blood (Gilbert, 1991;
Gaudette, 1995).

3. **Never set out to prove, verify, or demonstrate the truth of
   something.** Rather, set out to test, document, or describe. In biology
   (and science in general), truth is elusive; it is important to keep an open
   mind when you begin a study and when you write up the results of that
   study. It is not uncommon to repeat someone else's experiment or observations and obtain a different result or description. Responses will
   differ with species, time of year, and other, often subtle, changes in the
   conditions under which the study is conducted. To show that you had
   an open mind when you undertook your study, you would want to revise the following sentences before submitting them to your instructor:

In this experiment, we attempted to demonstrate induction of preference in larvae of *Manduca sexta*.

This study was undertaken to verify the description of feeding behavior given for *Manduca sexta*
by Jones (1903).

This experiment was designed to show that pepsin,
an enzyme promoting protein degradation in the
vertebrate stomach, functions best at a pH of 2, as
commonly reported (Bernheim and Cochrane, 1983).

The first example might be modified to read:

In this experiment, we tested the hypothesis that
young caterpillars of *Manduca sexta* demonstrate
the phenomenon of induction of preference.

How would you modify the other 2 examples to show that you approached the studies without prejudice?

4. **Be brief.** Include only the information that directly prepares readers for the statement of intent, which will appear at the end of the Introduction section as already discussed. If, for example, your study was undertaken to determine which wavelengths of light are most effective in promoting photosynthesis, there is no need to describe the detailed biochemical reactions that characterize photosynthesis. As another example, consider these few sentences taken from a report describing an induction-of-preference study. Caterpillars were reared on one diet for 5 days and tested later to see if they chose that food over foods that the caterpillars had never before experienced.

```
In this experiment, we explored the possibility
that larvae of Manduca sexta could be induced to
prefer a particular diet when later offered a
choice of diets. The results of this experiment
are important because induction of preference is
apparently linked to (1) the release of electro-
physiological signals by sensory cells in the an-
imal's mouth and (2) the release of particular
enzymes, produced during the period of induction,
that facilitate the digestion and metabolism of
secondary plant compounds (laboratory handout,
2001).
```

The entire last sentence does not belong in the Introduction. The work referred to in this example was a simple behavioral study; students did not make electrophysiological recordings, nor did they isolate and characterize any enzymes. Although a consideration of these 2 topics might profitably be incorporated into a discussion of the results obtained, these issues should be excluded from the Introduction because they do not explain why this particular study was undertaken. Include in your Introduction section only information that directly prepares the reader for the final statement of intent. You might, on a separate piece of paper, jot down other ideas that occur to you for possible use in revising your Discussion section, but if they don't make a contribution to your Introduction, don't let them intrude. Be firm. Stay focused.

5. **Write an Introduction for the study that you ended up doing.** Sometimes it is necessary to modify a study for a particular set of

conditions so that the observations actually made no longer relate to the questions originally posed in your laboratory handout or laboratory manual. For example, the pH meter might not have been working on the day of your laboratory experience, and your instructor modified the experiment accordingly; perhaps the experiment you actually performed dealt with the influence of temperature, rather than pH, on enzymatic reaction rates. In such an instance, you would not mention pH in your Introduction section since the work you ended up doing dealt only with the effects of temperature.

A Sample Introduction

The following paragraphs satisfy all the requirements of a valid Introduction. This Introduction section is brief but complete—and effective:

> It is well known that plants are capable of using sunlight as an energy source for carbon fixation (Ellmore and Reed, 1993). However, all wavelengths of light need not be equally effective in promoting such photosynthesis. Indeed, the green coloration of most leaves suggests that wavelengths of approximately 550 nm are reflected rather than absorbed so that this wavelength would not be expected to produce much carbon fixation by green plants.
>
> During photosynthesis, oxygen is liberated in proportion to the rate at which carbon dioxide is fixed (Ellmore and Reed, 1993). Thus relative rates of photosynthesis can be determined either by monitoring rates of oxygen production or by monitoring rates of carbon dioxide uptake. In this experiment, we monitored rates of oxygen production using special filters to test the hypothesis that wavelengths differ in their ability to promote carbon fixation by *Elodea canadensis*.

Note how, in this Introduction, the material progressed from a rather general statement (plants photosynthesize), to more specific statements, and finally to the specific research objectives of the study. You will see the same progression in the Introduction sections of most published studies. Your instructor should also see it in yours.

TALKING ABOUT YOUR STUDY ORGANISM OR FIELD SITE

If your study organism or field site was deliberately chosen because it was ideally suited to investigating the particular problem that you addressed, conclude your Introduction with a brief paragraph explaining your choice. Otherwise, that information would be more appropriate in your Materials and Methods section, as on p. 155. Here is an example of how the material presented on pp. 155–156 could be rewritten as a fine ending to an Introduction:

> *Hydroides dianthus* is an excellent organism for such a study, as its larvae can be obtained in great numbers almost year round and reared in the laboratory with greater than 90% survival (Qian, 2000; Toonen and Pawlik, 2001). Moreover, the larvae become capable of metamorphosing within 4–6 days at 25°C (Scheltema, 1981; Bryan and Qian, 1997) and can be readily induced to metamorphose by simply elevating the potassium concentration of seawater by 15 mM* (Bryan and Qian, 1997).

DECIDING ON A TITLE

A good title summarizes, as specifically as possible, what lies within the Introduction and Results sections of the report. Your instructor is a captive audience. In the real world of publications, however, your article will vie for attention with articles written by many other people; the busy potential reader of your paper will often glance at the title of your report and promptly decide whether to stay or move on. The more revealing your title is, the more easily your potential audience can assess the relevance of your paper to their interests. A paper that delivers something other than what is promised by the title can lose you considerable good will when read by the wrong audience and may be overlooked by the audience for which the paper was intended. Indeed, many potential readers will miss your paper entirely since indexing services such as *Biological*

°millimolar = 10^{-3} moles per liter.

Abstracts and *Current Contents* use key words from a paper's title in preparing their subject indexes.

Here is a list of mediocre titles, each followed by 1 or 2 more revealing counterparts:

No: Metabolic rate determinations

Yes: Exploring the relationship between body size and oxygen consumption in mice

No: Plankton sampling in Small Pond

Yes: Species composition of the spring zooplankton of Small Pond, MA

No:

1. Measuring the feeding behavior of caterpillars
2. Eating habits of *Manduca sexta*
3. Food preferences of *Manduca sexta* larvae

Yes:

1. Measurements of feeding preferences in tobacco hornworm larvae (*Manduca sexta*) reared on 3 different diets
2. Can larvae of *Manduca sexta* (Arthropoda: Insecta) be induced to prefer a particular diet?

No: Effects of pollutants on sea urchin development

Yes: Influence of Cu^{++} on fertilization success and gastrulation in the sea urchin *Strongylocentrotus purpuratus*

No: Protozoan behavioral responses

Yes: Studies on the response of the protozoan *Paramecium aurelia* to shifts in light and temperature

The original titles are too vague to be compelling. Why go out of your way to give potentially interested readers an excuse to ignore your paper?

Of more immediate concern in writing up laboratory reports rather than journal articles is this suggestion: why not use a title that demonstrates to your instructor that you have understood the point of the exercise? Win your reader's confidence right at the start of your report. (By the way, the title should appear on a separate page, along with your name and the date that your report is submitted.)

WRITING AN ABSTRACT

The Abstract, if requested by your instructor, is placed at the beginning of your report, immediately following the title page. Yet it should be the last thing that you write since it must completely summarize the essence of your report: why the experiment was undertaken; what problem was addressed; how the problem was approached; what major results were found; what major conclusions were drawn. And it should do all this in a single paragraph. Despite its unimpressive length, a successful abstract is notoriously difficult to write. In compact form, your abstract must present a complete and accurate summary of your work, and that summary must be fully self-contained; that is, it must make perfect sense to someone who has not read any other part of your report, as in the following example. Note that Abstracts are typically written in the passive voice:

This study was undertaken to determine the wavelengths of light that are most effective in promoting photosynthesis in the aquatic plant *Elodea canadensis* since some wavelengths are generally more effective than others. Rate of photosynthesis was determined at 25°C, using wavelengths of 400, 450, 500, 550, 600, 650, and 700 nm and measuring the rate of oxygen production for 1-h periods at each wavelength. Oxygen production was estimated from the rate of bubble production by the submerged plant. We tested 4 plants at each wavelength. The rate of oxygen production at 450 nm (approximately 2.5 ml O_2/mg wet weight of plant/h) was nearly 1.5X greater than that at any other wavelength tested, suggesting that light of this wavelength (blue) is most readily absorbed by the chlorophyll pig-

```
ments. In contrast, light of 550 nm (green) pro-
duced no detectable photosynthesis, suggesting
that light of this wavelength is reflected rather
than absorbed by the chlorophyll.
```

Note also that the sample Abstract is informative. The author does not simply say that "Oxygen consumption varied with wavelength. These results are discussed in terms of the wavelengths that chlorophyll absorbs and reflects." Rather, the author provides a specific summary of the results and what they mean. Be sure that your Abstract is equally informative. Clearly, this section of your report will be easiest to write if you save it for last.

PREPARING AN ACKNOWLEDGMENTS SECTION

Most biologists are aided by colleagues in various aspects of their research, and it is customary to thank those helpful people in an Acknowledgments section, the penultimate section of the report. Here is an example that might be found in a typical student report:

```
I am happy to thank Sigrid Smith and Jennifer
Hsieh for sharing their data with me, and Wei Li
for late night discussions concerning the effects
of temperature on metabolic rate. Professor C.
Orians made me aware of the crucial Lesser and
Schick (1989) reference. Finally, I am also in-
debted to Jean-François Vilain for lending me his
graphics software, and to Professor J. Jarrett
for teaching me how to use it.
```

As in the example above, you must include the last names of the people you are acknowledging and indicate the specific assistance received from each person named.

PREPARING THE LITERATURE CITED SECTION

In the Literature Cited section, the final section of your paper, you present the complete citations (in alphabetical order, according to last name of the first author of each paper or book) for all the factual material you refer to in the text of your report. This presentation provides a convenient way for readers to obtain additional information about a particular topic, as well as a means of verifying what you have written as fact. Detailed directions for citing sources are given in Chapter 4.

PREPARING A PAPER FOR FORMAL PUBLICATION

Papers submitted to an editor for possible publication must conform exactly to the requirements of the specific journal you have targeted. Before beginning a manuscript, you must determine which is the most appropriate journal for your work and read carefully that journal's Instructions for Authors, typically found at the front or back of each issue or, in some cases, at the front or back of several issues each year. Many journals also make this material available online. It also helps to study similar papers published in recent issues of the targeted journal. How are references cited in the text? How are they listed in the Literature Cited section? Does the journal permit (or require) subheadings in the Materials and Methods or Results sections? If you fail to follow the relevant instructions, your paper may be returned unreviewed; at the least, you will annoy the editor and reviewers.

Do not incorporate figures and tables into the text of the manuscript, unless required to do so (as for some online journals). Instead, put tables (in numerical order, and including the table legends) after the Literature Cited and Acknowledgments sections. Then insert a page of figure captions (in numerical order, with multiple captions per page), and finally include the figures themselves, with the authors' names and the figure designations (e.g., "Moy et al., Fig. 4") in the upper right corner.

Before mailing your manuscript to the journal's editor, go through your work one last time and be certain that every reference cited in the text is listed (and correctly so) in the Literature Cited section, and that the Literature Cited section contains no references not actually mentioned in the text. You should also indicate, in the left margin, where each figure and table is first referred to, writing something like, "Fig. 2 near here." This helps the publisher know where best to place each element.

Your manuscript should be accompanied by the correct number of copies, as specified in the Instructions to Authors section of the journal, along with a brief cover letter, which should read something like this:

Dear Dr. Shumway:

    Please consider the enclosed manuscript enti-
tled "Avoidance of drilled gastropod shells by
the hermit crab *Pagurus longicarpus* at Nahant,
Massachusetts" by J.A. Pechenik and S. Lewis for
publication in the *Journal of Experimental Marine
Biology and Ecology.* Dr. Dan Rittschof (Duke
University Marine Laboratory) and Dr. P. Y. Qian
(Hong Kong University of Science and Technology)
would be especially suitable reviewers for this
manuscript. I can send the original figures immediately upon request.

    My contact information follows:
> phone (617-627-9999)
> fax (617-627-3805)
> e-mail: jan.pechenik@tufts.edu

    Thank you for your attention.

See the book by R. A. Day about preparing professional manuscripts (Appendix E). Send original graphs only after the manuscript has been accepted for publication; this reduces the chance of damage or loss prior to the manuscript being sent to press for printing. Photographs should be included with the manuscript since the editor will need to determine how well they will reproduce. Although editors are happy to have you suggest appropriate reviewers, they won't necessarily take all of your suggestions. Recommend experienced people to give honest and carefully considered reviews—if the manuscript has problems, you want them found out before publication. Once the paper is published, it's out there forever.

CHECKLIST FOR THE FINAL DRAFT

Title

❑ Title gives a specific indication of what the study is about (p. 207)

Abstract

❑ Background stated in 1 or 2 sentences (p. 208)

❑ Clear statement of specific question addressed and of specific hypotheses tested (p. 208)

❑ Methods summarized in no more than 3 or 4 sentences (p. 208)

❑ Major findings reported in no more than 2 or 3 sentences (p. 208)

❏ Concluding sentence relates to statement of specific question addressed (pp. 208–209)

❏ Abstract is a single paragraph; if not, can it be rewritten as one paragraph? (p. 208)

Introduction

❏ Clear statement of specific question or issue addressed (p. 200)

❏ Logical argument provided as to why the question or issue was addressed (p. 202)

❏ Specific hypotheses are indicated, if appropriate, and a rationale for those expectations is provided (pp. 192, 201)

❏ Every sentence leads to the statement of what was done in this study (p. 204)

❏ All statements of fact or opinion are supported with a reference or example (p. 202)

❏ If appropriate, the rationale for choosing the study system or organism is given (p. 206)

Materials and Methods

❏ Methods are presented in the past tense (p. 154)

❏ Design of study or experiment is clear and complete (pp. 152–155)

❏ Rationale for each step is self-evident or clearly indicated (p. 154)

❏ Each factor mentioned is likely to have influenced the outcome of this study, and all factors likely to have influenced the outcome are mentioned (pp. 153, 157)

❏ Precision of all measurements is indicated (p. 155)

❏ Includes brief description of how data were analyzed (calculations made, statistical tests used) (pp. 155, 157)

❏ If appropriate, the field site or study organism is described (p. 155)

Results

❏ Text summarizes important trends in the data; does not simply repeat raw data from the graphs or tables (pp. 183–184)

❏ Results are presented in the past tense (p. 184)

❏ Results are presented in active terms whenever possible, for example, in terms of what organisms or enzymes did (pp. 95–96)

❏   All general statements are supported with reference to data (and by results of statistical analysis when possible) (p. 183, 185)

❏   Major results are presented in words, but their implications are not discussed (p. 158)

❏   No raw data are presented (pp. 159–161)

❏   Figures are referred to as "Figures," not as graphs, drawings, or photographs (pp. 182, 186)

❏   The same data are not presented in both tabular and graphical form within the same report (p. 161)

❏   Every table or graph makes an important and unique contribution to the report (p. 166)

❏   Each figure or table has an informative caption or legend, correctly placed (below figure, above table) (pp. 162, 181)

❏   Symbols are used consistently in all figures, and are chosen to facilitate interpretation when possible (pp. 162, 164)

❏   Tables and figures are numbered in the order in which they are first referred to in the paper (p. 182)

❏   Each figure or table is self-sufficient; readers can tell what question is being asked, the major aspects of how the question was addressed, and what the most important results are without reference to the rest of the paper (pp. 23–25, 163, 181–182)

❏   Numbers of individuals and numbers of replicates are clearly indicated in the graph, table, caption, or legend (pp. 167, 173, 182)

❏   The meaning of error bars on figures is clearly indicated in the caption; for example, one standard error about the mean (pp. 172–173, 182)

Discussion

❏   Data are clearly related to the expectations and hypotheses raised in the Introduction (p. 191)

❏   Facts are carefully distinguished from speculation (p. 194)

❏   Unusual or unexpected findings are discussed logically, based on biology rather than apology (p. 193)

❏   All statements of fact or opinion are supported with references to the literature, data, or an example (pp. 190–191)

❏   Discussion suggests further studies that should be conducted, additional questions that should be posed, or ways that the present study should be modified in the future (pp. 194, 196–197)

Literature Cited

❏   Citations are provided for every reference cited in the report and are in the correct format (pp. 70–74, 209)

❏   Section includes no references that are not cited in the report (p. 210)

❏   Each citation includes names of all authors, title of paper, year of publication, volume number, and page numbers (pp. 70–74)

Acknowledgments

❏   People are mentioned by first and last names, and their specific contributions are noted (p. 209)

General

❏   Text of report is double-spaced

❏   First page shows name of author, name of lab section or instructor, and date submitted (p. 208)

❏   All information is presented in the appropriate section of the report

❏   All pages are numbered

TECHNOLOGY TIP   5
Graphing with Excel

Excel was designed for business people, not biologists, and for graphing it is less flexible and intuitive than some other programs, such as GraphPad Prism (See Appendix F). However, Excel is so widely used (and misused) by students in biology courses that it is worth pointing out some tips for using it effectively. I assume here that you already have some familiarity with the program.

Entering data. Enter your data in a new spreadsheet. For bar charts, enter the treatment names (the independent variable; e.g., human, dolphin, sea lion, etc. if you were plotting Figure 25) in the first row. Enter your data starting with the second row.

If you are plotting data for a scatter plot (e.g., Figs. 15, 17, 19), enter data for your x-axis (usually the independent variable, e.g., temperature in Fig. 19) in the first column. In Figure 19, feeding rate data would then be entered in the adjacent column. For Figure 15, you would enter feeding rate data for each of the 3 treatments in adjacent columns. Do not leave space between columns.

Save your worksheet frequently. I recommend including the date the study was conducted as part of the title you give the project.

Transforming data. You may wish to transform your data before plotting it. For example, you may need to convert your measurements to different units, or you may wish to plot the logarithms of the data collected. To transform a column of data, first click on an empty column. Click in the first box of the new column and type an equal sign, which tells the program that you are about to enter a formula. Then select "Function" within the "Insert" command on the menu bar. The transform functions you need are found under the "Math" option. Once you select the desired function, specify the row and values to be transformed. For example, suppose you have 8 values in Column B of your spreadsheet. To take the log (base 10) of those 8 data points and put those new values in Column D, first click in space D1 and type "=". Then select the Log10 function, enter A1 within the parentheses, and click OK. Then click on the button in the lower right of the rectangle around space D1 and drag down to space D8. You should see the transformed values in all 8 rows of column D.

Calculating statistics. First click on an empty rectangle below the column of numbers you wish to work with and type an equal sign in the box, which instructs the program that you are about to insert a formula. Then select "Function" within the "Insert" command on the menu bar and choose the correct option (e.g., Average—for calculating the mean, or StDev—for calculating the Standard Deviation). Next specify the range of values to use (e.g., B1:B8) and click OK. Once you have calculated your statistic for one column of data, drag the calculation into adjacent columns to calculate the same statistics for those columns.

(Continued)

Making graphs. One of the many endearing idiosyncrasies of Excel is the terminology it uses, which agrees hardly at all with that used by biologists. I present an Excel decoder in Table 8.

Note the tool bar above the worksheet that contains your data. To plot a graph, first highlight the data you wish to plot. Usually you will highlight all the numbers entered (by holding the left mouse button and dragging over the screen), but sometimes you will want to select certain columns (columns of transformed data, for example). Then alert Chart Wizard (hereafter referred to as CW) of your intentions to plot a graph by clicking on the CW icon (a small but colorful bar chart) toward the right side of the tool bar.

- If you wish to plot a bar graph or histogram, select the "Column" option. Do not plot 3D graphs, which can be difficult to read.

- If you wish to produce a scatter plot (e.g., Figs. 15 and 19), choose "XY Scatter."

- Do not select "Line" even when you wish to plot a line graph. Your x-axis values will not be properly spaced.

- For scatter plots, you have several suboptions to choose from. Usually you will want either to just plot the points

Table 8. The Excel decoder.

What It Means	What Excel Calls It
Graph	Chart
x-axis	Category axis
y-axis	Value axis
Area inside the axes of the graph	Plot area
Area outside the axes of the graph but inside the frame	Chart area
Scatter plot (a point graph)	XY (Scatter)
Don't use this!	Line (under Chart Type)
Key (for on-graph explanation of symbols used in graph)	Legend

without any lines (you can add a regression line later) or to connect the points with straight lines. Occasionally you will want to include smooth curves. **Never choose the options for plotting curves without data points**.

- To add a regression line to a scatter plot, first click on any point in the graph, to identify the data set, and then select "Add Trendline."

- Use white as a background color for all graphs, to maximize contrast and clarity. To do so, double-click anywhere inside the graph, and select the white icon (the default option is gray!). At the same time, select None for "Area," and None for "Border" (to remove the frame that Excel otherwise draws around each graph).

- If you will include a key to symbols used in your graph (i.e., if you are displaying more than one treatment, requiring the use of at least 2 symbols), use white as the background color for that as well. Double-click anywhere within the key area, and follow the instructions given above.

- If space is available in the figure, move the key into the figure by clicking on it once, and then dragging it into the figure.

- In the Chart Options of the Chart menu, leave "Chart Title" blank. You will enter your title as part of your figure caption later. Be sure to enter the units (in parentheses) after the labels for the x- and y-axes.

- To add error bars to a point or bar, double-click on the point or bar to obtain the "Format Data Series" menu and then select the "Y Error Bars" option. Enter the values of the error bars to be added (e.g., the standard errors, calculated on the spreadsheet using the Function button), in sequence and separated by commas (e.g., 8.4, 12.5, 5.5), in the Custom rectangle on the menu. Choose the type of display you want, at the top of the menu (usually "plus" for bars, "both" for points).

- To change the size of the points plotted in a scatter plot, double click on any point and change the size in the Patterns part of the menu.

(Continued)

- To modify a graph at a later time, click anywhere inside the graph and then select the desired option from the "Chart" item in the menu bar. If you wish to add or remove particular data points, do so first on the spreadsheet, and then use either the "Add data" or "Source Data" options in the Chart menu.

- If you correct a data entry in the spreadsheet, the correction will appear automatically in your graph.

9

WRITING RESEARCH PROPOSALS

Research proposals are commonly assigned in advanced biology courses in place of the more standard "term paper"; the 2 assignments have much in common, and you should read, or reread, Chapter 7 before proceeding with this chapter. Research proposals, essays, and term papers all require critical review and synthesis of the primary literature—that is, papers presenting detailed, original results of research rather than articles and books presenting only summaries and interpretations of that research. In addition, however, a research proposal includes a written argument in which you propose to go beyond what you have read; you propose to do a piece of research yourself and seek to convince the reader that what you propose to do should be done and can be done, and should in fact be done exactly how you propose to do it.

Research proposals are perhaps the best vehicle for developing your reasoning and writing skills as biologists. This assignment, more than any other, gives you a chance to be creative and to become a genuine participant in the process of biological investigation. Writing a good research proposal is no trivial feat, and the sense of accomplishment you feel once you are finished is indescribably nice.

Research proposals have 2 major parts: a review of the relevant scientific literature and a description of the proposed research. In the first part, you review the primary literature on a particular topic, but you do so with a particular goal in mind: you wish to lead your reader to the inescapable conclusion that the question you propose to address follows logically from the research that has gone before. Writing a research proposal rather than a term paper thus helps you avoid falling into the book report trap; once you develop a research question to ask, you should have an easier time focusing your literature review on the development of a single, clearly articulated theme. Developing that theme will take some time and thought, but your writing will then have a clear direction.

In addition to providing you with a convenient vehicle for exploring and digesting the primary scientific literature and for focusing your discussion of that literature, you may find that the research you propose to

219

do can actually be done—and can be done by you. Your proposal could turn out to be the basis for your own summer research project, senior thesis, or even master's or Ph.D. thesis.

RESEARCHING YOUR TOPIC

Proceed as you would for researching a term paper or essay (see Chapter 7). For this assignment especially, you must have a firm grasp of your subject before plunging into the original, primary scientific literature, so read the appropriate sections of several recent general textbooks before you look elsewhere. The next step should be to browse through recent issues of appropriate scientific journals; your instructor can suggest several that are particularly appropriate to your topic of interest.

Before you roll up your sleeves and prepare to wrestle in earnest with a published scientific paper, read it through once for general orientation. Once you begin your second reading of the paper, don't allow yourself to skip over any sentences or paragraphs you don't understand. Keep a relevant textbook by your side as you read the primary literature so that you can look up unfamiliar facts and terminology.

I mentioned previously that the results of any study depend largely on the way the study was conducted (p. 151, 193). We have also seen that although the results of a study are real, the interpretation of those results is always subject to change (pp. 157–158). The Materials and Methods section and the Results section of research papers must therefore be read with particular care and attention, as discussed in Chapter 2. Scrutinize every table and graph until you can reach your own tentative conclusions about the results of the study before allowing yourself to be swayed by the author's interpretations. Read with a questioning, critical eye (see Chapter 2).

As you carefully read each paper, pay special attention to the following:

1. What specific question is being asked?
2. How does the design of the study address the question posed?
3. What are the controls for each experiment? Are they appropriate and adequate?
4. How convincing are the results? Are any of the results surprising?
5. What contribution does this study make toward answering the original question?
6. What aspects of the original question remain unanswered?

Reread the paper until you can answer each of these questions. Then ask yourself the following additional question:

7. What might be a next logical question to ask, and how might this question be addressed?

Continue your library research using the references listed at the end of the recent papers you are reading, and perhaps by consulting *Biological Abstracts*, The Web of Science, or one of the other indexing services discussed in Chapter 2. One particularly convenient thing about preparing a research proposal is that it's relatively easy to tell when your library work is finished; it's finished when you know what your proposed research question will be and when you know exactly why you are asking that question.

WHAT MAKES A GOOD RESEARCH QUESTION?

You need not propose to cure or prevent any particular disease, rid the world of hunger or parasites, or single-handedly solve any other major humanitarian problem. Rather, **your goal is to pose a specific question that follows in some logical way from what has already been published in your area of interest and that can be addressed by available techniques and approaches** (Figure 32). This can be tricky to accomplish. On the one hand, you might ask a perfectly valid question but come up with no good way to address it convincingly. It is more common, however, for students to pose addressable questions that are difficult to justify. A question such as "Does music influence plant growth?" can certainly be addressed, but you will have great difficulty convincing readers that the question is worthwhile because it has no foundation in

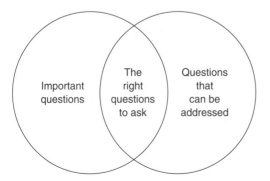

Figure 32. The trick of developing a valid research question. Many questions are easy to answer but are meaningless or too trivial to be worth asking. Many other questions are important but unapproachable by existing methods.

the scientific literature. What you propose to do must not only be doable; it must also seem like the next most logical question to ask in the area in which you are proposing to work, based on previously published research.

The question you propose must also be within your realm of expertise. You cannot write a convincing proposal on a topic that you do not fully understand.

The trick to asking a good question is to write down lots and lots of questions as you read and as you think about the topic. Many of the questions won't lead anywhere, or won't lead anywhere that interests you, but eventually you will come up with something that fits the bill.

WRITING THE PROPOSAL

Divide your paper into 3 main portions: Introduction, Background, and Proposed Research.

Introduction

Give a brief overview of the research being considered, and indicate the nature of the specific question you will pursue, as in the following example*:

> Endurance exercises such as running and swimming can affect the reproductive physiology of women athletes. Female runners (Dale *et al.*, 1979; Wakat *et al.*, 1982), swimmers (Frisch *et al.*, 1981), and ballet dancers (Warren, 1980) menstruate infrequently (i.e., exhibit oligomenorrhea) in comparison with nonathletic women of comparable age, or not at all (amenorrhea). The degree of menstrual abnormality varies directly with the intensity of the exercise. For example, Malina *et al.* (1978) have shown that menstrual irregularity is more common, and more severe, among tennis players than among golfers.
>
> The physiological mechanism through which strenuous activity disrupts the normal menstrual

---

*Modified from a student paper written by A. Lord.

```
cycle is not yet clear; inadequate fat levels
(Frisch et al., 1981), altered hormonal balance
(Sutton et al., 1973), and physiological predis-
position (Wakat et al., 1982) have each been im-
plicated.
     In the proposed research, I will study 200 fe-
male weight lifters in an attempt to determine
the relative importance of fat levels, hormone
levels, and physiological predisposition in pro-
moting oligomenorrhea and amenorrhea.
```

Notice that the author of this proposal has not used the Introduction to discuss the question being addressed or to describe how the study will be done. The Introduction provides only (1) general background to help the reader understand why the topic is of interest, and (2) a brief but clear statement of the specific research topic that will be addressed.

It helps to write the last sentence of your Introduction first, stating the specific question to be addressed; then write the rest of your Introduction, giving just enough information for the reader to understand why anyone would want to ask such a question. Limit your introduction to 2 or 3 paragraphs. A detailed discussion of prior research belongs in the Background section of the proposal, and a detailed description of the proposed study belongs in the Proposed Research section of the proposal. Idea Mapping (Chapter 5, pp. 76–81) can also be an excellent aid to organizing your Introduction.

Notice in the above example that every factual statement (for example, "Female runners . . . menstruate infrequently.") is supported by a reference to one or more papers from the primary literature. These references enable the reader to obtain, painlessly, additional information on particular aspects of the subject and to verify the accuracy of statements made in the proposal (Chapter 4). Backing up statements with references also protects the author of the proposal by documenting the source of information; if the author of your source is mistaken, why should you take the blame?

Background

In this section, you demonstrate your complete mastery of the relevant literature. Discuss this literature in detail, leading up to the specific objective of your proposed research. This section of your proposal follows the format of a good term paper or essay, as already described in Chapter 7 (pp. 134–140). In a proposal, however, the Background section will end with a brief summary statement of what is now known and what is not yet known about the research topic under consideration, and a clear, specific description of the research question(s) you propose to investigate. Here are 2 examples. The author of Example 1 has already spent nearly 3 pages of the Background section describing documented effects of organic pollutants on adults and developmental stages of various marine vertebrates and invertebrates.

EXAMPLE 1

Thus many fish, echinoderm, polychaete, mollusc, and crustacean species are highly sensitive to a variety of fuel oil hydrocarbon pollutants, and the early stages of development are especially susceptible. However, many of these species begin their lives within potentially protective extra-embryonic egg membranes, jelly masses, or egg capsules (Anderson *et al.*, 1977; Eldridge *et al.*, 1977; Kînehcép, 1979). The ability of these structures to protect developing embryos against water-soluble toxic hydrocarbons has apparently never been assessed.

The egg capsules of marine snails are particularly complex, both structurally and chemically (Fretter, 1941; Bayne, 1968; Hunt, 1971). Such capsules are typically several mm to several cm in height, and the capsule walls are commonly 50-100 μm* thick (Hancock, 1956; Tamarin and Carriker, 1968). Depending on the species, embryos may spend from several days to many weeks developing within these egg capsules before emerging as free-swimming larvae or crawling juveniles (Thorson, 1946).

Little is known about the tolerance of encapsulated embryos to environmental stress, or about the permeability of the capsule walls to water and solutes. Kînehcép (1982, 1983) has found that

---

°μm = micrometers (10^{-6} meters).

the egg capsules of several shallow-water marine snails (*Ilyanassa obsoleta, Nucella lamellosa*, and *N. lapillus*) are permeable to both salts and water, but are far less permeable to the small organic molecule glucose. Capsules of at least these species are thus likely to protect embryos from exposure to many fuel oil components.

In the proposed study, I will (1) document the tolerance of early embryos of *N. lamellosa* and *N. lapillus*, both within capsules and removed from capsules, to the water soluble fraction of Number 2 fuel oil; (2) determine the general permeability characteristics of the capsules of these 2 gastropod species to see which classes of toxic substances might be unable to penetrate the capsule wall; and (3) use radioisotopes to directly measure the permeability of the capsules to several major components of fuel oil.

The next, shorter example, concerns the hormonal control of reproductive activity in sea stars. The author of this proposal has already spent 3 pages of the Background section discussing experiments demonstrating that (1) gamete release (spawning) is under hormonal control; (2) the response to the hormone varies seasonally; and (3) the variation in response seems to reflect changing concentrations of an inhibitory hormone called shedhibin.

EXAMPLE 2

The present evidence suggests, therefore, that the influence of the excitatory hormone is regulated by seasonal fluctuations in the secretion of shedhibin, although seasonal changes in the concentrations of this inhibitory hormone have not yet been documented.

In the proposed research, I will:

1. identify the time of year during which gamete release is inhibited in mature sea stars (*Asterias forbesi*);

2. develop a monoclonal antibody to the inhibitory substance shedhibin; and

```
3. use immunofluorescent techniques to quantify
   the amount of shedhibin produced and se-
   creted at different stages of the reproduc-
   tive cycle of A. forbesi.
```

This section of your proposal has the potential to lead a double life: It can later serve as the basis for the Introduction and Discussion sections of a thesis or research article.

Proposed Research

This portion of your proposal has 2 interrelated parts: (1) what specific question(s) will you ask? and (2) how will you address each of these questions? Different instructors will put different amounts of stress on these 2 parts. For some of us, the formulation of a valid and logically developed question is the major purpose of the assignment, and a highly detailed description of the methods will not be required. For such an instructor, you may, for example, propose to extract and separate proteins without actually having to know in detail how this is accomplished. But other instructors may feel that your mastery or knowledge of methodological detail is as important as the validity of the questions posed. Both approaches are defensible, depending largely on the nature of the field of inquiry, on the level of the course being taken, and on the amount of laboratory experience you have had. Be sure you understand what your instructor expects of you before preparing this section of your paper.

Before you begin to write this section of your proposal, I strongly recommend that you sketch a flowchart of your proposed study, as shown in Figure 12 (p. 146). This will help to organize your thinking and will also serve as a template for your writing. Often it is helpful to include such a flowchart in your proposal, making it easy both for the reader to grasp the complete experimental design and for you to write about it.

As you describe each component of your proposed research, **indicate clearly what specific question each experiment is designed to address**, as in the following 3 examples:

```
To see if there is a seasonal difference in the
amount of hormone present in the bag cells that
induce egg-laying in Aplysia californica, bag
```

cells will be dissected out of mature individuals each month and. . . .

Before the influence of light intensity on the rate of photosynthesis can be documented, populations of the test species (wild columbine, *Aquileqia canadensis*) must be established in the laboratory. This will be done by. . . .

To monitor seasonal changes in the relative abundance of macroalgae at different levels in the rocky intertidal zone at Nahant, MA, I will inspect each of the 10 boulders at monthly intervals for a 12-month period. At each inspection, I will. . . .

If the proposed research has several distinct components, it is helpful to separate them using subheadings. Your first subheading might read, for example, "Collecting and maintaining *Aplysia californica* adults," while a second subheading might read, "Isolating and homogenizing bag cells," and a third might read, "Assaying for hormonal activity" (see Chapter 8, pp. 155–157, for additional examples).

Citing References and Preparing the Literature Cited Section

Cite references directly in the text by author and year, as in the examples given earlier in this chapter (see also pp. 66–70). The Literature Cited section of your proposal is prepared as described in Chapter 4 (pp. 70–74).

TIGHTENING THE LOGIC

Read your proposal aloud, slowly and thoughtfully, before deciding that your work is finished. If you listen as you read, you can often catch logical and typographical errors that you might otherwise miss.

In rereading your description of what you propose to do and how you propose to do it, try to envision the specific objections that an interested but critical reviewer would raise. Can you argue those objections away? Do so in your presentation, if possible. If not, can you modify your approach or add additional components to the study that will address those specific objections? Perhaps you need to add additional controls or additional experiments, or to modify your experimental design. In some cases, you may need to modify the question that you are proposing to address.

It is the reviewer's job—and your instructor's—to find flaws in your proposal. Try to be your own harshest critic and find and fix as many as you can before anyone else judges your work.

THE LIFE OF A REAL RESEARCH PROPOSAL

This is no idle exercise; the formal proposals written by practicing biologists are prepared exactly as described, except that each proposal must adhere strictly to the particular format (major headings, page length, type size, width of margins, number of copies to be submitted) requested by the National Science Foundation, National Institutes of Health, or other targeted funding agency. Proposals must be submitted by specified due dates or they will not be considered—no excuses are accepted. Copies of the proposal are then sent out to perhaps 6 to 10 other biologists for anonymous reviews. A panel of still other biologists then meets to discuss the proposal and the reviews, and to then make its own evaluation. If your case is well argued, you may receive funding; if it is not well argued, there is little hope. Learning to write a tightly organized and convincing proposal now will surely make your life easier later, no matter what career ultimately attracts you: sooner or later you will probably need to convince someone of something, in writing.

CHECKLIST

(see also the checklist at the end of Chapter 5, on revising)

- ❏ Title gives specific indication of the proposed work (pp. 141, 206–207)
- ❏ Introductory material leads to a clear statement of the specific goal(s) and hypotheses (pp. 222–223)
- ❏ The questions posed follow logically from previous work in the area of interest (pp. 219, 221–222)
- ❏ The logic behind all hypotheses presented is made clear (pp. 192, 201)

❑ Final paragraphs of the Introduction and Background sections address the issues raised in the introductory paragraphs (p. 223)

❑ All statements are supported by reference, data, or example (pp. 7–8, 66–69)

❑ Proposed methods will address the questions posed, and are designed to distinguish among all alternative hypotheses

❑ A rationale is provided for each step proposed (pp. 226–227)

❑ Controls are appropriate and clearly indicated

❑ Samples sizes and number of replicates per treatment are indicated

❑ Plans for data analysis are clear (p. 157)

❑ Each sentence follows from the preceding sentence and leads logically to the one that follows (pp. 99–103)

❑ Work has been carefully proofread and revised according to the guidelines presented in Chapter 5 (pp. 119–120)

❑ Citations are provided for every reference cited in the report

❑ Each listing in the Literature Cited section includes names of all authors, title of paper, year of publication, volume number, and page numbers, in the correct format (pp. 70–74)

❑ Text of report is double-spaced (p. 14)

❑ All pages are numbered (p. 14)

10

ANSWERING ESSAY
QUESTIONS

BASIC PRINCIPLES

Answering essay questions on examinations differs from the other forms of scientific writing already discussed in only 2 respects: the essay examination must be completed within a short time, usually from 15 to 50 minutes, and you have no choice in the subject of the essay. A winning answer to an essay question will follow all the guidelines outlined in Chapter 1. Your performance on essay questions can be strengthened by keeping in mind a few additional points:

1. **Read the question carefully before writing anything.** You must answer the question posed, not the question you would have preferred to see on the examination. In particular, note whether the question asks you to list, discuss, or compare. A list will not satisfy the requirements of a discussion or comparison. A request for a list tests to see whether you know all components of the answer; a request for a discussion additionally examines your understanding of the interrelationships among these components.

   Consider this list of the characteristics of a Big Mac and a Whopper, based on a tax-deductible study conducted in Boston, Massachusetts, in January 2003:

BIG MAC	WHOPPER
2 beef patties	1 beef patty
patties 3.25″ diameter	patty 3.75″–4″ diameter
fried beef	broiled beef
3-part bun (3 slices)	2-part bun (top and bottom)

sesame seeds on top bun	sesame seeds on top bun
slice of pickle	slice of pickle
chopped onion	slices of onion
slice of cheese	2–3 slices of tomato
lettuce	ketchup
sauce	mayonnaise
$2.51	$2.49
surrounded by a cardboard ring and wrapped in paper	packed in styrofoam box

Suppose you are asked to write an essay presenting the features of both items. Your essay might look like this:

```
     The Big Mac consists of 2 patties of fried
ground beef, each patty approximately 3.25 inches
in diameter, with lettuce, chopped onion, sliced
pickle, a slice of cheese, some reddish sauce,
and a 3-part bun, with the 2 patties separated
from each other by one of the bun slices. The top
slice of the bun is covered with sesame seeds.
The Big Mac sells for $2.51 and is served in a pa-
per wrapper, with a cardboard ring inside to hold
the sandwich together.
     The Whopper consists of 1 patty of broiled
ground beef (approximately 4 inches in diameter),
with mayonnaise, ketchup, several slices each of
tomato, pickle, and onion, and a 2-part bun, with
the upper half of the bun covered with sesame
seeds. The Whopper sells for $2.49 and is served
in a styrofoam box.
```

If you are asked to compare, or to compare and contrast, the 2 products, your essay must be written differently. All too often, when asked to "compare and contrast" A and B, students first write everything they know about A, then everything they know about B, and then conclude with something like, "And so you can see that A and B have many similarities and many differences." That is unacceptable. You are asking your instructor to make the comparisons! To make them yourself requires a thorough understanding of the information—an overview of the subject that goes beyond what is needed to simply list facts. The instructor's question is designed to see if you've got that understanding.

Here is an example, comparing the characteristics of the Big Mac and the Whopper:

> Both the Big Mac and the Whopper contain ground beef and are served on buns. The 2 hamburgers differ, however, with regard to the way the meat is cooked, the way the meat and bread are distributed within the hamburger, the nature of accompanying condiments, and how the sandwiches are served.
>
> The meat in the Big Mac is fried, and each sandwich contains 2 patties, each approximately 3.25 inches in diameter and separated from the second patty by a slice of bun. In contrast, the meat in the Whopper is broiled, and each sandwich contains a single, larger patty, approximately 3.75-4 inches in diameter. The top bun of both sandwiches is dotted with sesame seeds. Both the Big Mac and the Whopper contain lettuce, onion, and slices of pickle. The Big Mac, however, contains chopped onion, whereas the onion in the Whopper is sliced. Moreover, the Big Mac has a slice of cheese, which is absent from the Whopper. On the other hand, the Whopper comes with slices of tomato, which are absent from the Big Mac. Both sandwiches contain a sauce: ketchup and mayonnaise in the Whopper and a premixed sauce in the Big Mac. The Big Mac, at $2.51, costs only about 1% more than the Whopper.

If you are asked for a comparison and respond with a list, you will probably lose points, not because your instructor is being picky but because you have failed to demonstrate your understanding of the relationship between the characteristics of the 2 products. **It is not the instructor's job to guess at what you understand**; it is your job to demonstrate what you know to the instructor. Note that the facts included are the same in the 2 essays. The difference lies in the way the facts are presented.

If asked for a list, give a list; this response requires less time than a discussion, giving you more time to complete the rest of the examination. When asked for a discussion, discuss: present the facts and support them with specific examples. When asked for a comparison, you will generally discuss similarities and differences, but the word *compare* can also mean that you should consider only similarities. Often an instructor will ask you to compare and contrast, avoiding any such ambiguity. If you have any doubts about what is required, ask your instructor during the examination.

2. **Present all relevant facts.** Although there are many ways to answer an essay question correctly, your instructor will undoubtedly have in mind a series of facts that he or she would like to see included in your essay. That is, the ideal answer to a particular question will contain a finite number of components; the way you deal with each of these components is up to you, but each of the components should be considered in your answer.

Before you begin to write your essay, then, list all components of the ideal answer, drawing both from lecture material and from any readings you were assigned. For example, suppose you are asked the following question:

> Discuss the influence of physical and biological factors on the distribution of plants in a forest.

What components will the perfect answer to this question contain? Begin by making a list of all relevant factors as they occur to you—don't worry about the order in which you jot these factors down.

PHYSICAL	BIOLOGICAL
amount of rainfall	competition with other plants
annual temperature range	predation by herbivores
light intensity	
hours of light per day	
type of soil	
pesticide use	
nutrient availability	

This list is not your answer to the essay question; it is an organizing vehicle intended for your use alone. Feel free to abbreviate, especially if pressed for time ("nutr. avail.," "pred. by herbs"), but be certain you won't misunderstand your own notes while writing the essay.

In preparing to write your answer to the essay question, arrange the elements of your list in some logical order, perhaps from most to least important or so that related elements are considered together; this grouping and ordering is most quickly done by simply numbering the items in your list in the order that you decide to consider them. You have now outlined your answer; the most difficult part of the ordeal is finished.

Incorporate into your essay each of the ordered components in your list. Avoid spending all of your time discussing a few of these components to the exclusion of the others. If you discuss only 4 of the 8 relevant issues, your instructor will be forced to assume you don't realize that the other issues are also relevant to the question posed. Show your instructor you know all the elements of a complete answer to the question.

3. **Stick to the facts.** An examination essay is not an exercise in creative writing and is not the place for you to express personal, unsubstantiated opinion. As with any other type of examination question, your instructor wishes to discover what you have learned and what you understand. Focus, therefore, on the facts, and, as with all other forms of scientific writing, support all statements of fact or opinion with evidence or example. You may wish to suggest a hypothesis as part of your essay; if so, be sure to include the evidence or logic upon which your hypothesis is based.

4. **Keep the question in mind as you write.** Don't include superfluous information. If what you write is irrelevant to the question posed, you probably won't get additional credit for your answer, and you will most likely annoy your instructor. If what you write is not only irrelevant but also wrong, you will probably lose points. By letting yourself wander off on tangents, you will usually gain nothing, possibly lose points, and probably lose your instructor's good will; certainly, you will waste time that might more profitably be applied elsewhere on the examination. Listing the components of your answer before you write your essay will help keep you on track.

Applying the Principles

To see how these principles are applied in a more realistic situation, consider this question: Compare and contrast the locomotion of a mobile polychaete worm and a sea urchin (Figure 33).

A good response might begin as follows:

> The locomotion of both polychaete worms and sea urchins involves many dozens of appendages that move in complex but highly coordinated patterns.

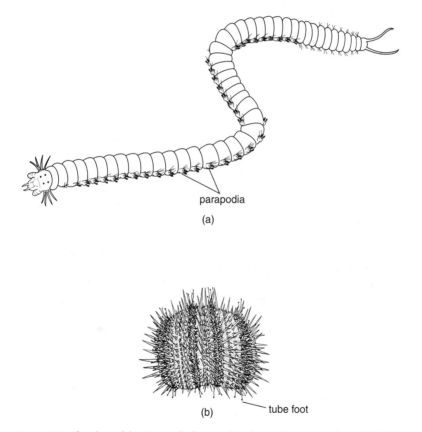

Figure 33. Sketches of the 2 animals discussed in the student's essay (pp. 235–236) (a) a polychaete annelid and (b) a sea urchin, showing locomotory appendages (parapodia and tube feet, respectively).

(The student might add a few sentences here about the pattern of movement in both groups.)

```
However, the 2 types of animal differ in the
skeletal systems they employ in moving the ap-
pendages, the manner in which the appendages form
temporary attachments to the substrate, the de-
gree of development of the nervous system direct-
ing and coordinating those movements, and the ex-
tent to which body wall musculature is also
involved in locomotion. Whereas the movements of
sea urchin appendages involve a fluid skeleton ex-
clusively, the muscles operating polychaete para-
podia act against each other through a rigid, in-
ternal skeleton, the acicula. . . .
```

The answer would continue in this vein, dealing with the topics in the order that they were listed in the second sentence. Note that the student includes no extraneous information, such as the names of the phyla the 2 animals are contained in, and that the student has listed *all* of the issues to be discussed early in the answer. You might want to leave a few lines of empty space in this part of your response so that you can add items that may occur to you as you keep writing, or as you work on other parts of the examination. Even if this student runs out of time before completing a thorough discussion of each issue, he or she will earn substantial credit by having at least indicated all of the specific areas of overlap and contrast. Also, **note that every sentence makes some sort of comparison**, indicating an impressive command of the information. This student has been *processing* information, not just storing it. You can't help but do well on an essay exam, on any topic, if you follow this model.

11

WRITING A POSTER PRESENTATION

Most biologists go to at least one scientific meeting each year to share their research progress with others in related fields. For many years, the standard meeting format has been a series of 10- to 15-minute individual presentations, followed by an additional 5 minutes for questions. However, as the number of meeting participants has been increasing dramatically, while meeting length has not, oral presentations have been giving way to poster presentations. In a poster session, displays (called posters) containing both text and data are lined up in rows, like billboards, for all to see. Each poster represents the research of one person or research team. Each group of posters is usually displayed for only an afternoon or evening, and 40 or more posters—sometimes several hundred—may be on display at any one time, each competing for the attention of meeting attendees.

Compared with oral presentations, poster presentations have the advantage that many biologists can be "talking" about their research simultaneously in a single room, and "listeners," as they stroll about the room browsing among the many posters, can have detailed conversations with the authors of the posters they find especially interesting. The disadvantage of poster presentations is that the "speaker" no longer has a captive audience: poster sessions are like flea markets, complete with all the noise and crowds. To be successful in "selling" your information, you must plan carefully to create a display that captures the attention of browsers and then leads them through an especially clear, logical, and interesting presentation of the research; otherwise, much of your potential audience will simply pass you by, lured elsewhere by another's more compelling presentation.

How do you create a poster that people will want to stop at and read, and from which even the casual reader will take away something of substance? Plan a 2-pronged attack:

1. limit the amount of information you present, and
2. arrange the information advantageously.

All too often, posters display what is essentially a full scientific manuscript—complete with formal Introduction, Materials and Methods, Results, and Discussion sections—enlarged and hung up for view, page by page. This is not a good way to attract a sizable audience for your work. It is simply not reasonable to expect people to read through 40 or more complete research papers during the hour or so they may spend at a particular poster session.

To be effective, your poster presentation should be streamlined to its essential findings. **An effective poster must include less detail than you would include in a formal publication or even in a talk.** Your poster should be designed to inform people both within and (largely) outside your immediate field about what you have done and what you have found, and it should provide a basis for discussion with those who wish to find out more about your work. It should highlight the major questions asked, the major results obtained, and the major conclusions drawn, and it should contain the least possible amount of text.

As an example of how to construct a successful poster, let's create one based on a paper published by Richard K. Zimmer-Faust and Mario N. Tamburri in 1994, in the journal *Limnology and Oceanography* (Volume 39: 1075–1087). Normally, one gives a poster or oral presentation before publishing the work; however, the interested reader will profit from comparing the published paper with the poster presentation that follows. The paper reports a series of experiments defining the chemical cue that causes the swimming, microscopic larval stages of oysters to stop swimming and settle to the bottom in preparation for metamorphosing to the more familiar immobile (and highly edible) juvenile stage.

Your key weapon in attracting an audience is your title, which appears in large letters at the top of your poster. The title of the published paper, "Chemical identity and ecological implications of a waterborne, larval settlement cue," contains too little specific information to be completely compelling as a poster title; moreover, the passerby who reads only the title leaves with nothing of substance. The poster will attract more attention and convey more information with a more revealing title, such as "Oyster larvae settle in response to arginine-containing peptides." **This title indicates clearly both the question that was addressed and the key finding of the study.**

The rest of the poster should focus on the Results. Only the most important results should be presented: the published paper contains 7 figures and 4 tables; our poster will display only 3 of the figures, and none of the tables. To make it as easy as possible for viewers to extract the essential information we wish to convey, **we want each of these**

figures to be self-sufficient. Each should have clearly labeled axes, contain definitions of any symbols used, and be accompanied with clear indications of the specific question being addressed and the major results found. These goals are easily accomplished, as we will see momentarily.

The bigger difficulty in achieving a completely self-sufficient figure is in explaining how the experiment was performed or how the observations were made. **Don't include a detailed, formal Materials and Methods section.** Instead, for each figure either (1) list the major steps taken, in numerical order, or (2) present a flowchart summary of the steps taken. You may wish to have a more detailed description of the methods available as a 1-page handout that particularly interested biologists may take with them, but the poster itself should not be cluttered with such detail. If you do accompany your poster with handouts, be sure the handout includes your name, mailing address, e-mail address, and poster title.

LAYOUT OF THE POSTER

Figure 34 shows a possible layout for the poster just described. Notice that it is divided into 3 major sections, each highlighting one key issue, and each section is clearly separated from the other sections by substantial space. The illustrated layout makes it easy for readers to follow the logic of the presentation by scanning left to right, section by section— there is never any question of where to look next—and makes it difficult for even a casual reader to miss the point of what they are looking at.

Let's fill in the entire top section of the poster, entitled "Oyster bath seawater stimulates larval settlement." Our Methods section might look like this:

Methods:
1. Incubate 8 adult oysters (*Crassostrea virginica*) in 16 liters of artificial seawater for 2 hours.
2. Adjust pH of oyster-conditioned seawater and control seawater to 8.0; adjust salinity to 25%.
3. Separate oyster-conditioned seawater and control seawater samples into 3 molecular size-fractions by dialysis.
4. Expose oyster larvae to both solutions.
5. Videotape larval behavior; determine number of individuals settling on bottom of containers by end of 3 minutes.

OYSTER LARVAE SETTLE IN RESPONSE TO
ARGININE-CONTAINING PEPTIDES

R. Zimmer-Faust and M. Tamburri, Univ. South Carolina

I.   Oyster bath seawater stimulates larval settlement

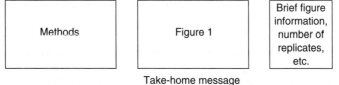

II.   The active component is degraded by proteases but not by other enzymes

III.   The active factor has arginine at the C-terminus of the peptide

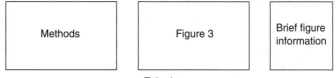

Figure 34. General layout of the poster. The goal is to make it easy for readers to see what was done and what was discovered.

Here is the same Methods information presented in flowchart format:

Methods

Incubate 8 adult oysters in 16 l of artificial seawater

↓ 2 hours

Adjust pH to 8.0, salinity to $25\%_{00}$

↓

Distribute conditioned water into a glass dish

↓

Distribute control seawater into another glass dish

↓

Add sixty 20-day-old oyster larvae to each dish

↓

Videotape for 3 minutes

↓

Assess numbers of larvae settling to bottom in control
and adult-conditioned seawater

↓

Repeat 7 more times, using another 120 larvae per test

The accompanying figure and associated take-home message are shown in Figure 35. Each section of the poster will contain a separate Methods section and accompanying graph, following the format just presented.

MAKING THE POSTER

Well in advance of the meeting you will be told the dimensions of your display area—typically 4 feet high by 6 feet wide. Your entire display must fit within the designated area. The title of your poster should be readable from 15 to 20 feet away, so plan on using letters about 4 cm (~1.5 inches) tall. You can use a slightly smaller font for the names of all authors and the institution(s) they are from. The rest of your poster should be readable from about 4 to 6 feet away, so text size should be about 1 cm (~3/8 inches) high. The easiest way to manipulate text size is

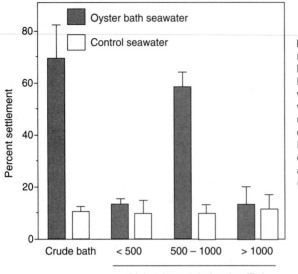

Figure 1. Each bar is the mean of 8 replicates with 60 larvae per replicate. Different molecular weight fractions were obtained by ultrafiltration through dialysis membranes. Error bars represent one standard error above the mean (SEM).

The active molecules have a molecular weight of 500-1000 daltons

Figure 35. The figure and take-home message for the first section of the poster shown in Figure 34.

by using an enlarging copying machine, although many computer software packages can also be used.

Some biology departments have the technology to print an entire poster on a single, very large sheet of paper. Otherwise, mount the individual items of your poster on colored paper or posterboard. **Use a single background color for the entire poster to unify the presentation**; you may wish to use different shades of that color to better distinguish the different sections of the poster. Choose a color that provides good contrast without being jarring or distracting; brown and blue are good choices. Thumbtacks and tape, for attaching the components of your poster to the display board, are generally provided at the meetings, but bring your own just in case.

When registering to present a poster or oral presentation at a meeting you are generally required to submit an Abstract of your work (see pp. 208–209), and you may be required to include the Abstract in the upper left-hand corner of your poster. If so, be sure to leave room for the Abstract in planning your layout.

Creating a successful poster takes considerable planning. But it is well worth the time and effort required: not only will you have a more productive and enjoyable meeting, you will also return from the meeting with something that can be displayed in your biology department for students and faculty to read at their leisure.

CHECKLIST FOR MAKING POSTERS

1. Poster includes all required information (such as institutional affiliation, names of all coauthors).

2. All components will fit within the space provided for display.

3. Title lettering is 4 cm tall, readable from a distance of at least 15 feet.

4. Text letters are 1 cm high (3/8").

5. The amount of text in each section is the minimum required and not excessive.

6. The flow of information on the poster is easy to follow.

7. Methods are presented in flowchart form or as a simple listing.

8. The Introduction states the specific issue that was addressed.

9. Each figure or table is self-sufficient.

10. The significance of each result is stated explicitly, as a take-home message.

11. The poster has been checked for typographical and grammatical errors.

12. If supplementary handouts are provided, they include the poster's title, names of all authors, and the mailing and e-mail addresses of the lead author.

12

WRITING FOR A GENERAL AUDIENCE: SCIENCE JOURNALISM

Explaining scientific advances to the general public is a worthwhile—even a noble—endeavor. If you have a substantial background in the subjects you are writing about you will have a real advantage over most journalists, who typically are trained in journalism rather than science. But the purpose of this chapter is not to prepare you for a career in newspaper or magazine publishing. Rather, I include this chapter because writing for a general audience can sharpen both your thinking skills and your writing skills.

Assimilating a piece of research published in the primary scientific literature and reorganizing that information to produce a successful piece of science journalism is an excellent exercise in summarizing information, simplifying complex material, and de-jargonizing your writing. Most important, writing for a general audience of intelligent nonscientists is a wonderful way to tell if you really understand something, and to show your instructor how much you have learned from what you have read. The science journalist is essentially a teacher. But as you may have discovered already, trying to teach something to someone else is one of the best ways of teaching it to yourself. It can also be fun—fun for you to write and fun for your instructor to read.

SCIENCE JOURNALISM BASED ON PUBLISHED RESEARCH

Science journalism differs from most of the other forms of writing discussed in this book in that the take-home message is always presented at the beginning of the article rather than at its end. That is, the article *begins* by summarizing what follows. By the end of the first or second short paragraph, for example, one typically finds sentences like these:

Scientists have now found that lobsters use an internal magnetic compass to navigate during their annual mass migrations into deeper waters.

In a recent report published in the journal *Nature*, Professors Tia-Lynn Ashman and Daniel J. Schoen present the remarkable finding that plants time their production of flowers in much the same way that people run efficient businesses.

According to Professors Graziano Fiorito and Pietro Scutto, working at their laboratories in Italy, the common octopus can not only be trained to distinguish between objects of different colors, but can in fact learn to make these distinctions more quickly from each other than from human trainers.

Researchers at the Dr. Seus School of Medicine and the Mt. Auburn Hospital have discovered an inherited molecular defect that makes some people naturally resistant to malaria, a disease affecting over 300 million people in tropical areas around the world.

Often such sentences begin the article. In other cases, summary sentences are preceded by one or a few sentences designed to stimulate additional reader interest in the topic. The opening sentences are known as the "lead." Leads tend to follow 1 of 4 major formats: the simple statement, the bullet lead, the narrative lead, and the surprise or paradox lead. Some of these leads allow the writer considerable room for creativity.

The first is a simple, but dramatic statement of the major finding, usually in a single sentence, as in the example about malaria given above. A more interesting lead, but one that is more challenging to write, is called the *bullet lead*. Actually, it consists of 3 bullets, which are always followed by the general summary statement. For example:

We all know people who have trained their dogs to fetch the daily newspaper without tearing it. Similarly, we all know that horses can be trained to respond to the slightest movement of their riders. And we all know that goldfish can be trained to come to the front of the fish bowl at the sound of a bell. Now it turns out that even

octopi (*Octopus vulgarus*) can be trained to perform certain simple tasks, and that they actually
learn those tasks more quickly from each other
than from a human trainer.

If the bullets are fired successfully, by the end of the third "shot," the
reader is wondering how the individual bullets are related and where
they are "leading." And just at that moment, the skillful writer answers
those questions; if done properly, the reader wants to read more.

Another common lead takes the form of a narrative; it tells a story of
some sort, and then follows up with the summary sentence:

Sitting at the bottom of a large glass tank is
a 2-pound octopus. The octopus has been trained
for several weeks to avoid balls of one color and
to pick up balls of a different color. Every day
for 6 hours he has been rewarded with food for
choosing the right balls, and punished with mild
electric shocks for choosing the wrong ones. Now,
he sits idly in the tank, his eyes apparently
following every movement of the researchers as
they prepare to set up the next experiment, his
mantle cavity filling and emptying in a consistent
respiratory rhythm.

The researchers bring over a tank containing
another octopus, one that was freshly collected
that morning from the warm and inviting waters
just outside the marine laboratory. The 2 octopi
quickly crawl toward each other in their respec-
tive tanks, peering through the glass with apparent interest. "Now watch this," one of the researchers says to the newcomer, as she puts the
trained octopus through his morning paces. The
newly collected octopus watches, and seems genuinely interested in what the other octopus is doing. Now the researchers offer the same choices to
the new octopus. Remarkably, after watching only 4
trials, the observing octopus chooses the correct
ball over the other one in every one of the trials.

The surprising finding that octopi can learn
from watching each other was recently published
in the research journal *Science* by 2 biologists

working at laboratories on the Italian coast,
Professors Graziano Fiorito and Pietro Scotto.

Finally, there is the lead that tries to arouse the reader's attention by making a surprising or paradoxical statement, and then follows up with the summary sentence. Here is an example:

Biologists have for years spent many tedious
hours training animals to perform simple tasks, by
rewarding the desired behavior and punishing the
undesired behavior. Now it seems that at least some
animals may learn far more quickly by simply watching each other than by being trained by humans.

Two Italian scientists, Professor Graziano
Fiorito and Professor Pietro Scotto, announced in
a recent issue of the research journal *Science*,
that the common octopus can not only be trained to
distinguish between objects of different colors,
but can in fact learn to make these distinctions
even more quickly by simply watching each other.

No matter how it begins, the rest of the article expands on the summary that has preceded it. For the article to be effective for a general audience, you must be careful to explain to the reader what was done, why it was done, what happened, and why the result is interesting, avoiding big words whenever possible and carefully explaining any terms that are essential to the story. Remember, you are not trying to impress or bamboozle others; you are trying to teach them something. Here is an example that further develops the story on octopus learning. If this was your own work, of course, you would submit it to your instructor double-spaced. Note that paragraphs tend to be shorter here than in other forms of writing in biology:

Two Italian scientists, Professor Graziano
Fiorito and Professor Pietro Scotto, announced in
a recent issue of the research journal *Science*,
that the common octopus can not only be trained to
distinguish between objects of different colors,
but can in fact learn to make these distinctions
even more quickly by simply watching each other.

They performed their study with *Octopus vul-
garis* collected from the Bay of Naples, Italy.
First they trained 30 individuals to grab a red
plastic ball and 14 individuals to prefer a white

plastic ball, by rewarding the animals with food if they chose correctly and mildly shocking the animals if they chose incorrectly. After 17–21 trials, the octopi all learned to make the correct choice, and no further training was necessary.

There is nothing unexpected so far: biologists have been successfully training octopi to exhibit simple behaviors for many decades. The surprising part of the experiment came when the researchers then let each trained octopus exhibit its acquired color preference 4 times to a freshly caught octopus that had received no prior training.

The observing octopi were then themselves given the opportunity to select either a white or a red plastic ball. Remarkably, all but a few of the 44 observers chose the color preferred by the octopus it had watched. Just as remarkably, the color preferences shown by the observing octopi persisted for at least 5 days, when they were tested again.

Clearly, the octopus is a quick learner. And it learns more quickly from simply watching what other octopi do than it does by being shocked or rewarded by humans in the standard laboratory experiment. One wonders about the extent to which octopi can learn more complex behaviors from each other, and about the things octopi might actually be learning by example in their natural environment. Learning by example is apparently not a uniquely vertebrate characteristic; octopus see, octopus do.

JOURNALISM BASED ON AN INTERVIEW

An alternative to writing a piece of science journalism based on a published research article is writing a piece based on research that someone in your biology department is currently performing. Obviously, you need to get the professor's permission and cooperation to do this, and you have to do some preparation beforehand by reading some general textbook references about the research area being investigated and perhaps by looking over a few papers that the professor has recently published. Allow about 1/2 hour for the interview, and have at least a half-dozen questions prepared in advance. Here are some possible questions to get an interview started:

What basic question are you asking in your research?

How did you start doing research in this area?

What do you enjoy most about doing research?

What is the most surprising thing you have found out so far?

How did you find that out?

Although biologists are generally eager to explain what they do and why they do it, most of us don't get much practice talking about our research to undergraduates—so don't be surprised if the biologist you interview is difficult to follow at first. If you don't understand something that the professor says to you, don't be embarrassed or afraid to ask for clarification. Any lack of understanding is sure to be apparent in what you write; you can't explain something to someone else that you yourself don't understand. And in science journalism, unlike some other forms of writing in biology courses, you can't hide your ignorance behind big words and convoluted sentence structures. **The success of your writing depends mightily on how hard you work to understand your source**. Along the way, you will learn a lot, meet some interesting people, and might even end up with something that you can publish in your campus newspaper.

One good way to prepare for the interview is to read examples of science journalism in major newspapers and magazines, such as the *New York Times* and *Newsweek*. For each article, ask yourself, "What questions did the interviewer probably ask his or her subject in conducting the interview?" and "What additional questions would I ask if I got to talk to this person myself someday?" That sort of thinking puts you in exactly the right frame of mind for the real thing.

Here is an example of interview-based science journalism. See if you can determine what questions the student asked the person he was interviewing:

> "Don't worry, I'm on the pill," he said, to allay her contraceptive concerns. Such male contraceptive pills may be available in the near future, resulting from research being conducted by Professor Norman Hecht at Tufts University.
>
> Over the past 20 years or so Professor Hecht has worked to understand how sperm develop, reasoning that the ability to block their normal development in the testis could lead to an effective contraceptive pill.

As sperm develop within the testis, many new proteins must be synthesized in a particular order, or the sperm will not be able to function properly.

Hecht and his coworkers—4 postdoctoral fellows, 1 graduate student, and collaborators in 5 other research laboratories around the world—have so far isolated 7 of these sperm-specific proteins and are now studying the expression of the genes responsible for producing them. What turns the expression of these genes on at the appropriate time in sperm development? What turns the expression of these genes off at the appropriate time in sperm development? If he can disrupt the normal expression of the genes coding for those proteins, abnormal—and ineffective—sperm should result.

Sperm production can be attacked at a number of points in their development (called spermatogenesis), by interfering with either the transcription of genes from DNA, the storage of the resulting gene messages (called messenger RNA, or mRNA for short), or the translation of those messages into the final proteins.

The genes coding for the testis-specific proteins that Professor Hecht is interested in are transcribed from their DNA templates early in spermatogenesis and are then stored in the cytoplasm for many days before being translated into proteins. "If we can prevent either the transcription of the genes or the subsequent translation of the mRNAs encoding these genes," says Professor Hecht with great enthusiasm, "we should be able to prevent the development of normal, functional sperm."

The great appeal of this approach, which Professor Hecht believes to be unique in the field, is that it should be possible to block sperm development without interfering with physiological processes elsewhere in the body.

One protein of particular interest to Professor Hecht is called contrin, which he and his coworkers discovered and isolated last year. Contrin binds to both DNA and mRNA. When it binds to DNA, it promotes transcription. Contrin also binds to mRNA, preparing it for long-term storage. Preventing germ cells from synthesizing contrin might therefore disrupt normal sperm development both by preventing certain transcriptional processes from occurring and by preventing the storage of mRNA molecules that are transcribed. No one yet knows how crucial contrin is for normal sperm development, but Professor Hecht expects to be the first to find out.

Professor Hecht has recently isolated the genes coding for mammalian contrin, and has successfully synthesized contrin in the laboratory using the cloned DNA sequences. With unlimited quantities of pure contrin in hand, the next step will be to determine the precise 3-dimensional structure of the contrin molecule. It should then be possible to create artificially other molecules that bind specifically to contrin and disable it. Then it should be possible to prevent contrin synthesis in male mice and determine what happens to spermatogenesis in the absence of contrin.

This could be a first exciting step toward deliberately blocking the synthesis of crucial sperm-specific proteins indefinitely.

How much longer do men (and women) have to wait before male contraceptive pills become available commercially? "It will probably happen eventually," says Professor Hecht, "but not immediately."

"There are those in the United States and abroad," he says, "who believe the time and technology are right for widespread use of male contraceptives." It looks as though his laboratory will remain active for quite some time.

It is not difficult to see that the writer of this piece understands his subject well. And one certainly gets the impression that he enjoyed the assignment. In fact, I happen to know that he did.

13

PREPARING ORAL PRESENTATIONS

Oral in-class presentations of published research papers are often assigned in conjunction with or in place of the written summaries or critiques discussed in Chapter 6. Research projects may also culminate in oral presentations. Although this book is about writing, I include this short chapter on talking because oral presentations are developed in much the same way as their written counterparts and can, in fact, provide an ideal framework for later expansion into written papers of any size. Indeed, in writing any paper—summary, critique, research report, research proposal, or literature review—it typically helps to think first in terms of giving a clear talk. Most of the advice that follows applies to any sort of oral presentation.

Despite some major similarities, an oral presentation must differ from a written presentation in one important respect: a typewritten page can be read slowly and pondered, and can be reread as often as necessary, until all points are understood; an oral report, however, gives the listener only one chance to grasp the material. An analogy can be made with music. Before about 1910, music, to be successful, had to be liked at the first hearing; composers knew that if their audience was not captivated by the first performance, that performance might well be the last. It was only with the invention of the phonograph that composers could sustain a career by intentionally delivering music intended to grow on its audience.

An oral presentation goes past the listener only once: for maximum impact, it must be very well organized, developed logically, stripped of details that divert the listener's attention from the essential points of the presentation, and delivered clearly, smoothly, and with enthusiasm.

TALKING ABOUT PUBLISHED RESEARCH PAPERS

A talk, like any written work, can be effective only if you fully understand your topic. As suggested in earlier chapters, it is wise to skim the paper that you are presenting or discussing once or twice for general orientation, consult appropriate textbooks for background information as neces-

252

sary, and pay particular attention to the Materials and Methods section and to the tables, graphs, drawings, and photographs included in the Results section. When you can summarize the essence of the paper in 1 or 2 sentences, you are ready to prepare your talk.

Preparing the Talk

The goal of your presentation is virtually identical to that of a written assignment: you seek to capture the essence of the research project—why it was undertaken, how it was undertaken, and what was learned—and to communicate that essence clearly, convincingly, and succinctly. Keep this goal in mind at all times, and obey the following rules:

1. **Do not simply paraphrase** the Introduction, Materials and Methods, Results, and Discussion sections of the paper or papers that you are presenting if you wish to keep your audience awake. To make an effective presentation, you must reorganize the information in each assigned paper. Begin your talk by providing background information, drawing from the Introduction and Discussion sections of the paper and from outside sources if necessary so that the listener can appreciate why the study was undertaken. End your Introduction with a concise statement of the specific question or questions addressed in the paper under discussion. Let the audience know where you are taking them, and why you are taking them there.
2. **Focus your talk on the methods and the results.**
3. **Draw conclusions as you present each component of the study** so that you lead in logical fashion from one part of the study to the next. Integrate the Materials and Methods and Results sections to form a continuous story. If you are discussing several experiments from a single paper, state the first specific question, briefly describe how it was addressed, present the key results, lead into the second specific question, describe how that question was addressed, present the key results, lead into the next question, and so forth. For example:

   The oyster larvae grew 20 mm/day when fed diet *A*, 25 mm/day when fed diet *B*, and 65 mm/day when fed a combination of diets *A* and *B*. This suggests that important nutrients missing in each individual diet were provided when the diets were used in combination. To determine what these missing nutrients might be. . . .

   Lead your audience by the nose from point to point.

4. **Be selective; delete extraneous details.** Much of what is appropriate in a research paper is not appropriate for a talk about that paper. Since the listener has only one chance to get the point, some of the details in the paper—particularly methodological details—must be pruned out in preparing the oral presentation. Streamline; include only the details needed to understand what comes later. If, for example, you will not discuss the influence of animal or plant age on the results obtained, do not burden the listener with such details in your talk. Similarly, is it important that the samples were mixed on a shaker table? If you never discuss this detail later in your talk, omit it at the outset. Tidbits such as these sometimes come out in the question period following your presentation but there is no reason to bring them into the presentation itself.

5. **Plan to use the blackboard or overhead transparencies.** A simple summary table or two is helpful when numbers are being discussed; numbers floating around in the air are difficult for listeners to keep track of. **A diagram or flowchart of experimental protocol can help the listener follow the plan of a study**, along the lines of Figure 12 (p. 146), for example (see also, p. 241). Data can often be effectively summarized in a few graphs, even when those data were presented in the original paper as complicated tables. Keep the graphs simple, and be sure to label both axes. You need not reproduce graphs exactly as given in the paper, and you need not display every entry from a particular table. Focus on showing the trends in the data, and omit anything that fails to help you make your point clearly; I discuss this more fully at the end of the chapter.

6. **Summarize the major findings of the research at the end of your talk**, driving the points home one by one. You may wish to end your talk with a brief discussion of the way the study could be improved or expanded in the future, but don't set out to discredit the authors. End on a positive note, reinforcing what you want your audience to remember.

7. **Be prepared for questions about methods.** Listeners often ask about interpretations of the data; to answer these questions, you must be thoroughly familiar with the way the study was conducted.

Giving the Talk

1. **Know what you're going to say and how you're going to say it.** Hesitation, vagueness, and searching for words will all suggest a lack of understanding and will lose the attention of your audience. Write

out your talk and practice it until you can produce a smooth delivery while maintaining eye contact with your listeners. Notecards can be an effective aid; be sure to number them in case they get dropped before or during your presentation.

2. **Don't rush.** Write on the blackboard or on overhead transparencies during your presentation when, for example, labeling the axes of graphs. This helps punctuate your statements and also gives the listener time to digest what you are showing as well as time to take notes. For the same reason, you should label curves as you draw and talk about them. It is often a mistake to put completed illustrations on the blackboard ahead of time; the listener generally gets deprived of the opportunity to absorb what is being presented.

   Even when showing completed graphs or tables, **take the time to orient viewers to the axis labels or column headings before plunging into the results**. You might say, for example, "Here we see adenylate cyclase activity on the y-axis, in picomoles of cyclic AMP produced per minute per milligram of heart tissue, as a function of time after adding the peptides, up to 1.5 hours." Remember, your audience has not seen these displays before; if you don't first orient your listeners, you will be blithely talking about how interesting the results are while your audience members are still busy figuring out what it is that they are looking at.

3. **Make the data work for you** by drawing the listeners' attention to specific aspects of the graphs and tables that represent the point you wish to make. Don't simply say, "This is clearly shown in the graph." Rather, say "For example, all the animals that were fed on diets A and B grew at comparable rates, but those fed on diet C . . ." and be sure to point to the data as you speak.

4. **Write unfamiliar terms on the blackboard or overhead transparency and avoid acronyms whenever possible**; there is no justification for referring to "NCAMs" instead of "neural cell adhesion molecules" when the term is used only once or twice in the talk. Remember, your goal is to communicate, not to impress or confuse.

5. **If using an overhead projector, point to the screen when you wish to highlight a detail, not to the transparency itself.** Transparency projectors magnify, and will transform the perfectly natural, barely noticeable nervous tremor of your hands into a highly distracting display of stage fright. It is not possible to seem at ease and self-confident when you appear to be experiencing an internal earthquake. When pointing to the screen, you are more likely to appear calm and collected.

6. **Avoid using laser pointers if you can.** Most are too weak to show up very well on the screen, especially against particular background colors. Moreover, even when the pointer can be seen, any nervousness you are feeling will translate into a very conspicuous tremor on the screen. In the hands of many speakers, laser pointers are more of a distraction than an aid, and pointed at the members of the audience they can even be dangerous. A physical pointer usually works fine.

7. **Don't put the text of your talk on your slides or overheads.** You want the audience to be *listening* to you, not reading your notes. (More on this point at the end of this chapter.)

8. **Don't mumble. Make eye contact with your listeners.** Don't talk to the blackboard.

9. **Try to sound interested in what you are saying**, no matter how many times you have practiced your talk. If you seem bored by your own presentation, you will most certainly bore the audience.

10. **Don't automatically refer to the author of a paper as *he*.** Many papers are written by women, and many are written by 2 or more researchers.

11. **Don't end abruptly.** Warn your audience when you are nearing the end of your talk by saying something like, "I would like to make one final point," or "Before I end, I wish to emphasize that. . . ." Such phrasings will prepare the listeners to receive your summary statements.

12. **End your talk gracefully.** A self-conscious giggle or a "Well, I guess that's it" isn't the best way to close an otherwise captivating presentation. I suggest that you first acknowledge any people who gave you advice, let you use their equipment and supplies, or helped in other ways, and then say something like, "Thank you. I would be happy to answer any questions."

13. **Do not allow your presentation to exceed the time allotted.** You will lose considerable goodwill by rambling on beyond your time limit. Here again, a few practice sessions come in handy.

14. **Paraphrase each question before answering it** so as not to lose the rest of the audience (and to buy yourself a few precious seconds to think). "The question is, does the technique used to isolate the DNA interfere with. . . ." Then address your answer to the entire audience, not just the person asking the question.

15. **Do not feel compelled to answer questions that you don't understand.** Politely ask for clarification until you figure out what is being asked.

16. **Do not be afraid to admit that you don't know the answer to a question.** You can easily work your neck into a noose by pretending you know more than you really do; nobody expects you to be the world's authority on the topic you are presenting. Simply saying, "I don't know" is the safest way to go.

TALKING ABOUT ORIGINAL RESEARCH

Follow the format just described for preparing and presenting your work. Again, begin by presenting the background information that listeners need to understand why you addressed the particular question or issue you chose to address; then clearly state the specific question or issue being considered. Focus on the results of previous studies when presenting the background information and on your own results when giving the rest of the talk. Draw your conclusions point by point as you discuss each facet of the study, showing how each observation or experiment led to the next aspect of the work. End the talk by summarizing your major findings with their potential significance, and perhaps with a brief suggestion of what you might do next to further explore the issue you raised at the start of your talk.

TALKING ABOUT PROPOSED RESEARCH

This is similar to presenting a research paper except that you have more literature to review. The preparation and delivery of your talk should follow all of the points detailed earlier in this chapter. Highlight a few key papers that show particularly clearly why the question you wish to address is a worthwhile and logical one, and focus on the results of the studies you discuss. Then state the specific question you plan to address in your own work, being sure this question follows logically from the work you have just summarized. Finally, describe the approach you will take, focus on what you will do, and make clear what each step of the study is designed to accomplish. Conclude by briefly summarizing how the proposed work will address the question under consideration.

THE LISTENER'S RESPONSIBILITY

Few things in life are more disappointing than putting your heart and soul into preparing and delivering a talk to an audience that shows apparent indifference. When you are a member of that audience, you bear a responsibility to listen closely, and to show the speaker that you listened closely. Try to formulate at least one question by the end of the talk, about something you didn't understand, something you thought was particularly interesting ("I was amazed by the ability of those polar fishes to keep from freezing. Do local fish produce the same kind of biological antifreezes in the winter?"), or something unusual you saw in the data ("In that table you showed us, why were the arsenic concentrations so high in the control animals' tissues?").

Even if the speaker can't answer your question, he or she will at least detect some interest in the talk and feel flattered that you cared enough about his or her development as a biologist and seminar speaker to have paid so much attention.

PREPARING EFFECTIVE
SLIDES AND OVERHEADS

A figure or table that works fine in a published paper may not work nearly as well as a visual aid for a talk. When reading a journal article, readers can scrutinize your data as long as required, over several cups of coffee if necessary. For a talk, however, you want the audience to understand the slide or overhead quickly so that you can concentrate on the results. If the slide is too complicated or too difficult to read, you may be finished talking about the results while your listeners are still trying to figure out what your axes are! Make your visual aids as simple and as clear as possible. They should ease communication, not hinder it.

Consider Figure 36, which was developed for publication. It concerns seasonal variation in initial carbon content and juvenile growth rate of an intertidal barnacle, *Semibalanus balanoides*. Combined with its caption, the figure is a perfectly acceptable, self-sufficient summary of the data. But it would not work well as a slide. For one thing, the lettering is too small; people sitting more than a few rows from the front of the room would likely be unable to read the axis labels, and they certainly wouldn't be able to read the caption. And you don't want them reading the caption while you're talking anyway: you want them to be listening to what you are saying. What's more, the listener must look back and forth to the left of the slide to interpret what the 2 curves represent.

Figure 37 shows how this presentation might be modified for conversion to an effective slide or overhead. By using 2 lines instead of one for the dates (*x*-axis) and the *y*-axis titles, and by shifting the *y*-axis titles

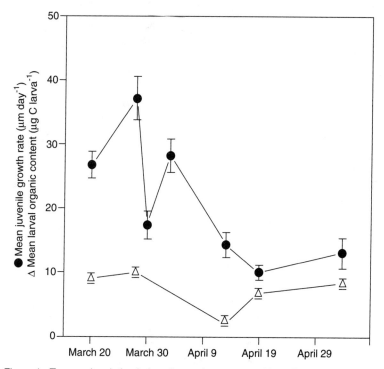

Figure 1. Temporal variation in larval organic content and juvenile growth rate of the barnacle, <u>Semibalanus</u> <u>balanoides</u>.   Larvae that attached to artificial substrates in the low intertidal zone were collected in the field at intervals during 1995; individual organic content was estimated by dichromate oxidation. Metamorphosed juveniles collected from the field were reared for 5–7 days in the laboratory under controlled conditions to determine growth rate.   Each point is the mean (± one standard error) of 13–33 individual measurements.

Figure 36. A graph with its figure caption, designed for publication in a formal research paper.

(Courtesy of J. Jarrett.)

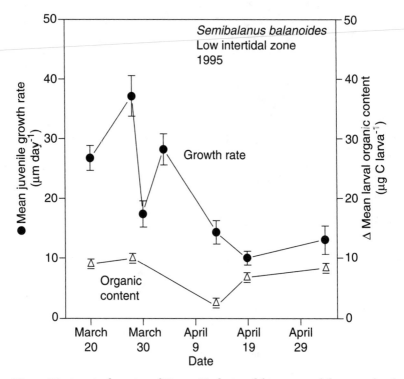

Figure 37. A revised version of Figure 36, designed for use as a slide or overhead during an oral presentation. Note that some of the information contained in the figure caption of Figure 36 is now placed directly on the graph.

(Courtesy of J. Jarrett.)

to separate sides of the graph, we can use a much larger, more readable typeface. I have also identified the 2 curves directly on the graph, and have added the name of the species and where and when the data were collected. Finally, the figure caption has been removed. A speaker will have a far easier time orienting his or her listeners to a slide or overhead made from this figure. Listeners should have little difficulty reading and understanding the illustrated data even if they are sitting in the back row. **In designing slides and overheads, always try to reach the person sitting at the back of the room.**

THE PROS AND CONS OF POWERPOINT PRESENTATIONS

More and more people are using computers to prepare and project graphs and other visual information for oral presentation. Some of these visual displays are very effective. Certainly they are spectacularly colorful, with palm trees in the background and words and phrases in a rainbow of hues zipping in from the left and right at the click of a button. The technology is impressive, and seductive, but it can work both for and against you.

Powerpoint presentations make it easy to show pictures of your study site and study organisms: you can insert photographs taken with a digital camera, photographs obtained from Web sites, or images scanned from books and magazines. And it's easy to add labels and pointers to the slides, to highlight particular features as you talk.

You can also show movies and animations with Powerpoint, bringing your animals to life for the audience. If you are studying aspects of animal behavior, you can show the audience examples of the actual behavior you've been studying. So, to the extent that you are using Powerpoint in ways that increase your ability to communicate your research, it's great. See Appendix H for more detailed information on giving Powerpoint presentations.

However, **you must not lose sight of your overriding goal: to communicate information**.

Many computerized presentations are in fact quite disappointing, and some are disastrous. Equipment problems aside, some slide backgrounds are simply distracting. Worse, many computerized presentations are unreadable: purple lettering on a blue background may look great to you on a computer screen, but for audience members sitting more than 5 feet from the screen, the words are illegible—or even invisible. Maximum clarity is achieved with maximum contrast, and the best contrast is achieved by putting black letters on a white background. Remember, too, that many people are colorblind, and will not be able to distinguish among some colors.

Also, I see more and more speakers putting their lecture notes into their Powerpoint presentations, word for word. First we see a detailed listing of goals, then a detailed listing of results, and finally a detailed listing of summary statements. If you give me all that material to read, I'll be reading; I won't be listening to you. If you're saying exactly what I'm reading, then I suppose it doesn't really matter that I've tuned you out . . . but then again, doesn't that make you superfluous? Talk to your audience.

That's hard to do if you're facing the screen reading your notes. Don't use Powerpoint as a teleprompter.

Perhaps an even more serious concern is that the hours you spend learning how to control the software and manipulate the color schemes and font options might be better spent analyzing your data or double-checking your analyses; thinking about what you did, why and how you did it, what the most important results are and what they mean; or reading more background information and more research papers, or reading them more carefully. Beware: Style is no substitute for substance. It's fine to be high-tech and colorful, but be sure you also have something to say. The fancier the presentation, the more suspicious I become as a listener—what is the speaker trying to hide? You can give an excellent talk using computer software. You can also give an excellent talk without it. Sometimes the simplest presentation style is the most effective. In one of the most compelling talks I've ever heard, the speaker spent 55 minutes talking about different aspects of a single slide that he projected at the start of his talk. It was masterful. **Make the substance of your talk the star of your show.**

CHECKLIST FOR BEING JUDGED

Many scientific societies give awards for the best student presentations at annual meetings. Knowing the criteria in advance can help you prepare a more effective presentation. I'll conclude this section by listing the sorts of things that judges and other listeners pay special attention to. Your instructor will probably be looking at the same sorts of issues in judging an in-class presentation.

❑ Was there a clear statement of the specific research question(s) addressed?

❑ Was all background information relevant? Was it sufficient to understand why the question was posed? Did it lead logically to the question(s) stated?

❑ Was the talk free of unnecessary and unexplained jargon?

❑ Did the speaker deal thoroughly with one issue at a time?

❑ Did the methods described follow logically from the questions posed?

❑ Were methods presented in the right amount of detail, including sample sizes, numbers of replicates, and use of controls? Too little detail? Too much detail? Was the design of the study easy to follow?

- ❏ Were procedures, concepts, and methods of data analysis presented clearly?
- ❏ Were graphs and tables easy to read, uncluttered, and easy to follow?
- ❏ Did the speaker take sufficient time to orient listeners to the data before describing the results?
- ❏ Did the speaker lead listeners through the results, to appropriate conclusions?
- ❏ Was the talk delivered clearly, at an appropriate pace, without reading word-for-word from notes, and without distracting mannerisms?
- ❏ Had the speaker clearly practiced the talk in advance?
- ❏ Did the speaker's talk fit the allotted time?
- ❏ Did the speaker maintain eye contact with audience members?
- ❏ Did the speaker respond well to questions from the audience?

14

WRITING LETTERS OF APPLICATION

An application for a job, or for admission to a graduate or professional program, will generally include a résumé and accompanying cover letter (both of which you write), and several letters of recommendation (which you generally never get to see). When applying to graduate or professional schools, and often when applying for jobs, you will also include a transcript of your college coursework and any special examination scores—for example, Graduate Record Examination (GRE) scores. You have no control over what your transcript and GRE scores say about you; what is done is done. But you can still influence the message transmitted through your résumé and supporting letters, and that influence works both ways: it can strengthen an otherwise weak case, or weaken an otherwise strong case.

Your résumé summarizes your educational background, relevant work experience, relevant research experience, goals, and general interests. The accompanying cover letter identifies the position for which you are applying and draws the reader's attention to the aspects of your résumé that make you a particularly worthy candidate. The recommendations will give an honest assessment of your strengths and weaknesses (we all have some of each) and offer the reader an image of you as a person and as a potential employee or participant in a professional program. In this chapter, I will consider the art of preparing effective résumés and cover letters, and of increasing the odds of ending up with effective letters of recommendation.

BEFORE YOU START

Always try to put yourself in the position of the people who will be reading your application. What will they be looking for? They will probably be considering your application with 3 main questions in mind:

1. Is the applicant qualified for this particular position?
2. Is the applicant really interested in our program or company?
3. Will the applicant fit in here?

Your application must address all 3 issues.

When you prepare your application, you should also consider that the number of applications received by a potential employer or professional or graduate school usually exceeds the number of positions available, and often by a considerable margin. Many applicants will be qualified for the position, yet not every applicant can be interviewed or offered admission. Whoever begins reading your application will necessarily be looking for any excuse to disqualify you from the competition; your goal, then, must be to hold the reader's interest to the end.

PREPARING THE RÉSUMÉ

The people who read your application will not spend hours scrutinizing your résumé; probably they will examine it for only 1 or 2 minutes at most. Therefore, an effective résumé is well organized, neat, and as brief as possible. Your résumé should not be longer than 2 pages.

There is no standard format for a résumé; the model given in Figure 38 should be modified in any way that emphasizes your particular strengths and satisfies your own esthetic sense. However, the résumé is no place to be artsy or cute; don't do anything that might suggest that you are not taking the application process seriously.

All résumés must contain the following 3 components:

1. Full name, address, telephone number (and e-mail address if you have one)
2. Educational history
3. Relevant work, teaching, and research experience, if any

In addition, you will want to add any other information that makes you look talented or well-rounded or both:

4. Honors received
5. Papers published
6. Special skills
7. Outside activities, sports, hobbies

Eileen Magnant

Address and phone number
  Until June 1, 2003:
    P.O. Box 029
    University Station
    Kingston, RI 02881
    (401) 201-1717

  After June 1:
    29 Lakeview Drive
    Narragansett, RI 02882
    (401) 788-0153

Date of Birth: September 13, 1981

Goals: To earn a Ph.D. in Conservation Biology and
    pursue a career in teaching and research.

Education

    University of Rhode Island, Fall 1999–Spring 2003.
    Major: Biology

Research Experience

    Conducted a one-semester research project (in Dr.
Oliver Hornbeam's laboratory) on the structure and
function of guard cells in lyre-leaved sage, *Salvia
lyrata* L., using transmission electron microscopy.
Presented the results of this research at the 38th New
England Undergraduate Research Conference, Siegel
University, Barnum, CT (May 2000).

Teaching Experience
    Undergraduate teaching assistant for introductory
    biology laboratory, Fall semester 2000.

Figure 38. Sample résumé

Honors

Elected to Phi Beta Kappa honor society, Spring 2002. Received Churchill Prize in Biology (for performance in introductory Biology course), Fall 1999. Dean's List seven out of eight semesters.
Selected for teaching assistant position noted above.

Work Experience

Summer 1997. Counselor, Lake Baker Summer Camp, AK
Summer 1998, 1999. Worked for Sweet Pea's Garden Center, Falmouth MA. Cared for all plants and shrubs, with one assistant.
Summer 2000. Assisted in the culture of oysters and hard shell clams. Mook Sea Farms, Damariscotta, ME.

Special Skills

Tissue preparation (fixation, embedding, sectioning) for transmission electron microscopy.
Operation of JEOL Model 100CX transmission electron microscope.
Developing 35-mm black and white film and TEM negatives; digital photography and image processing.

Outside Activities

Piano. URI Jazz band, 1999-2001
Swim team (1999-2001, captain 2001)
Campus tour guide Fall 1999, Fall 2002
Vegetable gardening (each summer since 1993)
Road racing (Boston Marathon 1998, 2001)

Figure 38 *(Continued)*. Sample résumé

Avoid drawing attention here to any potential weaknesses; if, for example, you lack teaching experience, do not write "Teaching experience: none." **Use the résumé exclusively to emphasize your strengths.**

You might also add a 1- or 2-sentence statement of your immediate and long-range goals, if known, and the names of people who have agreed to write references on your behalf; this material is often incorporated into the cover letter instead, as discussed shortly.

You are not required to list age, race, marital status, height, weight, sex, or any other personal characteristic. Be self-serving in deciding what to include. If you think your youth might put you at a disadvantage, omit this information. If you think your age, race, or sex might give you a slight competitive edge, by all means include that information.

Do not be concerned if your first résumé looks skimpy; it will fill out as the years go by. It is better to present a short, concise résumé than an obviously padded one.

You should alter your résumé for each application completed to focus on the different strengths required by different jobs or programs. If, for example, Eileen Magnant, whose résumé appears in Figure 38, were applying to a marine underwater research program, she might add under Special Skills that she is a certified SCUBA diver. If she were applying for a laboratory job in a hospital, she would probably omit the information about diving certification.

PREPARING THE COVER LETTER

The cover letter plays a large role in the application process and is usually the first part of your application read by an admissions committee or prospective employer. A well-crafted letter of application can do much to counteract a mediocre academic record. A poorly crafted letter, on the other hand, can do much to annihilate the good impression made by a strong academic performance. Keep revising this letter until you know it works well on your behalf. Have some friends, or perhaps an instructor, read and comment on your letter; then revise it again. Be sure to type or computer-print the final copy; neatness counts, and typing also conveys seriousness of purpose. The time you put into polishing your cover letter is time well spent. The cover letter should be about 1 or, at most, 2 typed pages.

Do not simply write,

P.O. Box 66

University Center

Medford, MA 02155

May 1, 2002

Dear M. Pasteur:

I am applying for the position advertised in the *Boston Globe*. My résumé is enclosed. Thank you for your consideration.

Sincerely,

Earl N. Meyer

Earl N. Meyer

Although the letter ends well, its beginning is vague and its midsection does little to further the applicant's cause. Use the cover letter to:

1. Identify the specific position for which you are applying (Monsieur Pasteur may have several positions open. Earl N. Meyer is applying for the position of research assistant, but how is M. Pasteur to know?).
2. Draw the reader's attention to the elements of your résumé that you feel make you a particularly qualified candidate.
3. Indicate that you understand what the position entails and that you have the skills necessary to do a good job.
4. Convince the reader you are a mature, responsible person.
5. Convey a genuine sense of enthusiasm and motivation.

Before you begin to write the letter, ask yourself some difficult questions, and jot down some carefully considered answers:

Why do I want this particular job or to enter this particular graduate program?

What skills would be most useful in such a job or program?

Which of these skills do I have?

What evidence of these skills can I present?

Your answers to these questions will provide the pattern and the yarn from which you will weave your cover letter.

Not everyone will have a résumé that looks like Eileen Magnant's (Figure 38). But you need not have made the Dean's List every semester or have had formal teaching or research experience in order to impress someone with your application. In your cover letter, focus on the experiences that you *have* had. In lieu of teaching, perhaps you have done formal or informal tutoring. In lieu of having had formal research experience, perhaps you have taken numerous laboratory courses. Perhaps some experience you had in one or more of these laboratory courses influenced your decision to apply for a particular job or program. Perhaps acquiring certain skills in one or more of these laboratory courses has prepared you for the program or position for which you are applying. Or perhaps you can draw from experience outside biology to document reliability, desire, and willingness to learn new things, or ability to learn new techniques quickly. We all have strengths; decide what yours are and which ones are appropriate for inclusion in your application.

Tailor each letter to the particular position or program for which it is being prepared. Try to find some special reason for applying to each program; if possible, your application should reflect deliberate choice and a clear sense of purpose. If, for example, you have read papers written by a faculty member at the institution to which you are applying and have become interested in that person's research, weave this information into your cover letter. Should you take this approach, you must say enough about that person's research or research area to make clear that you understand what you are writing about. On the other hand, if your major reason for wanting a particular job or wanting to attend a particular graduate program is the geographical location of the company or school, be careful not to state this as your sole reason for applying; as you write, and as you reread what you have written, try to put yourself on the receiving end of the cover letter and consider how your statements might be interpreted.

Back up all statements with supporting details. Avoid simply saying that you have considerable research experience. Instead, briefly explain what your research experience has been. Do not state that you are a gifted teacher; describe your teaching experience. State the facts and let the reader draw the proper inferences.

Sign the letter with your given name, not a nickname; again, don't run the risk of not being taken seriously.

Here is an example of a weak cover letter. Similar letters have, unfortunately, been submitted by people with very good grades, test scores, and letters of recommendation. The author is applying for admission to a Ph.D. program in Biology.

P.O. Box 666

University Center

Medford, MA 02155

May 1, 2002

To the admissions committee:

I have always been fascinated by the living world around me. I marvel at the details of the way biology works, and I would now like to fulfill my curiosity and passion for biology in pursuing a Ph.D. in your program.

As you can see from my transcript, I have taken 12 courses in biology (2 more than the number needed for graduation) and have done well in most of them. I am especially interested in plant physiology and did a one-semester research project on this subject during my senior year.

I would also like to apply for the teaching assistantship award. I have always liked helping people learn about science, and I am eager to

communicate my enthusiasm for biology to others.
I have requested that my GRE scores be sent
directly to you.

I look forward to your reply.

Sincerely,

Variola Major

Variola Major

Remember, the admissions committee is looking for any excuse to disqualify applicants; this letter may give the committee just that excuse regardless of what the rest of the application looks like. The letter does convey enthusiasm, but it is a very naive enthusiasm. What does the student find interesting about the physiology of plants? What was the research project? What question was asked? How was the question addressed? What results were obtained? Did the student learn anything from the experience? Does the student really know anything about plant physiology? What makes the student think that she would be an effective teacher? Has she had any teaching experience? Does she understand what teaching entails?

The rest of the application letter is equally uninformative. Why is the student applying to this particular program? All biology majors take biology courses, and the student's grades are already on the transcript. What has the student learned from these courses that makes her want to pursue advanced study?

The same student could have written a much more effective letter by thinking about what admissions committees might be looking for and by documenting her strengths. Here is an example of the way this student might have rewritten her letter*:

---

*The research described in her letter is based on a paper by Orians, C. M. and Floyd, T. (1997). *Oecologia, 109,* 407–413.

P.O. Box 666
University Center
Medford, MA 02155
May 1, 2002

To the admissions committee:

Please consider my application for admission
to your Ph.D. program in Biology. I will be
graduating from Mordor University in May with a
B.S. in Botany. I believe that I have the
experience and motivation to make a contribution
to your program.

I became interested in plant physiological ecology
through a seminar course taught by Professor
Mendel. This was my first experience reading the
original scientific literature, but by the end of
the semester I was able to present a well-received
research proposal on the subject of root growth,
based largely upon my own library research.

Dr. Mendel later invited me to participate in a
research project examining the relationship
between plant nutrition and resistance to attack
by 4 insect species. I conducted this research in
the field using 2 common willow species (*Salix
eriocephala* and *S. sericea*). The goal was to
determine whether the well-documented variation in

susceptibility to attack might be explained by
differences in soil nutritional quality, which we
manipulated by applying different amounts of
fertilizer.

To begin, we distributed cuttings from each
species among 3 treatments differing in the
concentration of fertilizer provided each week,
with 9 replicates per treatment. At intervals over
the next 4 months, I counted the number of leaves
and shoots on each plant and measured their
average sizes, to document the effects of the
nutrient treatments on plant growth rates. On 2
occasions we also quantified the degree of damage
caused to the plants by 2 species of leaf-mining
caterpillar, a leaf-folding sawfly, a leaf-chewing
beetle, and a fungal pathogen.

It turned out that for both willow species, the
more fertilizer the plants received, the faster
they grew and the more susceptible they were to
attack by most of the pests. I also discovered,
somewhat surprisingly, that the 2 plant species
differed dramatically in their susceptibility to
the different pests. Our working hypothesis is
that the 2 willow species probably differ in the
amounts of phenolic glycosides and other defensive
compounds contained in their leaves, and that
within a species, these compounds are produced at
lower concentrations in faster growing plants.

Through this study, I learned the importance of careful experimental design and data analysis, and, more important, that I have the patience to do research. I do not wish to commit myself to a specific field of research at this time, believing that I would benefit from an additional year of literature and laboratory exploration, but I believe that I would like to explore the potential trade-offs between faster plant growth and reduced chemical defense. During my first year, I would hope to take your 2 upper-level courses in plant physiology and biochemistry and an additional statistics course (in analysis of covariance).

During my last semester at Mordor University, I have been acting as an undergraduate teaching assistant for the introductory biology laboratory. I find that having to explain things to other students forces me to come to grips with what I do and do not know. I am enjoying the challenge greatly, and I look forward to doing additional teaching in the future; I am learning a lot about biology through teaching.

I have asked the following faculty members at Mordor University for letters of recommendation:

Professor G. Mendel (Biology Dept.)
Professor N. Eyster-Smith (Biology Dept.)
Professor A. Gardulski (Geology Dept.)

```
Thank you for considering my application.
I look forward to receiving your response.
```

Sincerely,

Variola Major

Variola Major

This letter, too, conveys enthusiasm, but it is an enthusiasm that reflects knowledge, experience, and commitment; the applicant seems to understand what research is all about and apparently knows how to go about doing it. Moreover, we see that Ms. Major thinks clearly and writes well.

Variola would write a somewhat different letter if she were applying for a job as a technician in a research laboratory. In this letter, she would want to emphasize her skills and reliability as a laboratory worker and her interest in the type of research being done in the laboratory to which she is applying. An example of such a letter follows:

```
P.O. Box 666
University Center
Medford, MA 02155
May 1, 2002
```

```
Dear Professor Hornbeam:


Please consider my application for the technical
position you advertised recently in the Boston
Globe. I will be graduating from Mordor
University this May with a B.S. degree in botany.
Although I eventually expect to return to school
```

to pursue a Ph.D., I would first like to work in a plant physiological ecology laboratory for 1 or 2 years to learn some additional techniques and to become more familiar with various research fields and approaches.

I first became interested in plant physiology through a seminar course with Professor G. Mendel at Mordor University. During the semester, we read 2 of your recent papers describing the effects of hybridization on leaf biochemistry in goldenrod.

Following this seminar, I began studying (under the direction of Dr. Mendel) the influence of soil nutrient quality on the susceptibility of willow plants (*Salix eriocephala and S. sericea*) to damage by leaf-mining caterpillars and fungi. We found that the more fertilizer the plants received, the faster they grew and the more susceptible they were to attack. The next step in the study will be to determine whether the differences in pest resistance can be explained by other chemical defenses by the plant's leaves.

Through this study, I learned a variety of general laboratory techniques (use of assorted balances, sterile culture methodology, how to digitize images for quantitiative analysis of leaf size, and how to use 2 major statistical programs

— GraphPad Prism and Systat). I also learned that I have the patience and motivation needed to do careful research. I have taken 6 laboratory courses in biology (General Genetics, Invertebrate Zoology, Comparative Animal Physiology, Plant Physiology, Cell Biology, and Developmental Biology), in which I learned several specialized laboratory techniques, including the pouring and use of electrophoretic gels, measurement of organismal and mitochondrial respiration rates, and use of a vapor pressure osmometer. I also learned to design quantitative field studies in terrestrial ecosystems.

In short, I am very much interested in your research and believe I can make a contribution to the work of your laboratory. I have requested letters of recommendation from the following faculty at Cerebral University:

Professor G. Mendel (Biology Dept.)
Professor P.-Y. Qian (Biology Dept.)
Professor T. Shank (Biology Dept.)

Thank you for considering my application; I look forward to hearing from you.

Sincerely,

Variola Major

Variola Major

Both of these letters convey knowledge of the position or program applied for, a sincere interest in biology, and a high level of ability and commitment. Your letter should do the same. Your credentials may not be as impressive as Ms. Major's, but if you think about the experience you have had in relationship to the skills required for the position or program, you should be able to construct an effective letter. Take your letter through several drafts until you get it right (see Chapter 5, on revising).

RECRUITING EFFECTIVE LETTERS OF RECOMMENDATION

Letters of recommendation can be extremely important in determining the fate of your application. Although you do not write these letters yourself and rarely even get the opportunity to read them, you can take steps to increase their effectiveness.

Getting an A in a course does not guarantee a helpful letter of recommendation from the instructor of that course. The most useful letters to admissions committees and prospective employers are those commenting on characteristics such as the following: laboratory skills, communication skills (written and oral), motivation, ability to use time efficiently, curiosity, maturity, intelligence, ability to work independently, and ability to work with others. Instructors cannot comment on these attributes unless you become more than a grade in their record books. Make an appointment to talk with some of your instructors about your interests and plans. We faculty members are usually happy for the opportunity to get to know students better.

When it is time to request letters of recommendation, choose 3 or 4 instructors who know something about your abilities and goals, and ask each of them if he or she would be able to support your application by writing a letter of recommendation. Give each person the opportunity to decline your invitation. If the people you ask agree to write on your behalf, make their task easier by giving them a copy of your résumé, transcript, and letter of application and, if appropriate, a copy of the job advertisement. **Be certain to indicate clearly the application deadline** and the address to which the recommendation should be sent.

It takes as much time and thought to write an effective letter of recommendation as it takes to write an effective letter of application. Don't lose goodwill by requesting letters at the last minute. **Give your instructors at least 2 weeks** to work on these letters. "It has to be in by this Friday" will probably annoy your prospective advocate and may not allow the recommender the time needed to prepare a good letter even if he or she is still in a cooperative mood. Moreover, last-minute requests don't speak favorably about your planning and organizing abilities, and they imply a lack of respect for your instructor. So be considerate, and thereby get the best recommendation possible.

Appendix A

The Disassembled Paragraph Reconstituted (from Chapter 5, Revising)*

It appears that all vertebrate, invertebrate, and perhaps even some plant eggs are activated by the generation of calcium transients in their cytoplasm (Roberts et al., 1994; Lawrence et al., 1997). In most cases these transients take the form of propagating calcium waves (Jaffe, 1985; Epel, 1990; Whitaker and Swamm, 1993), which appear to be essential for activating the eggs. It is becoming clear, however, that although wave propagation is a common feature of activation, there are both subtle and significant differences in this response when comparing eggs from different species. For example, in fish (Gilkey et al., 1978), echinoderms (Stricker et al., 1992), and frogs (Busa and Nuccitelli, 1985; Kubota et al., 1987), a single calcium wave is propagated across the activating egg. In contrast, activation triggers a series of repetitive calcium waves or oscillations in annelids (Stricker, 1996), ascidians (Albrieux et al., 1997), and mammals (Kline and Kline, 1992), including humans (Homa and Swann, 1994; Tesarik and Testart, 1994).

---

*Modified from the Introduction to a paper by Lee, K.W., Webb, S. E. & Miller, A. L. (1999). A wave of free cytosolic calcium traverses zebrafish eggs on activation. *Devel. Biol.*, *214*, 168–180.

Appendix B

Revised Sample Sentences

1. ~~To perform this experiment there had to be a low tide.~~ We conducted the study at Blissful Beach on September 23, 1991, at ~~2:30 PM.~~ *at low tide*

2. In *Chlamydomonas reinhardi*, a single-celled green alga, there are two mating types, + and -. The + and - cells mate with each other when starved of nitrogen and form a zygote.

3. Protruding from this carapace is the head, bearing a large pair of second antennae.

4. The order in which we think of things to write down is rarely the order we use when ~~we~~ explaining what we did to a reader.

5. ~~The purpose of~~ Professor Wilson's book ~~is the~~ examines questions of evolutionary significance.

6. The mechanics of Swimming ~~in fish~~ have been carefully studied in fish for only a few species.

7. One example of this capacity is ~~observed in~~ the ~~phenomenon of~~ encystment exhibited by many fresh water and parasitic species.

8. In a sense, then, the typical protozoan is ~~may be regarded as being~~ a single-celled organism.

9. An estuary is a body of water nearly surrounded by land and whose salinity is influenced by freshwater drainage.

10. The résumé ~~presents a~~ summarizes ~~of~~ your educational background, research experience, and goals.

11. In textbooks and many lectures, ~~you are being~~ presented you with facts and interpretations.

12. The human genome contains 50,000 genes; however, there is enough DNA in the genome to form nearly 2×10^6 genes.

13. ~~It should be noted that~~ The data were analyzed ~~analyses were done~~ to determine whether the caterpillars chose the different diets at random.

14. These experiments ~~were conducted to~~ test~~,~~ed whether the ~~condition of the~~ biological films ~~on the substratum surface~~ triggered larval settlement ~~of the larvae.~~ surface

15. ~~Various species of sea anemones live throughout the world.~~
    (Sentence deleted for lack of content.)

16. Thi~~s~~ese data clearly demonstrate~~s~~ that growth rates of the blue mussel (mytilus Edulis) vary with temperature.

17. Hibernating mammals mate early in the spring ~~so that~~ As a consequence, their offspring ~~can~~ reach adulthood before the beginning of the next winter.

18. This study ~~pertains to the investigation of~~ describes the effect of this pesticide on the orientation behavoir of honey bees.

19. ~~The results reported here have lead the author to the conclusion that~~ thirsty flies ~~will~~ apparently show a positive response to all solutions, regardless of sugar concentration ~~(see figure 2).~~

20. Numbers ~~are difficult for listeners to keep track of when they are~~ floating around in the air.

21. Those seedlings ~~possessing a quickly growing phenotype~~ genetically programmed for faster growth will be selected for, whereas. . .

22. ~~Under~~ using a dissecting microscope~~,~~ a slide with a drop of the culture was examined at 50x.

23. Measurements of salamander respiration ~~by the salamanders~~ typically took one-half hour each.

24. ~~The~~ results suggest that ~~some local enhancement of~~ pathogen-specific antibody produc~~tion~~ed at the infection site ~~exists,~~ ies are and thus are enhanced locally.

25. ~~Usually it has been found that higher temperatures (30°C) have resulted in the production of females, while lower temperatures (22-27°C) have resulted in the production of males. (e.g., Bull, 1980; Mrosousky. 1982)~~
    The turtles are typically born female when embryos are incubated at 30°C, and male when incubated at lower temperatures (22-27°C) (e.g., Bull, 1980; Mrosovsky, 1982).

26. Octopus have been successfully trained to distinguish between red and white balls of ~~varying~~ different size~~s~~.

Appendix C

The Revised Sample Sentences in Final Form

1. We conducted the study at Blissful Beach at low tide on September 23, 1991.
2. In *Chlamydomonas reinhardi*, a single-celled green alga, there are two mating types, + and −. When starved of nitrogen, the + and − cells mate with each other and form a zygote.
3. Protruding from this carapace is the head, bearing a pair of large second antennae.
4. The order in which we think of things to write down is rarely the order we use when explaining to a reader what we did.
5. Professor Wilson's book examines questions of evolutionary significance.
6. The mechanics of swimming have been carefully studied for only a few fish species.
7. One example of this capacity is the encystment exhibited by many freshwater and parasitic species.
8. In a sense, then, the typical protozoan is a single-celled organism.
9. An estuary is a body of water nearly surrounded by land and whose salinity is influenced by freshwater drainage.
10. The résumé summarizes your educational background, research experience, and goals.
11. Textbooks and many lectures present you with facts and interpretations.
12. The human genome contains at least 50,000 genes; however, there is enough DNA in the genome to form nearly 2×10^6 genes.
13. The data were analyzed to determine whether the caterpillars chose the different diets at random.
14. These experiments tested whether the biological surface films triggered larval settlement.
15. (Sentence deleted for lack of content.)
16. These data clearly demonstrate that growth rates of the blue mussel (*Mytilus edulis*) vary with temperaure.

17. Hibernating mammals mate early in the spring. As a consequence, their offspring reach adulthood before the beginning of the next winter.

18. This study describes the effect of this pesticide on the orientation behavior of honey bees.

19. Thirsty flies apparently show a positive response to all solutions, regardless of sugar concentration (Fig. 2).

20. Numbers floating around in the air are difficult for listeners to keep track of.

21. Those seedlings genetically programmed for faster growth will be selected for, whereas. . . .

22. A slide with a drop of the culture was examined at 50× using a dissecting microscope.

23. Measurements of salamander respiration typically took one-half hour each.

24. Results suggest that pathogen-specific antibodies are produced at the infection site, and thus are enhanced locally.

25. The turtles are typically born female when embryos are incubated at 30°C, and male when incubated at lower temperatures (22–27°C) (e.g., Bull, 1980; Mrosousky, 1982).

26. Octopus have been successfully trained to distinguish between red and white balls of different sizes.

Appendix D

Commonly Used Abbreviations

	ABBREVI-ATION	EXAMPLE
Length		
meter	m	3 m
centimeter (10^{-2} meter)	cm	15 cm
millimeter (10^{-3} meter)	mm	4.5 mm
micrometer (10^{-6} meter)	μm	5 μm
Weight		
gram	g	10 g
kilogram (10^{3} grams)	kg	15 kg
milligram (10^{-3} gram)	mg	16 mg
microgram (10^{-6} gram)	μg	4 μg
nanogram (10^{-9} gram)	ng	8 ng
picogram (10^{-12} gram)	pg	11 pg
femtogram (10^{-15} gram)	fg	10 fg
Volume		
liter	l, or L	3 l, or 3 L
milliliter (10^{-3} liter)	ml or mL	37 ml or 37 mL
microliter (10^{-6} liter)	μl or μL	13 μl or 13 μL
Time		
months	mo	6 mo per year
weeks	wk	4 wk
days	d	2 d
hours	h	Wake me up in 24 h
minutes	min	20 min
seconds	s	60 s
Concentration		
milliosmoles/liter	$mOsmL^{-1}$	650 $mOsmL^{-1}$
mole	mol	0.13 $g\ mol^{-1}$
molar	$mol\ L^{-1}$	a 0.3 molar solution
salinity (parts per thousand)	‰ S, ppt	31‰ S seawater, or 31 ppt

parts per million	ppm	0.2 ppm copper
parts per billion	ppb	200 ppb copper
Statistics		
mean	$\overline{X}$	$\overline{X}$ = 27.2 g individual^{-1}
standard deviation	SD	SD = 0.8
standard error	SE	SE = 0.3
sample size	N	N = 16
p-value	p	$p < 0.01$
Other		
newton (a measure of force)	N	26.1 N
joule (a measure of work or energy)	j	25.5 j (= 25.5 N·m)
photoperiod (h light: h dark)	L:D	10L:14D
1 species	sp.	*Crepidula* sp.
2 or more species	spp.	*Crepidula* spp.
approximately	c., $\approx$	c. 25°C, or $\approx$25°C

Appendix E

Suggested References for Further Reading

GENERAL BOOKS ABOUT WRITING

Barnet, S., Stubbs, M., & Bellanca, P. (1999). *Practical guide to writing* (8th ed.). New York: Addison-Wesley.

Elbow, P. (1998). *Writing with power* (2nd ed.). New York: Oxford University Press.

Hacker, D. (2003). *A writer's reference* (5th ed). Boston: Bedford/St. Martin's.

Hall, D., Birkerts, S.P., & Birkerts, S. (1998). *Writing well* (9th ed.). New York: Longman.

Lanham, R. (2000). *Revising prose* (4th ed.). Boston: Allyn and Bacon.

Strunk, W., Jr., & White, E.B. (1979). *The elements of style* (3rd ed.). New York: Macmillan.

Williams, J.M. (2000). *Style: Ten lessons in clarity and grace* (6th ed.). New York: Longman.

BOOKS AND ARTICLES ABOUT SCIENTIFIC WRITING

Davis, M. (1997). *Scientific papers and presentations*. New York: Academic Press.

Day, R.A. (1998). *How to write and publish a scientific paper* (5th ed.). Phoenix: Oryx Press.

Day, R.A. (1992). *Scientific English: A guide for scientists and other professionals*. Phoenix: Oryx Press.

Gopen, G.D., & Swan, J.A. (1990). The science of scientific writing. *American Scientist, 78*, 550–558.

King, L.S. (1978). *Why not say it clearly? A guide to scientific writing*. Boston: Little, Brown.

Kniseley, K. (2002). *A student handbook for writing in biology*. Sunderland, MA: Sinauer Associates and W.H. Freeman.

O'Connor, M. (1991). *Writing successfully in science*. New York: Chapman & Hall.

Penrose, A.M., & Katz, S.B. (1998). *Writing in the sciences: Exploring conventions of scientific discourse*. New York: St. Martin's Press.

Wilkinson, A.M. (1991). *The scientist's handbook for writing papers and dissertations*. Englewood Cliffs, NJ: Prentice Hall.

Zinsser, W. (1995). *On writing well: An informal guide to writing nonfiction* (4th ed.). New York: HarperCollins.

TECHNICAL GUIDE FOR BIOLOGY WRITERS

CBE Style Manual Committee, Council of Biology Editors. (1994). *Scientific style: The CBE manual for authors, editors, and publishers* (6th ed.). New York: Cambridge University Press.

Davis, E.B., & Schmidt, D. (1995). *Using the biological literature* (2nd ed.). New York: Marcel Dekker.

ADVICE ON ANALYZING DATA AND CONSTRUCTING EFFECTIVE GRAPHS

Cleveland, W.S. (1985). *The elements of graphing data*. Monterey, CA: Wadsworth Advanced Books and Software.

Motulsky, M. (1995). *Intuitive biostatistics*. New York: Oxford University Press.

Parkhurst, D.F. (2001). Statistical significance tests: Equivalence and reverse tests should reduce misinterpretation. *BioScience, 51,* 1051–1057.

Quinn, G.P., & Keough, M.J. (2001). *Experimental design and data analysis for biologists* (Chapter 19, pp. 494–510, on graphing data). New York: Cambridge University Press.

Tufte, E.R. (2001). *The visual display of quantitative information* (2nd ed.). Cheshire, CT: Graphics Press.

BOOKS ABOUT WRITING FOR A GENERAL AUDIENCE

Gastel, B. (1983). *Presenting science to the public*. Philadelphia: ISI Press.

Nelkin, D. (1987). *Selling science: How the press covers science and technology*. New York: Freeman.

Appendix F

Some Computer Software for the Biological Sciences

These are just some of the most popular of the many software programs available. Newly available software is reviewed at the back of each issue of the *Quarterly Review of Biology*, which is published 4 times each year. Additional information is readily available at each company's Web site.

GRAPHING PROGRAMS

DeltaGraph

SPSS Science
233 S. Wacker Drive, 11th floor
Chicago, IL 60606–6307
http://www.spssscience.com/deltagraph/

Prism

GraphPad Software
10855 Sorrento Valley Road, Suite 203
San Diego, CA 92121
http://www.graphpad.com/
(This program was designed by biologists, for use by biologists; it
includes both statistical and graphing functions.)

SigmaPlot

SPSS Science
233 S. Wacker Drive, 11th floor
Chicago, IL 60606–6307
http://www.spssscience.com/sigmaplot/

BIBLIOGRAPHIC SOFTWARE

Papyrus

Research Software Design
617 SW Hume Street
Portland, OR 97219–4458
http://www.researchsoftwaredesign.com/

Endnote, ProCite, and Reference Manager
ISI ResearchSoft
3501 Market Street
Philadelphia, PA 19104
http://www.isiresearchsoft.com/

STATISTICAL PACKAGES

Instat, Prism

GraphPad Software
10855 Sorrento Valley Road, Suite 203
San Diego, CA 92121
http://www.graphpad.com/
(These packages were developed by a biologist, for use by biologists.)

JMP

SAS Institute Inc.
JMP Software
SAS Campus Drive
Cary, NC 27513
www.jmp.com

Systat

Systat Software Inc.
501 Suite F
Point Richmond Tech Center
Canal Boulevard
Richmond,CA 94804-2028
www.systat.com

Minitab

Minitab Inc.
Quality Plaza
1829 Pine Hall Road
State College, PA 16801-3008
http://www.minitab.com/

Appendix G

Sample Form for Peer Review

This form was developed for evaluating the first draft of a research proposal. It can easily be modified for other uses.

Peer Response Guide

Writer's Name: _____ Reviewer's Name: _____ Date: _____

Introduction

1. In one or two sentences, state what you think is the major issue being addressed by the author. If you had trouble determining the specific question being addressed, can you indicate what caused the problem for you?

2. Are all statements of fact or opinion well supported by reference, data, or example? Give specific examples of cases in which you think the argument or point is not adequately supported, or where you can cite counter evidence that the author did not consider.

3. At the end of the introductory material, does the author of the proposal indicate specific hypotheses to be tested, or specific questions to be answered?

4. What do you find most interesting about the direction that this proposal is taking? Is there anything the author can do to increase its interest for you, or to better convince you of the study's value?

5. Is the introduction well organized? Do the ideas flow smoothly from sentence to sentence, and from paragraph to paragraph? Does any of the information seem excessive, inadequate, or irrelevant?

6. Is there anything in the introduction that seems confusing or unclear?

7. What would you like to know more about? What questions do you still have?

8. Is the title appropriate? Is it suitably specific and instructive?

Proposed Methods

1. Will the proposed study fully address the questions posed in the Introduction and Background sections? Are controls adequate? Will the design of the study allow the author to distinguish between all competing hypotheses?

2. Are there important features missing, such as the names of species to be studied, locations to be sampled, the sizes of areas to be sampled, and so forth?

3. Are you clear about the numbers of individuals to be used in the study, and the numbers of replicates?

4. Do you understand the reasons for each step proposed? If not, what issues confuse you?

5. Do you understand how the data will be analyzed? If not, explain why.

Appendix H

Some Useful Web Sites

WRITING CONVENTIONS IN BIOLOGY

http://www.councilscienceeditors.org
(Click on "Publications," and then "Scientific Style and Format")
http://www.councilscienceeditors.org/pubs_ssf_numberstyle.
shtml
(writing about numbers)

ADVICE ON GRAMMAR AND PUNCTUATION

http://owl.english.purdue.edu
(select "Grammar, spelling, punctuation")
http://writing-program.uchicago.edu/resources/grammar.htm

LOCATING USEFUL REFERENCES

http://middletownpubliclibrary.org/tutor.htm
(How to Search the World Wide Web: A tutorial for beginners
and nonexperts)
http://www.ase.tufts.edu/biology/bguide/
(A Biologist's Guide to Library Resources)
http://daphne.palomar.edu/tgsearch
(How to Search the Web: A Guide to Search Tools)
www.lib.berkeley.edu/TeachingLib/Guides/Internet/FindInfo.
html
(How to Choose the Search Tools You Need, from UC Berkeley)
http://lii.org
(Librarian's Index to the Internet)

EVALUATING WEB SITES

http://lib.nmsu.edu/instruction/evalcrit.html
http://library.albany.edu/internet/evaluate.html
http://www2.widener.edu/Wolfgram-Memorial-
Library/webevaluation/webeval.htm

http://www.vuw.ac.nz/~agsmith/evaln/index.htm
http://www.ithaca.edu/library/Training/hott.html
http://www.vuw.ac.nz/~agsmith/evaln/evaln.htm
http://www.library.tufts.edu/tisch/webeval.htm

CITING WEB SOURCES

http://www.councilscienceeditors.org/pubs_citing_internet.
    shtml
http://www.bedfordstmartins.com/online/cite8.html

PEER REVIEW GUIDELINES

http://instruct1.cit.cornell.edu/courses/taresources/peer.html
http://srv2.lycoming.edu/~newman/courses/bio22298/
    peerreview.html

WRITING LABORATORY REPORTS

http://www.uncg.edu/~jcbundy/genbio/labreprt.htm

UNDERSTANDING AND USING STATISTICS

http://www.graphpad.com/
    (Click on "GraphPad Library")

GIVING EFFECTIVE POWERPOINT AND OTHER ORAL PRESENTATIONS

http://www.swarthmore.edu/NatSci/cpurrin1/powerpointadvice.
    htm
    (Courtesy of Professor Colin Purrington)
http://www.kumc.edu/SAH/OTEd/jradel/effective.html
    (Courtesy of Professor Jeff Radel, Univ. Kansas Medical Center)

PREPARING EFFECTIVE POSTER PRESENTATIONS

http://www.swarthmore.edu/NatSci/cpurrin1/posteradvice.htm
    (Courtesy of Professor Colin Purrington)

http://www.kumc.edu/SAH/OTEd/jradel/effective.html
    (Courtesy of Professor Jeff Radel, Univ. Kansas Medical Center)

Appendix I

Using the Paper Versions of Leading Indexing Services*

Using *Science Citation Index*

To use *Science Citation Index*, you must first have discovered at least one paper (a "key" paper) from the primary literature pertinent to your quest. You then consult the Citation volume for the particular year you wish to search. For example, your key paper might have been published in 1965, and you wish to locate papers that cited the key paper in 1972. You then look up the author's name in the 1972 Citation volume. Below that author's name you will find a listing of references, one of which should be your key paper. Beneath the listing for that reference you will find a list of all the papers that have cited your key paper during the year covered by the index volume consulted. You might find, for example, a listing that looks like this:

> ICHINOSE, M. BRAIN RES 549: 146 72

This would tell you that a paper citing your key paper was published in 1972 by M. Ichinose in Volume 549 of the journal *Brain Research*, beginning on page 146 (an explanation of journal abbreviations is given at the beginning of each volume of *Science Citation Index*). A paper that cites your key reference is probably appropriate to your topic and worth consulting. If you locate an appropriate reference you can often retrieve an informative abstract of that paper in *Biological Abstracts* (see below), summarizing the paper's contents. That will help you to decide whether or not to get the entire paper.

Using *Zoological Record*

Each volume of *Zoological Record* is devoted to a particular animal phylum or group of related phyla. At the front of each volume is a section

---

*Abbreviated from Pechenik, J. A. (1997). A short guide to writing about biology (3rd ed.) New York: Longman.

arranged by subject, such as "Feeding," "Reproduction" and "Pollution." Turning to the indicated page on the subject of interest you will find a variety of references on that topic. You can then look up the complete reference for any research paper listed, either by the first author's last name, or by the reference number given in parentheses at the right side of the entry. In addition to the author and subject indexes, *Zoological Record* also contains a Geographical Index (presenting references arranged by geographical region and country), a Systematic Index (presenting references arranged by taxonomic group), and a Paleontological Index covering animals known only as fossils (arranged by geological epoch and era). If you locate an appropriate reference using *Zoological Record* you can often retrieve an informative abstract of that paper in *Biological Abstracts* (see below), summarizing the paper's contents. That will help you to decide whether or not to get the entire paper.

Using *Biological Abstracts*

Begin searching *Biological Abstracts* by selecting volumes for a particular year and then looking up key words relevant to the topic being researched, such as "prolactin" or "milk." You may see many lines below the key word; each line represents a different paper relevant to the key word. To the left and right of the key word you will see additional words drawn from each paper's title, sometimes with additions by the editors of the index. If a paper looks potentially useful to you, turn to the reference number given at the right side of the entry. This leads you to the complete citation for that particular paper, along with an informative abstract summarizing the paper's contents.

Index

abbreviations, scientific, 67, 187–188
    list of commonly used, 286–287
abstract, of a laboratory report, 208–209
acknowledgments section, 209
active voice, 97–98
affect and *effect*, 107–108
Agricola, using, 42
ambiguity, 9–11, 84–90
among and *between*, 105
anthropomorphism, 103–104
applications, preparation of, 264–280
arguments
    developing, 133–134
    supporting, 133, 192–195, 201
audience, 7, 84

background section, of a research proposal,
    223–226
Baggins, Bilbo, 69
bar graphs, 165–167, 173–175
between and *among*, 105
Big Mac, 230–232
Biological Abstracts, use of, 42–43, 296
BIOSIS, 42–43
book report format, 131
brain-on reading, 21–23
breaks, on graph axes, 168

captions. *See* figure captions
caution, in data interpretation, 8–9, 83–84,
    185
checklists
    for laboratory and research reports,
        211–214
    for oral presentations, 262–263
    for poster presentations, 243
    for research proposals, 228
    for revising, 119–120
Chi-Square test, 56–60
choosing a topic, for term papers, 131–133
citations, *See* sources
citing sources, 7–8, 66–70, 140, 190–191

clarity, 7, 10–11, 84–90
clauses, restrictive and nonrestrictive, 106
coherence, revising for, 10–11, 76–81,
    91–103
comma splice, 109
commas, use before scientific names,
    110–111
commandments, of concise writing, 94–99
compare and contrast, 231–233
completeness, revising for, 90–92
computer database, use of, 40–43
computers
    use in revising, 14–16, 76, 104
    use in graphing, 19, 166, 291
concentration, versus density, 109–110
conciseness, revising for, 11–12, 92–99
confidence interval, statistical, 51
content, revising for, 11–12, 81–84
contractions, in formal writing, 107
correlation, 55, 64
Council of Biology Editors, 187, 289
cover letter, of application, 268–279
    components of, 269
    supporting details in, 270–271
    tailoring of, 270
criticism
    giving, 112–114
    receiving, 114–116
critiques, preparation of 126–129
    example of, 127–129
    format of, 126–127
Current Contents, use of, 41–42

data
    as a plural noun, 14
    excluding from analysis, 186
    fabrication of, 168, 186
    reading, 23–28
    summarizing of, 158–161
data sheets, 53, 188–190
defining clause, 106
defining terminology, 7, 202–203